Fathers' Rights Activism a ...
Persp...

The legal status, responsibilities and rights of men who are fathers—married or unmarried, cohabiting or separated, biological or social in nature—is a topic with a long and well-documented history. Yet recent developments in a number of countries suggest a growing politicisation of the relationship between law and fatherhood. In some countries, an increasingly vocal, visible and well-organised fathers' rights movement has been credited with influencing perceptions of the politics of family justice. Fathers, it is argued, have become the new victims of family law systems that have swung 'too far' in favour of mothers. Armed with such claims, fathers' rights activists have set out to achieve a range of legal reforms, most notably in the areas of child support law and contact and residence rights following separation.

This book presents an attempt to understand these developments. Bringing together leading international commentators it provides a careful, critical and comparative analysis of the work of fathers' rights activists, the role law has played in their campaigning, their legal strategies, their success (or otherwise) in achieving legal reform, similarities and divergences with the women's movement, and the relationship between fathers' rights movements and the societies that frame them.

Fathers' Rights Activism and Law Reform in Comparative Perspective

Edited by

Richard Collier and Sally Sheldon

·HART·
PUBLISHING

OXFORD AND PORTLAND, OREGON
2006

Published in North America (US and Canada) by
Hart Publishing
c/o International Specialized Book Services
920 NE 58th Avenue, Suite 300
Portland, OR 97213-3786
USA
Tel: +1 503 287 3093 or toll-free: (1) 800 944 6190
Fax: +1 503 280 8832
E-mail: orders@isbs.com
Website: www.isbs.com

Hart Publishing, 16C Worcester Place, Oxford, OX1 2JW
Telephone: +44 (0) 1865 517530 Fax: +44 (0) 1865 510710
E-mail: mail@hartpub.co.uk
Website: http://www.hartpub.co.uk

British Library Cataloguing in Publication Data
Data Available

ISBN-13: 978-1- 84113- 629-5 (paperback)
ISBN-10: 1- 84113- 629- 8 (paperback)

Typeset by Compuscript Ltd. Shannon
Printed and bound in Great Britain by
TJ International Ltd, Padstow, Cornwall

Acknowledgements

The first drafts of the papers contained in this volume were presented at a well attended workshop, *Fathers' Rights Activism and Legal Reform*, held in Keele on 9 September 2005 and funded by the ESRC (RES-451-26-0121). The workshop was the last in a series of six seminars held at Keele, Kent and Westminster Universities to examine the theory/practice divide in the context of issues relating to gender, sexuality and law. We are extremely grateful to the workshop's audience for their rigorous and lively engagement with the papers, and stand particularly indebted to our four discussants: Anne Bottomley, Didi Herman, Oliver Phillips and Carol Smart. We learnt greatly from their involvement and their impact on the final shape of this book should be clear to them.

This volume comes at the end of a very fulfilling period spent working in Keele Law School for one its editors. Sally Sheldon would like to thank her colleagues there for their active involvement in the ESRC programme of seminars which gave rise to this volume and, more generally, for their unstinting collegiality, friendship, support, intellectual stimulation and inspiration. The influence they have had on her over the last twelve years will stay with her for a long time to come.

Finally, we would like to thank Richard Hart for his enthusiastic support of this book project.

Richard Collier, Newcastle University
Sally Sheldon, Kent Law School

Preface

CAROL SMART

The papers in this timely and important collection present rigorous analyses of the rise and influence of fathers' rights movements in major post-industrial societies. The papers are unified by a core set of questions which focus on why there are now so many fathers' movements, what demands they make, and how their demands are changing the landscapes of family law and policy. Perhaps one of the most significant questions discussed is why, given the ongoing privileged position of men (politically, economically and culturally) in western societies, there is now an expressed need by men to (re)assert their position and status as fathers. Although there are important differences between the ways in which fathers in different countries seek to make claims in relation to children (most notably between Sweden and Australia for example) there is nonetheless a shared policy backcloth in all these places that now insists that fathers must be made more central to the emotional lives of their (biological) children, most particularly after separation or divorce. The fact that very similar debates are going on in places like Sweden, the USA, England, Canada and Australia (as well as other countries not included here) suggests that a global movement is afoot or, at the very least, a set of shared political goals amongst men in a wide range of countries. Moreover, the fact that governments are listening to these demands is indicative of significant cultural shifts in perceptions of fathers and of the needs of children. In this sense, we are living in interesting times and this scholarly collection provides a much needed sustained engagement with these complex social, cultural and legal challenges. It is extremely important to develop an understanding of these changes in an international perspective to see what these fathers' movements share in common but, at the same time, the value of this collection is that it provides an understanding of each national movement in its own legal and social context, thus allowing for a more nuanced understanding of fathers' demands for recognition and status.

It is interesting to note of course that while the demands of fathers have become more vociferous, there has been a relatively muted response from the women's movement regarding these developments. The most outspoken response has been in relation to the ongoing problem of domestic violence (for women and for children) and the extent to which this has been overlooked in the rush to acknowledge the emotional significance of fathers to children. But outside this sphere it has been hard for an organised feminist response to find a voice, except in terms of pointing to the irony of fathers' demands for equality of contact and residence of children when women have nowhere yet achieved equality in terms of employment, earnings, benefits, wealth and so on. But it is possible to go only so far in pointing to this irony. It tends to have a distasteful quality about it because mothers are not supposed to use their responsibilities towards children as part of a political or economic argument against fathers. So there does not appear to be a legitimate way in which mothers can enjoin the debate because they appear to be arguing against the rights of their children to maintain proper relationships with their fathers. This means that the debate has become rather one-sided, with the experiences of fathers weighing heavily in balance of considerations that are currently influencing policy. Moreover, 'common sense' seems to support separated fathers' claims that they are being discriminated against in the courts because, of course, wherever one looks children are still primarily in the care of their mothers. This everyday evidence is no longer interpreted as an indication that mothers rather than fathers take on the bulk of child care, rather it is now re-interpreted as a sign that mothers exclude fathers from the caring roles they would otherwise adopt. In this context, evidence about mothers' care work makes little headway against fathers' personal anecdotes and stories of emotional pain on living apart from their children. That evidence should make such little headway against emotion in the heat of political debate and argument (the example provided by Rhoades in this volume is a classic case study of just this issue) undoubtedly carries an important lesson about how politico-legal systems operate, the nature of 'progress', and also about the workings of power,[1] and it is precisely these workings that are explored so carefully in the chapters that follow.

While all the chapters in this book reflect the current and growing concern that the interests and needs of mothers (and also perhaps of children) may be about to be crushed by the popularist juggernaut of fathers' demands for equal treatment, there is also a recognition that the rise of the fathers' movements (especially the more militant variety) has both expressed the felt needs of (some) men and captured the attention of an audience that is prepared to be sympathetic. In other words, it is accepted that these voices would not be heard unless there was something significant going on in terms of cultural and historical shifts in understanding about fathers and fatherhood. Moreover, from where I stand on these issues,[2] it would seem that many of the things that these fathers are claim-

---

[1] It should of course be noted that feminist campaigners have also used this method widely. It was the particular tool of Caroline Norton in the mid-19th century when she started what might be seen as the first feminist campaign to improve mothers' access to and guardianship rights over children in England.

[2] As a Second Wave feminist who remembers the demands of the Women's Liberation Movement in the UK in the 1970s which included the demand that men took greater responsibility for child care.

ing are precisely the sort of things that mothers and children have long demanded (and still do demand) of fathers: namely closer emotional involvement, greater commitment, shared care and shared responsibility. The problem therefore would seem to reside in the context and the timing of these demands, rather than solely in a rejection of men's desire to father in a new way. By this I mean that it is not intrinsically a problem for feminist analyses—or mothers in general—that fathers wish to become more involved with their children, rather it is that they are agitating to do so primarily after they have separated from their partners rather than during the course of their relationship (a point I develop more fully below). This means that the shape of fathers' demands in the early 21st century is not about reconfiguring parenthood as a whole in order that both parents can share the responsibilities and disadvantages—as well as benefits; rather it is a campaign against mothers and a reassertion of paternal privilege which can be exercised at will. So what I propose to do here is give brief consideration to what I shall call the micro-politics of child contact because, although the issue of contact is not the sole concern of all fathers' movements (see for example Crowley in this volume), this is one of the most significant issues they have raised in recent years.

The New Micro-Politics of Child Contact

1. The most obvious problem to be faced when contemplating the demands of fathers for more contact with their children is that this collective demand raises its voice at the point when men's relationships with their children's mothers have broken down. Of course, from the point of view of many fathers there has been no urgency about raising their voices before this point. Arguably the system whereby mothers carry the main responsibility for children and suffer the consequences in the labour market and in terms of later benefits such as pensions, is not a problem for the majority of fathers who can fit even quite 'active' fathering in around their employment and other leisure commitments. This gendered division of labour only becomes a problem for fathers on divorce and separation when the emotionally powerful position of mothers is revealed to them in a meaningful way. But the fact that this realisation comes at the moment of separation inevitably means that the demand for more contact or even residence becomes part of the (inevitable) conflict that surrounds separation and, indeed, even intensifies this conflict.

2. The next element in these micro-politics involves the interwoven nature of 'care' and 'love'. It is empirically established that mothers do most of the caring for children—even if some fathers do a substantial amount (particularly in the UK where there are high levels of part-time maternal employment and low levels of state provided child care). Moreover, caring for children is often

an expression of love and it provides a context in which love can thrive and develop. This has two consequences. <u>For mothers, reducing the amount of caring for children that they do is associated with guilt and loss,</u> and the majority of mothers experience anguish when they return to work or when their children first go to school. So, giving up 'caring time' has emotional connotations for mothers. For fathers, love may not be so bound up with caring activities and responsibilities, but this does not mean that they do not love their children. However, as a consequence the love they evince may be perceived to be rather superficial (he does all the fun things while she does all the laundry!) and so less weighty or emotionally significant compared with a mother's love. This means that the demand by fathers for caring time to be taken away from mothers creates emotional pain (especially if it is the father's new partner or mother who will do the work of caring) while the demand itself can appear to be based on trivial or superficial emotions and motives.

3. This problem ties in with a third issue which concerns the nature and quality of fathering in the absence of maternal guidance and supervision. As I have noted, the dominant pattern in heterosexual parenting in most post-industrial societies is that <u>mothers</u> take overall responsibility for care for children, but they <u>may *delegate* certain activities to fathers.</u> This cultural arrangement is obviously open to change and variation (compare Sweden with the UK for example), but it is still the prevailing pattern in most post-industrial societies. This means that after divorce or separation it is <u>difficult for mothers to trust fathers with full-time care</u> (at least of young children) because they are <u>perceived as occupying the status of a partially trained apprentice in the sphere of</u> childcare work. This of course is just as much a source of men's anger as it is of women's anxiety. Take, as examples of this problem, the statements quoted below which are extracted from a study on post-divorce parenthood. The first comes from a mother whose ex-husband wanted to have the children live with him. The last two are from angry fathers who were enraged by the control that mothers continued to exercise in relation to the children after divorce.

The mother's case:

Jessica: So I put this to Alec. I said "Look, if you really, really feel that you can look after these kids on a full time basis, don't you think you ought to give yourself a weekend with them and then just see how it feels and then maybe after a weekend maybe progress onto say you're having them for a full week and see how you cope with them". He just absolutely hit the roof because he's got this thing in his head that he'd be baby-sitting for me, so he said "No". I said, "Look, in that case I'm not even prepared to discuss it with you because I feel you just don't know how hard it is, you haven't had the children on a full time basis for three years, I do feel that you're just out of it a little. [I feel you should have them] in a normal everyday routine, bringing them to school, picking them up from school, cooking, cleaning, washing and ironing for them, helping them with their homework, if they're sick, nursing them. And then we will re-discuss, re-assess the situation".[3]

The father's case:

> Jack: They hold all the cards and you're the one who's got to crawl back. I wanted to give her a good hiding or shake her. I couldn't even upset her. You've got no choice, you've got to go by what they say.

> George: I can't go up and see [my son] any time I want to, it's got to be done through an appointment, so where do your parental rights come into it?[4]

These different perspectives from mothers and fathers are, at a micro level, the foundations of the 'gender wars' that are referred to in several of the papers in this collection. The conflict arises directly from different experiences of the gendered division of labour. The problem, however, is that while fathers' anger has found a 'legitimating' political voice, mothers' anger has not.

4. The final ingredient to add to this rather toxic mix is the ambiguous view that many fathers apparently have of their role as economic provider for children after divorce or separation. This ambiguous relationship sits uneasily with the often stated aspiration of becoming emotional carers and more involved in the lives of their children. In other words there is an apparent lack of ethical congruence between the political demand to care/love and the common refusal to provide adequate financial support for children. This ambiguity was clearly captured in a notable English case known as *R v Secretary of State for Social Security ex p W*.[5] In this case the father had previously applied for parental responsibility in relation to the children of his partner in order that he should have a degree of social and legal recognition of his status as father of the children. However, when his relationship with their mother ended he refused to pay child support and, notwithstanding his previous application for parental responsibility, he reclaimed his status as a non-father (because he was not the biological father) and declined to accept any responsibility for financial support of the children. This case epitomises the situation where it is culturally available to fathers to have an 'opt-in/opt-out' style of relationship with their children, causing much resentment to the parent who cannot/would not opt out. It also gives weight to the impression that men's claims to fatherhood are not serious, altruistic or responsible, but are generated by a desire for personal gratification and sometimes by a desire to spite mothers who are seen as too powerful.

There are undoubtedly other micro-political elements that could be included here, however it is perhaps enough to see how these four key ingredients can

---

[3] Mother quoted in C Smart and B Neale, *Family Fragments?* (London, Polity, 1999) 125.
[4] Fathers quoted in *ibid*, 145.
[5] [1999] 2 FLR 604.

interweave with one another to produce a toxic mix which is hardly conducive to generating new co-operative styles of parenting after separation. This means that claims by men that they wish to embrace new forms of fathering cannot be accepted by many feminists and mothers alike as genuine feelings, and are seen more as opportunistic claims which will do little to improve the lives of children, and will do much to damage the lives of mothers.

The fathers' movements have taken their experiences of these interpersonal conflicts and reframed them as issues of justice and inequality. In so doing they have obscured the structural basis of the gendered division of labour that supports and sustains women's greater role in child care, and have turned mothers' objections into an apparently self-interested, child-harming defence of the status quo. In framing the issues as ones of justice, they have also turned to law (especially judges and the courts) to demand 'fairness', while claiming much moral high ground through the emotive vehicle of personal accounts and anecdotes. In a sense they are seeking the help of meta-political or legal sanctions (eg penalties against mothers) to solve micro-political disputes in their favour. They have not sought to redistribute the burdens of working and caring. In this endeavour they might achieve some of the sanctions they wish for, but almost any analysis of the power of law to change people's perceptions and behaviours—especially in the realm of intimate relationships—would suggest to these fathers that they will not succeed in finding the remedy they imagine the law can provide. There is discussion in the papers that follow about the ways in which these fathers' groups present themselves as latter-day suffragettes or even civil rights campaigners, and the ways in which they seek to enhance their cause by taking on the mantle of an oppressed group. But this is a strategy based on an analysis of law (and what law can achieve) which is also located in the past. In other words, their understanding of what law can do is ill informed. Their appeal to law is misplaced, not because the law is indifferent to their 'plight' but because family law does not address itself to underlying structural problems, nor does it have the tools that might be required to manage interpersonal hostility which is grounded in gender divisions. Unfortunately, this does not mean that there will not be attempts to regulate mothers,[6] nor does it mean that some children will not be required to divide their time equally between parents (at least until they are old enough to make their own decisions). But these measures do not constitute solutions, they simply redistribute emotional pain and the practical problems associated with living and caring across households. As this book makes particularly clear, if contemporary fathers' movements were really to learn from the women's movements and the civil rights movements of previous decades, they might also learn that there are no easy solutions to be found through law reform.

---

[6] For example, there was a brief period in England when the electronic tagging of mothers who were seen to be resisting or undermining contact was contemplated. It is not at all clear what this might have achieved.

Author Biographies

Susan B Boyd is a law professor and holds the endowed Chair in Feminist Legal Studies at the University of British Columbia where she teaches courses in family law and feminist legal studies. Professor Boyd researches gender and sexuality issues in the fields of child custody law and family law. Her latest book is *Child Custody, Law, and Women's Work* and her current research involves an exploration of the influence of fathers' rights, feminism and neo-liberalism on family law reform.

Richard Collier is Professor of Law at the University of Newcastle Upon Tyne. He has published extensively in the areas of law and gender, family law, crime and legal education and is author of *Masculinity, Law and the Family* (1995), *Masculinities, Crime and Criminology: Men, Heterosexuality and the Criminal(Ised) Other* (1998) and the forthcoming *Essays on Law, Men and Gender* (2007). Richard is the British Academy Thank-offering to Britain Senior Research Fellow (Jan 2007–Jan 2008).

Jocelyn Elise Crowley is an Associate Professor of Public Policy, a member of the Graduate Faculty in the Department of Political Science, and an Affiliated Faculty Member of the Department of Women's and Gender Studies at Rutgers, The State University of New Jersey. She has written extensively on the topic of family policy, including a book, *The Politics of Child Support in America*. Professor Crowley has also written on the subject of women and politics, and is currently working on a book related to the fathers' rights movement in America.

Maria Eriksson, PhD, is a sociologist and researcher in the Department of Gender Studies at Göteborg University, Sweden. Previously she was the programme co-ordinator of the Nordic Council of Ministers' research programme, *Gender and Violence* (2000–4), which sponsored 16 research networks and 13 individual projects across the Nordic counties. Her current research concerns violent fathers' everyday life after separation or divorce; and abused children as social actors in legal processes regarding contact, custody and residence. She is also one of the lead researchers in a *Coordination Action on Human Rights Violations (CAHRV)*, funded by the EU 6th framework programme.

Keith Pringle is Professor of Social Work at Aalborg University, Denmark, and holds visiting professorships in sociology and social policy respectively at Mälardalens Högskola, Sweden and Warwick University. His main research fields are comparative welfare analysis and power relations—especially regarding gender, ethnicity and age. He has authored or co-authored three books and edited two more on these topics. Currently he is co-editing two books arising from a recently completed European-funded transnational project on men which he co-ordinated, as well as the *Routledge International Encyclopaedia on Men and Masculinities*.

Helen Rhoades is a Senior Lecturer in Law at the University of Melbourne, Australia. She teaches and publishes in the field of family law, and has conducted socio-legal studies on a wide range of family law issues, including family property division, parenting disputes, family law reform and dispute resolution developments.

Sally Sheldon will take up a Chair at Kent Law School in October 2006. She has written widely on issues relating to law and gender, has been general editor of *Social & Legal Studies: An International Journal* and was series editor (with Anne Bottomley) of the Cavendish *Feminist Perspectives on Law* series. She is currently an ESRC Research Fellow (RES-000-27-0111) working on a socio-legal analysis of fatherhood. As part of this research, together with Richard Collier, she is writing a monograph, *Fatherhood: A Socio-Legal Study*, which will be published by Hart in 2007.

Carol Smart is Professor of Sociology and Co-Director of the Morgan Centre for Study of Relationships and Personal Life at the University of Manchester. She is currently writing a book on new sociological perspectives on relationships and personal life for Polity and is managing an ESRC-funded research project on civil partnerships and the importance of legal/social recognition for same sex couples. She is also involved in the ESRC National Centre for Research Methods Node based at Manchester and Leeds, and particularly with two research projects: one is a study of the meaning and significance of family resemblances and the other deals with ceremony and ritual in everyday life.

Contents

1

Fathers' Rights, Fatherhood and Law Reform—International Perspectives

RICHARD COLLIER AND SALLY SHELDON

Introduction

Fathers, it is sometimes said, have become the new victims of legal systems that have moved too far in favour of mothers. Groups claiming to represent the interests of fathers have mobilised in a number of countries to protest against such changes. Their demands seem seductively simple, often involving little more than a request for formal equality with mothers or, put quite simply, 'justice for fathers'.[1] There is no doubt that the simplicity of this request has sharpened the point with which it has bored its way into the public consciousness, and contributed greatly to its success in being heard across a range of policy making forums. Internationally, the Fathers' Rights Movement (FRM), like the broader men's movements with which it is often associated,[2] has established an increasingly vocal, visible, organised and powerful presence in debates about family law reform across jurisdictions, albeit one which is deeply marked by the social and cultural specificities of the national contexts within which the FRM operates.

This volume offers a snapshot of the work of the FRM in a number of countries at the current time: a historical moment that, it will be suggested, is particularly

---

[1] This is reflected in the names of these groups: eg DADS (Dads Against Discrimination); Equal Parents of Canada; Fathers For Equality; Mouvement pour l'Egalité Parentale, the Equal Parenting Council, Parents and Children for Equality. Organisations operating under the name Fathers 4 Justice have established an international presence (albeit one which is not necessarily officially sanctioned by the original UK group: see further below, also n 22). This focus on 'justice' is not a new phenomenon: in Ontario, Canada, for example, a group called Fathers For Justice existed in the 1980s and 1990s: RA Kennedy, *Fathers For Justice: The Rise of a New Social Movement in Canada as a Case Study of Collective Identity Formation* (Ann Arbor, MI, Caravan Books, 2004). We are grateful to Susan Boyd for this point.

[2] See generally MA Messner, *Politics of Masculinities: Men in Movements* (Thousand Oaks, CA, Sage, 1997); M Flood, 'Men's Movements' (1998) 46 *Community Quarterly* 62; R Collier, '"Coming Together?": Post-Heterosexuality, Masculine Crisis and the New Men's Movement' (1996) 4(1) *Feminist Legal Studies* 3.

significant both for the evolution of the FRM and for the politics of law reform in the field of family law more generally. The contributors assess the diverse discourses, strategies and impact of fathers' rights groups (FRGs) in seeking to set reform agendas in family law in five national contexts, highlighting important commonalities and significant diversity in their operation. Their work ranges from a close examination of FRM members' claims 'in their own words' to detailed assessments of the success of activists in achieving specific goals within these jurisdictions. It encompasses an analysis of the reasons *why*, at the present moment, the issue of fathers' rights should have assumed such a high political and public profile. A central issue is the extent to which, and why, law should have become a focal point of the FRM. This involves questions of how legal strategies have been deployed; the success (or otherwise) which the FRM has had in achieving legal reform; the commonalities and points of difference which exist between the FRM and other social movements (particularly feminism); and the question of what, if anything, the FRM may have learnt from other such movements and organisations.[3]

In this introductory chapter, we aim firstly to sketch some of the broad structural factors that shape the present contours of the FRM and current debates about fathers' rights; secondly, to outline some of the general themes that emerge from the analysis of the chapters to follow; thirdly, to explore some of the questions which, it will be suggested, the FRM raises for feminist audiences; and, finally, we seek to draw some conclusions from the other chapters regarding the relative success, or otherwise, of the FRM in effecting and affecting legal reform. Before moving on, however, some explanation is necessary regarding, firstly, terminology and, secondly, the choice of countries within which we study the work of the FRM.

Terminology

In this volume, we use the term 'fathers' rights group' to refer to individual groups within the countries under discussion and the broader 'fathers' rights movement' to refer collectively to these groups, as they exist either within national boundaries or across them. However, this terminology itself begs a number of questions as each of these words—'fathers', 'rights' and 'movement'—suggests its own problems.

---

[3] The issues of what the FRM has taken from other social movements is most explicitly addressed by Crowtly, see below.

Firstly, to what extent can the FRM claim to represent (all) fathers?[4] Fathers, of course, are a hugely disparate group, divided by race and ethnicity, sexuality, class, education, and every shade of political opinion. They are married and unmarried, gay and straight, living in intact families, in families that are separated across households following marriage or cohabitation, or have never lived with their children or their children's mother as a family. Fathers are sometimes involved simultaneously in parenting a number of children born of different mothers and living in several households. Their relationships with children may be grounded in genetic links, or in social relationships with a child or that child's mother. Fathers as a group are themselves unlikely to agree on very much. The idea that we can isolate a particular set of interests as belonging to all fathers or that any one group can speak for them, should thus be greeted with considerable scepticism.[5] More generally, it cannot be assumed that the majority of men accept the aims and objectives of the FRM either in general or in relation to any particular fathers' rights group or organisation. Most strongly, it has even been suggested that the FRM may be actively harmful to the interests of fathers.[6]

Further, the precise content of what is included in the FRM's demand of 'rights for fathers' is often unclear. Typically, as is evident from the analysis of this book, such groups have focused on a number of narrowly defined problems and have addressed quite specific constituencies of fathers.[7] Their membership, it has been argued, may itself be often drawn from limited sections of society.[8] The very fact that some FRGs have secured a high public and media profile, and have done so, in some instances, in a relatively short space of time, might be taken as evidence of the relative sophistication of leading group members in dealing with the media, an issue which raises further questions about the broader social profile of such

[4] On the importance of differentiating the views of FRGs from those of 'fathers' in any more general sense, see further A Gavanas, 'The Fatherhood Responsibility Movement: The Centrality of Marriage, Work and Male Sexuality in Reconstructions of Masculinity and Fatherhood' in D Hobson, *Making Men into Fathers: Men, Masculinities and the Social Politics of Fatherhood* (Cambridge, Cambridge University Press, 2002).

[5] This mirrors the classic problem for feminism of grounding a mandate to speak for 'women'. See further below.

[6] See M Flood, 'Separated Fathers and the Fathers' Rights Movement' presented at *Feminism, Law and the Family*, workshop held at Melbourne Law School, 24 February 2006. Flood suggests that FRGs may incite fathers to anger, blame and destructive strategies of litigation.

[7] Demands have typically centred, for example, upon post-separation genetic/(quasi) marital fathers and issues of (quantum of) child support to be paid and contact with their children. The FRM has typically not directed resources into other issues such as, for example, immigrant fathers' putative rights to live in the same country as their children, the rights of unmarried fathers to pass on citizenship to their children, or gay men's right to parent.

[8] This is a point deserving of further analysis. It has been suggested, for example, that there may be differences between the social class background of 'rank and file' group members compared with that of the 'leaders' who are more likely to engage with the media and policy makers. See further Collier, this volume, Messner, above n 2; C Betroia and J Drakich, 'The Fathers' Rights Movement: Contradictions in Rhetoric and Practice' (1993) 14(4) *Journal of Family Issues* 592.

groups.[9] Moreover, and as is frequently emphasised by FRGs themselves, their membership does not consist entirely of fathers but also contains female partners and other members of the wider kin networks within which they are located, in particular grandparents.[10] This raises both questions of women's agency, motherhood and parenting in the context of a social movement ostensibly based on shared interests and goals, and complex issues of age and generation. Finally, distinctions can be drawn between FRGs and certain government-funded bodies such as, in the UK, the organisation *Fathers Direct* or government appointed advisory groups, such as Sweden's 'Daddy Group';[11] and between the FRM and the broader men's movement. The interactions between such groups are complex, shifting, and influenced by a range of factors both external and internal to the dynamics of the organisations themselves.

Secondly, to what extent does it make sense to describe the focus of the FRM as a quest for 'rights'? It will be seen in the chapters to follow that a focus on achieving reform through the acquisition of formal legal rights for fathers (and sometimes for children) has been a notable feature of the work of FRMs.[12] Indeed, it has been suggested that this kind of focus on rights might itself be characterised as a distinctively masculine form of engagement with law.[13] Moreover, aspects of what has been called the 'new fatherhood' may themselves be seen to correlate with this tendency for men to frame their engagements with law in terms of a rights-based framework.[14] However, it is important to note that the activities of the FRM extend significantly beyond a demand for legal rights or, indeed, a focus on legal reform.[15] The FRM plays a significant non-campaigning role, offering practical and emotional support to its members. This help may be of particular value to individual men in the process of divorce given the well-documented psychological strains which can be faced at the time of separation.[16]

---

[9] *Ibid.*

[10] An issue stressed in FRM websites and literature. This points to a wider point of great significance: when we talk about recognising 'fathers', children's relationships with a whole kin network can also be at issue: see M Griffiths, *Feminisms and the Self: The Web of Identity* (London, Routledge, 1995).

[11] See respectively *Fathers Direct: The National Information Centre on Fatherhood* (http://www.fathersdirect.com); Eriksson and Pringle, this volume.

[12] This focus on 'rights' also figures heavily in the names that such groups have chosen for themselves: eg Fathers' Rights and Equality Exchange, Fathers' Rights Network, Aktion Recht des Kindes auf beide Eltern, Association of Fathers' Rights Protection, Ligue des Droits du Père.

[13] T Arendell, *Fathers and Divorce* (Thousand Oaks, CA, Sage, 1995).

[14] As Fathers 4 Justice put it: 'We are driven by a sense of duty, responsibility and the need to create change and bring about justice': http://www.fathers-4-justice.org/pledge/index.htm. See further below.

[15] See particularly Crowley, this volume. It is also important to recognise that contact law reform is not the sole object of this engagement with law.

[16] See Crowley, this volume. As is noted above, it is also possible that participation in FRGs might have negative effects for men themselves, as well as women and children: see Flood, above n 6.

That many FRM members might participate primarily in order to gain such support, dipping 'in and out' of activities, or might have what is at best a partial commitment to the political aims of the organisation, makes any depiction of the groups' primary or sole aim as the promotion of a fathers' legal rights agenda extremely problematic.[17] It is also noteworthy that other kinds of discourse are also at play in the language of the FRM and, as Smart has argued, that the discourse of FRGs can shift register *between* different voices, appealing at various moments, for example, to ideas of welfare, care and caring, as well as justice and rights.[18]

Finally, given the diversity of approaches and political views encompassed in what is—at best—a loose coalition of organisations, does it make sense to talk of a Fathers' Rights 'Movement' at all? The issue of what constitutes a social movement itself remains heavily contested. Further, while our use of the singular 'FRM' suggests sufficiently powerful commonalities between the goals, rhetoric and strategies of different FRGs for them to be considered as part of one movement, as will become clear from the analysis of this book, the groups are marked by significant diversity due, not least, to the pull of the different national contexts in which they operate.

In the light of the above, the terms 'FRM' and 'FRG' must be deployed with caution and with due regard to their shortcomings. While they are used throughout this book as convenient shorthand for what we want to argue is an important social phenomenon (and as terms which are often adopted by the fathers' rights activists themselves), the caveats entered here should nonetheless be borne in mind.[19]

Choice of Countries

The chapters that follow discuss the work of the FRM in Australia, Canada, Sweden, the United Kingdom and the United States of America. This is obviously not a comprehensive list of countries where the FRM is active[20] and we do not

[17] Participants who drop in and out of organisations can be considered 'single shot' as opposed to 'long term' players. This issue of transient membership also raises important questions about the strength and durability of individual groups. See further M Olson, *The Logic of Collective Action: Public Goods and the Theory of Groups* (Cambridge, MA, Harvard University Press, 1965). We are grateful to Jocelyn Crowley for this observation.

[18] C Smart, 'Equal Shares: Rights for Fathers or Recognition for Children?' (2004) 24(4) *Critical Social Policy* 484. See also Rhoades' chapter in this volume describing the deployment of a 'softer discourse' of fairness rather than rights in recent Australian debates.

[19] The term 'fathers' rights activist' must also be deployed with caution as many FRM members will not be involved in any form of activism.

[20] Groups exist in a large number of other countries, particularly in Europe, including eg Ligue des Droits du Père and Fédération des Mouvements de la Condition Paternelle (France); Väter für Kinder (Germany), Père pour Toujours (Switzerland), Associazione Padre Separati (Italy), Pais (e Filhos) Para Sempre (Portugal), Asociacion de Padres de Familia Separados (Spain).

have the space here to attempt an explanation of why such groups may not have coalesced in the same way elsewhere.[21] Further, we make no claim that the countries discussed below offer in any way a representative sample of the international scene regarding the range of debates now taking place about fathers' rights and law reform. What the chapters below do present is, firstly, significant recent comparative data on the shifting discourses and strategies of some of the most active FRGs, and the ways in which they have sought to influence law reform in the countries and distinctive legal systems in which they operate. As such, the volume is a step towards providing an understanding and critical assessment of some of the FRM's more important recent campaigns.

Secondly, the volume offers the possibility of discerning the extent to which there may be a transplantation of ideas and strategies occurring between FRGs across national borders. For example the UK group, Fathers 4 Justice, although distinctive in a number of respects in terms of the methods of direct action it has adopted, does appear to have influenced the debate in each of the national contexts studied in this volume, where branded websites have emerged publicising and advocating what is described as a distinctive 'fathers 4 justice' form of protest and agenda.[22] It is unclear at the time of writing whether the reported disbanding of the UK group by its founder, Matt O'Connor, will also result in the end of these satellites.[23] Recent developments in the UK around the emergence of the group 'the Real Fathers 4 Justice' suggest it is unlikely that the protests themselves will stop.

Thirdly and perhaps most importantly, taken together, the chapters of this volume provide ample evidence of the growth of a significant social movement in western countries, and one characterised by both powerful commonalities and considerable diversity. While the chapters clearly demonstrate important similarities between FRGs, they also illustrate the role of national and cultural factors in shaping their focus, priorities and strategies. Such considerations include the relative strength of religious factors within a particular country,[24] the role and impact of key individuals,[25] the influence of the media,[26] the presence of a

---

[21] One issue deserving of further research is the extent to which such groups are themselves a phenomenon of the west or the economic north.

[22] See: http://www.fathers-4-justice.org; http://www.fathers-4-justice.us; http://www.fathers-4-justice.ca; http://www.f4joz.com; http://www.f4j.se/eng. The group also has websites in Italy and the Netherlands: http://www.fathers-4-justice.it and http://www.f4j.nl/index3.php respectively. Although see further n 3 above and Collier, this volume.

[23] See further Collier, this volume.

[24] Crowley this volume; A Gavanas, above n 4.

[25] See, for example, Collier's discussion of the role of key individuals in fathers' rights politics in the UK, this volume; M Kaye and J Tolmie, 'Fathers' Rights Groups in Australia and their Engagement with Issues in Family Law' (1998) 12 *Australian Journal of Family Law* 19, 22.

[26] Compare, for example, the enthusiasm with which the UK media have reported the F4J's 'superhero' stunts and the Swedish media's virtual ignoring of a similar event: Collier, and Eriksson and Pringle, this volume.

national disposition towards anti-intellectualism,[27] as well as culturally contingent understandings of gender roles, children and childhood[28] and the specific cultures and practices of the national legal systems themselves.

In such a context it is, inevitably, difficult to generalise. In the remainder of this introductory chapter we will, nonetheless, seek briefly to set out some of the broad factors that have underpinned the evolution of the FRM over recent years. While dispute and contestations regarding fathers' legal rights have a long history, it is our suggestion that the last thirty years has seen a marked intensification of activity in this area, with FRMs becoming more militant and currently enjoying a previously unparalleled media and political profile.[29] With this analysis in place, we go on to outline some key themes to emerge from the discussion of the chapters of this volume.

Beyond Backlash: The Evolution Of The FRM

The extent to which the emergence of the FRM is a new phenomenon is contested. Activism and social concern around the issue of fathers' rights have been in evidence for some time and can be traced, for example, to the 19th century (and, indeed, earlier periods).[30] What has become evident over the last thirty years, however, is an increased intensity to these debates alongside a heightened media presence. FRGs have also become far more focused and organised in their engagement with issues of legal reform and have secured a greater political prominence. Why has this occurred?

A number of authors have sought an explanation for this phenomenon in the compelling picture of 'backlash', most famously painted by the US author, Susan Faludi. In *Backlash*, Faludi traces 'a powerful counter-assault on women's rights, a backlash, an attempt to retract the handful of small and hard-won victories that the feminist movement did manage to win for women', a trend which she locates as beginning in the very late 1970s and which gathered momentum throughout the 1980s.[31] In her subsequent book, *Stiffed*, Faludi goes on to explore what she

---

[27] See Rhoades' discussion in this volume of the influence of ideas of 'class war' in Australian politics, citing FRGs' hostility towards court personnel and the legal professions; the rise of a 'new populism'; and growing antipathy to knowledge-elites (a new class of university educated, inner city dwellers with progressive opinions, who are seen as contemptuous of the values of 'ordinary people').

[28] See Eriksson and Pringle, this volume, on the relevance of Swedish attitudes towards childhood.

[29] An intensification which was perhaps especially marked during the 1990s. On the possible reasons for this see further Collier, this volume. This is not to claim that it is inevitable that these groups will grow in strength and membership. Many FRM members, in the US at least, are worried about recruiting others to the movement and, indeed, express uncertainty as to whether it is appropriate to talk about a 'movement' at all in this context: JE Crowley, 'Organizational Responses to the Fatherhood Crisis: The Case of Fathers' Rights Groups in the United States' (forthcoming 2006) 39 *Marriage and Family Review*.

[30] See, for example, R Collier, *Masculinity, Law and the Family* (London, Routledge, 1995).

[31] S Faludi, *Backlash: The Undeclared War Against Women* (London, Chatto and Windus, 1991) 12.

identifies as a broader trend whereby men have been pushed out of the labour market and undermined in the family:

> at the end of the millennium it is men who are in crisis. Even in the world that they are supposed to own and run ... men just as much as women are at the mercy of cultural forces that distort their lives and plague our culture.[32]

Following Faludi, a number of commentators have suggested that increased demands for men's legal rights can usefully be understood as a reaction to increased female power within and beyond the family. Within this framework, it is argued, as women gain more influence outside of the household, in particular in relation to paid employment, men are somehow seen as being disadvantaged, losing their traditional role and authority both within and outside of the home.[33] The inevitable result, it is suggested, is that men will 'fight back' and 'gender wars' will result:

> to the degree that the economic inequality between men and women is decreased ... *fathers become aware of their disadvantage*, naturally and partially legally. The woman has *possession* of the child as a product of her womb ... The men who free themselves from the 'fate' of a career and turn to their children come home to an empty nest.[34]

These themes map to broader notions of the 'contemporary crisis of masculinity', which has been discussed extensively across a range of literatures (in particular within critical studies of men and masculinities).[35]

In the context of debates around family law reform, some FRGs more closely allied to a broader men's movement have undoubtedly embraced and advocated a distinctively anti-feminist—and, in some cases at least, openly misogynistic—politics.[36] The rhetoric of 'sex wars' has become a common theme both in the rhetoric of such groups and in much of the media reporting of debates and issues concerning fathers' rights.[37] However, other commentators have questioned the

---

[32] Faludi's argument is summarised in this revealing passage on the inside cover of her book: S Faludi, *Stiffed: The Betrayal of the Modern Man* (London, Chatto and Windus, 1999). Compare, in the UK, M Phillips, *The Sex-Change Society: Feminised Britain and the Neutered Male* (London, The Social Market Foundation, 1999).

[33] See further, in the context of Canadian FRGs, S Boyd, 'Backlash Against Feminism: Custody and Access Reform Debates of the Late 20th Century' (2004) 16(2) *Canadian Journal of Women and the Law* 255.

[34] U Beck, *Risk Society: Towards a New Modernity* (London, Sage, 1992) 113, emphasis in original. For an interesting discussion of Beck's approach, see C Smart and B Neale, *Family Fragments?* (Cambridge, MA, Polity, 1999) 13–19.

[35] Earlier discussions of this idea within this literature can be found, for example, in A Brittan, *Masculinity and Power* (Oxford, Blackwell, 1989) 25–36; RW Connell, *Gender and Power*, (Cambridge, Polity, 1987) 183–6; T Carrigan, R Connell and J Lee, 'Towards a New Sociology of Masculinity' (1985) 14 *Theory and Society* 551, 598. Compare J Hearn, 'A Crisis in Masculinity, or New Agendas for Men?' in S Waldby (ed), *New Agendas For Women* (London, Macmillan, 1999).

[36] See Boyd, below n 64.

[37] This is explored in a number of the chapters to follow.

accuracy of this portrayal of backlash, suggesting that to view the FRM as a reaction to women's social, political and economic gains in the 1960s and 1970s—gains which are themselves contested—is to deny the long history of struggles over rights and responsibilities in relation to the family.[38] It is also, significantly, to ignore the grounding of these developments in more complex, and at times contradictory, social changes. This is a point that each of the contributors to this volume seeks to make in different ways. Further, it has been suggested, such an account tends to evoke a univalent form of power, one constructed around a central binary of the powerful/powerless mother/father, where male and female interests are somehow locked within what has been described as a 'zero sum game'.[39] A growing body of research suggests, however, that the complex realities of contemporary family life and family practices are not easily reducible to a framework in which, it is assumed, as women gain power, influence and rights men somehow proportionately 'lose' them and vice versa.[40]

While we would accept that there are times when it does make sense to talk in terms of an opposition of male and female interests in this way, there are surely other occasions where powerful commonalities of interest can exist. This remains true even, for example, within debates regarding post-divorce/separation contact where the interests of mothers and fathers are often seen as most starkly opposed. Far from it being the case that most mothers seek to oppose fathers' contact time with their children, empirical studies suggest that the majority of mothers would welcome fathers spending *more* time with their children.[41] It is also important to remember in this context that the great majority of contact or custody arrangements are themselves uncontested. At issue here, therefore, are complex questions about how, psychologically, separation is negotiated and experienced; how both men and women come to take on or invest in certain subject positions, such as that of the 'good' mother or father (or, indeed, 'fathers' rights activist'); and how ideas of good fatherhood can themselves shift within the individual life course. These issues are much more complex than the idea of backlash idea can, by itself, recognise.

Finally, the chapters in this volume suggest that the idea of 'gender wars' may itself resonate in some national contexts more than in others. In their contribution to this volume, Eriksson and Pringle follow Eduards in questioning whether, in contemporary Sweden, political encounters regarding gender and power can ever

---

[38] See, for example, R Collier, 'From "Women's Emancipation" to "Sex War"?: Beyond the Masculinized Discourse of Divorce' in SD Sclater and C Piper (eds), *Undercurrents of Divorce* (Aldershot, Dartmouth, 1999); DE Chunn, SB Boyd and H Lessard (eds), *(Re)Action and Resistance: Feminism, Law and Social Change* (Vancouver, UBC Press, forthcoming).

[39] On the 'zero-sum' conception of power implicit in this kind of argument see R Collier, *ibid.*

[40] DHJ Morgan, *Family Connections* (Cambridge, Polity, 1996).

[41] M Maclean and J Eekelaar, *The Parental Obligation: A Study of Parenthood Across Households* (Oxford, Hart, 1997).

play out in a way that assumes mutually acknowledged and respected differences of interest between men and women. Conceptualising men as a political category and interested group in a power relationship with women is, they suggest, something of a taboo in the Swedish democratic order.[42] Any attempt to 'name men as men' in the debate about fathers' rights must thus take account of questions of context and cultural specificity. The ideas of gender wars and backlash therefore can, at best, be seen as culturally contingent caricatures of a more complex reality. Further, they are caricatures that, much as they may have entranced some national media, would appear to have failed greatly to capture the imagination of legislators.[43] The chapters in this volume illustrate what Boyd has termed, writing in the Canadian context, the 'uneven influence' and contradictory nature of recent law reform processes in this area.[44] Other contributors note similar patterns and what appears to be, in certain key respects at least, the noticeable failure of the FRM to direct and shape national policies, at least in the way they would wish.

While there are limits to the ideas of backlash and 'gender wars' in seeking to understand the rise of the FRM, we would suggest that it is possible to point to three broad interrelated trends that underpin the new prominence of the FRM internationally: firstly, complex shifts in household and familial arrangements; secondly, changes in understandings of fatherhood, motherhood and, importantly, childhood; and, finally, a shift in how legal regulation relates to the family. Each of these factors is considered in more detail below.

Shifting Household Demographics

A rise in cohabitation and a general decline in marriage and rising rates of divorce/separation have led to more fathers living apart from their genetic children. This process, described by Smart and Neale as a 'fragmentation' of families, rests in one sense upon a fragmentation of fatherhood itself.[45] Following the breakdown of a relationship, children in each of the countries discussed in this volume remain overwhelmingly likely to live with their mothers. Men who retain parental roles and responsibilities post-separation will thus do so whilst living in a different household, possibly sharing the role of social father with the mother's new partner.[46] As Smart and Neale note:

---

[42] See below, citing M Eduards, *Förbjuden Handling* (Forbidden Action) (Malmö, Liber, 2002).

[43] See below.

[44] This volume. See also C Smart, 'Feminism and Law: Some Problems of Analysis and Strategy' (1986) 14 *International Journal of the Sociology of Law* 109.

[45] Smart and Neale, above n 34.

[46] *Ibid.* According to the last census, 87% of step-families involve households made up of a couple with children from the woman's previous relationship, 11% have children from the man's previous relationship, with 3% including children from both partners' previous relationships: *Living in Britain: General Household Survey 2002*, http://www.statistics.gov.uk, table 3.10.

fragments of families are found in various households linked by biological and economic bonds, but not necessarily by affection or shared life prospects. We might say that family law is trying to hold the fragments together through the imposition of a new normative order based on genetics and finances, but not on a state-legitimated hetero-sexual union with its roots in the ideal of Christian marriage.[47]

The shifting familial relationships, combined with changes to the economic relationship between men and women—not least as a result of more women working outside the home, albeit in many cases part-time[48]—has required a complex and ongoing renegotiation of the rights and duties of all parties, played out partly through family law.[49] In a context where fathers increasingly have never been married to their children's mothers, and where marital ties are themselves less secure, the question of the fragility of men's relationships with their children has become more pressing.

Evolving Expectations of Fatherhood

It is significant that this fragmentation of fatherhood is occurring at a time of growth of the phenomenon of the so-called 'new fatherhood'. Expectations of men as fathers have expanded from requiring a commitment to the traditional male breadwinner role to include a more 'hands-on', caring model of fatherhood. Such a model involves, in particular, greater levels of emotional engagement with children.[50] While the extent of real change in men's parenting behaviour remains contested, there is reason to believe that the aspirations for, and expectations of, fathering for many men have, across each of the jurisdictions discussed in this book, changed significantly.[51] The findings of therapeutic, psychological and sociological research suggest a qualitative shift in men's physical and emotional relationships to children and childcare, as well as in men's own self-identification around ideas of commitment to 'family life'.[52] At the very time when fatherhood

---

[47] Smart and Neale, above n 34, 181, references omitted.

[48] M O'Brien, *Shared Caring: Bringing Fathers into the Frame* (Manchester, Equal Opportunities Commission, 1995).

[49] See further, and generally, A Diduck, *Law's Families* (London, LexisNexis, 2003).

[50] D Lupton and L Barclay, *Constructing Fatherhood: Discourses and Experiences* (London, Sage, 1997).

[51] See, for example, in the UK context, D Smeaton and A Marsh, *Maternity and Paternity Benefits: Survey of Parents 2005: Employment Relations Research Series No 50* (London, Department of Trade and Industry, 2006), which suggests that fathers are taking more parental leave than was previously thought around the time of the birth of a child.

[52] See further C Lewis, *A Man's Place in the Home: Fathers and Families in the UK* (York, Joseph Rowntree Foundation, 2000); J Warin, Y Solomon, C Lewis and W Langford, *Fathers, Work and Family Life* (York, Joseph Rowntree Foundation/Family Policy Studies Centre, 1999); G Dench, *Exploring Variations in Men's Family Roles: Joseph Rowntree Foundation Social Policy Research Findings No 99* (York, Joseph Rowntree Foundation, 1996); P Moss (ed), *Father Figures: Fathers in the Families of the 1990s*, (London, HMSO, 1995).

becomes less secure, then, cultural, economic and legal imperatives are reframing the debate about what it means for men to become 'good fathers' and more 'involved' parents.[53]

These 'new fatherhood' norms are, it will be argued, reshaping many aspects of men's interpretation and experiences of separation, an issue that has a bearing on understandings of the rise of the FRM. The convergence of cultural and legal exhortations for men to be more involved fathers with the greater fragility of their connections to their children is one which has ploughed fertile ground for the growth of fathers' rights agendas. For example, Crowley's analysis of various FRGs in the United States notes that what often unites them is a common belief in the capacity of all men to renew their commitment to the moral and legal enterprise of fatherhood. The influence of ideas of 'new fatherhood' on the rhetoric of the FRM is, in this context, particularly clear. Collier, meanwhile, writing on the UK, notes significant common ground between the discourse of 'new fatherhood' and the language of the FRM. Both, for example, tend routinely to distinguish the 'good father' from those other men deemed 'bad', 'feckless' or 'deadbeat'.[54] The ideal of 'new fatherhood' proclaimed by many FRGs can be one which itself often tends to deny, minimise or normalise any paternal conduct that might be subject to criticism. Significantly, both also include a belief that such a 'good father' would and should 'fight for' his children given the messages conveyed within the new post-divorce/separation contact culture in family law.[55] Each of these discourses frequently deploys images of the 'bad mother' as a figure who, in failing her children, further necessitates the presence of the father, if necessary by recourse to law.[56] Crucial to these arguments is the idea of the father as an active presence in his children's lives, an idea which mirrors a growing concern across western governments about how to facilitate forms of 'active' desirable fathering.[57] This issue raises complex questions about the specific economic, cultural and legal contexts in which men become subjectively committed to and experience fatherhood.

The growing militancy of parts of the FRM, in particular in the area of post-divorce/separation contact law reform, can be linked to two further interrelated processes: a broader rise of individualisation within society (the decline of various forms of collective solidarity, a move to an ethos of self-absorption and

---

[53] Although precisely what being 'involved' means in this context is itself open to question.

[54] Compare G Furstenberg, 'Good Dads—Bad Dads: Two Faces of Fatherhood' in AJ Cherline (ed), *The Changing American Family and Public Policy* (Washington, DC, The Urban Institute Press, 1988).

[55] J Dewar, 'The Normal Chaos of Family Law' (1998) 61 *Modern Law Review* 467. Dewar suggests, for example, that the concerns about justice expressed by FRGs appear to be shared by many men who have expressed a growing dissatisfaction with the perceived limits of a broad discretionary system in the family law field.

[56] See further Boyd, this volume and 'Demonizing Mothers', n 64.

[57] See, for example, R Collier, 'Feminising the Workplace? (Re)constructing the "Good Parent" in Employment Law and Family Policy' in A Morris and T O'Donnell (eds), *Feminist Perspectives on Employment Law* (London, Cavendish, 1999).

self-improvement)[58] and a refiguring of understandings of children and the idea of childhood.[59] These shifting visions of childhood have considerable significance when seeking to understand the growth in prominence of the FRM more generally. Understandings of childhood vary not just across time, but also across cultures. Eriksson and Pringle provide an example of how different understandings of childhood in the Swedish context (specifically the failure to understand children as possible objects of abuse and therefore institute relevant regimes of protection) have had a marked impact on the evolution of legal reforms. This is a salutary reminder that the renegotiation of fathers' rights and responsibilities is inevitably highly culturally specific, playing out in different ways in different national contexts. Nonetheless, within both the shifting demographics described above and the rich cultural specificity implied by national contexts, the FRM can be seen as part of a far broader renegotiation of the parameters, not only of fatherhood but also of motherhood and childhood—a process occurring in a context in which the rights and responsibilities ascribed to each role are themselves becoming ever less clear cut.

Law, State and Governance

It is in the light of these shifting adult investments that the perceived sense of loss of the relationship with one's child experienced by many men in the processes of divorce and separation is so keenly felt. This does not explain, however, why the consequences of these personal tragedies should then be projected with such force and vehemence onto the perceived failings of the legal process. Why should law have emerged as such a clear target for FRM members' feelings of disappointment, anger and frustration? As noted above, some men are likely to join FRGs in order to find a range of practical and emotional supports at the time of separation. It seems plausible that the men likely to approach FRGs at such a moment are those who are experiencing the more negative separation experiences and are possibly already in conflict with their former partners regarding issues such as contact and child support. Membership of an FRG allows for discussion with other separated men with similar experiences and there is evidence to suggest that participation is itself likely to provide scope not only for generalising one's emotions but also for locating individual problems as part of broader, structural factors: a situation due, say, not merely to the fault of one's own partner or one's own circumstances but as related, rather, to more generalised issues such as the

---

[58] U Beck and EA Beck Gernsheim, *Individualisation* (London, Sage, 2002). See also J Lewis, *The End of Marriage? Individualism and Intimate Relations* (Cheltenham, Edward Elgar, 2001).
[59] See further Collier, this volume.

changing role of women, the biased nature of legal norms or the discriminatory practices of legal agents and law reform processes.[60]

This brings us on to the third broad factor that underlies the increased profile of the FRM: the shifting nature of the regulation and governance of family practices within certain jurisdictions. In the UK, for example, it has been suggested that, within a broader context of a political refocusing on ideas of citizenship and responsibility,[61] there has been a clear and determined attempt to effect 'social engineering' in the area of the family by changing the very nature of post-divorce family life. The repositioning of fatherhood has been a central element in this process, with ideas of 'good' fatherhood being reconstructed in complex ways in the legal regulation of post-divorce family life.[62] The way in which the divorce process is negotiated and experienced here, however, has been seen as part of the development of a broader 'project of the self' involving a repositioning of ideas of 'good citizenship' and social responsibility. But this process can itself run counter to the psychological realities of separation and divorce for many women and men. Each of the following chapters questions, in different ways, how ideas of child welfare have been understood within the context of the shifting legal regulation of post-divorce family life; and, in particular, how related assumptions about the desirability of contact between fathers and children might be more complex and, at times, problematic than the apparent policy consensus around the desirability of co-parenting would indicate.

We hope that, from what has necessarily been a brief sketch, it is clear that describing the rise of the FRM in terms of a 'backlash' to increased female power is, at best, a caricature which fails to capture the multifaceted, fast changing, complex realities of men's and women's experiences of family breakdown and shifting gender roles. The greater prominence of the FRM might be better understood as one aspect of a complex renegotiation of understandings of men's role as parent in the light of shifting gender relations, household forms, discourses of parenting and childhood, legal norms and modes of governance. All of these factors, it will be seen, can play out in different ways in different contexts, being more or less significant, and interacting with other cultural and legal factors in a complex, dynamic and evolving manner. The simplicity of an understanding rooted in 'backlash' can thus be no substitute for the detailed and grounded analyses of the processes of FRM strategies and law reform contained in the contributions that follow. These chapters reveal the differing strengths and importance of FRGs in national contexts, as well as highlighting how culturally contingent factors can, in turn, influence their popularity, the kinds of strategies and discourses they deploy,

---

[60] See further Crowley, this volume; Flood, above n 6.
[61] See H Reece, *Divorcing Responsibly* (Oxford, Hart, 2003).
[62] See generally Collier, this volume and the literature discussed therein.

their popular appeal and chances of success in achieving legal reform. We move now to outline some of the points of commonality and contradiction to emerge from these chapters.

The FRM: Formal Equality and Beyond - Commonality and Contradiction

It is clear from the contributions to this volume that fathers' rights agendas play out in different ways across jurisdictions.[63] While recognising this diversity it is possible, nonetheless, to detect within the now rich literature[64] that has emerged in this field the presence of some common rhetorical devices being employed by the fathers' rights movement internationally. [65] These include:

— the embrace of the language of formal equality.[66] This is evident in the UK context, for example in the case of Fathers 4 Justice and their depiction of fathers' rights activists as 'suffra*gents*', with a campaign branding using the colour purple;

---

[63] On differences between Canada and Australia see H Rhoades and S Boyd, 'Reforming Custody Laws: A Comparative Study' (2004) 18 *International Journal of Law, Policy and the Family* 119; H Rhoades, 'Posing as Reform? The Case of the Family Law Reform Act' (2000) 14(2) *Australian Journal of Family Law* 142; H Rhoades, R Graycar and M Harrison, *The Family Law Reform Act 1995: The First Three Years* (Sydney, University of Sydney/Family Court of Australia, 2000).

[64] Kaye and Tolmie, above n 25; M Kaye and J Tolmie, 'Discoursing Dads: The Rhetorical Devices of Fathers' Rights Groups' (1998) 22 *Melbourne University Law Review* 162; J Arditti and K Allen, 'Distressed Fathers' Perceptions of Legal and Relational Inequities Post-Divorce' (1993) 31 *Family and Conciliation Courts Review* 461; S Boyd and CF Young, 'Who Influences Family Law Reform? Discourses on Motherhood and Fatherhood in Legislative Reform Debates in Canada' (2002) 26 *Studies in Law, Politics and Society* 43; R Graycar, 'Law Reform by Frozen Chook: Family Law Reform for the New Millennium?' (2000) 24 *Melbourne University Law Review* 737; A Melville and R Hunter, 'As Everybody Knows: Countering Myths of Gender Bias in Family Law' (2001) 1(1) *Griffith Law Review* 124; C Bertoia, 'An Interpretative Analysis of the Mediation Rhetoric of Fathers' Rightists: Privatization versus Personalization' (1998) 16(1) *Mediation Quarterly* 15; S Boyd, 'Demonizing Mothers: Fathers' Rights Discourses in Child Custody Law Reform Processes' (2004) 6(1) *Journal of the Association for Research in Mothering* 52; M Kaye and J Tolmie, '"Lollies at a Children's Party" and Other Myths: Violence, Protection Orders and Fathers' Rights Groups' (1998) 10(1) *Current Issues in Criminal Justice* 52.

[65] See, in addition to the chapters in this volume, Rhoades and Boyd, above n 63; R Collier, 'Fathers 4 Justice, Law and the New Politics of Fatherhood' (2005) 17(4) *Child and Family Law Quarterly* 1; L Neilson, 'Demeaning, Demoralizing and Disenfranchising Divorced Dads: A Review of the Literature' (1999) 31(3/4) *Journal of Divorce and Remarriage* 129.

[66] Kaye and Tolmie, 'Discoursing Dads', above n 64, 164.

— the deployment of, and appeal to, formal legal rights (what Smart and Neale characterise as evoking a self-interested, individualised form of power);[67]
— a claim to victim status,[68] supported by what critics suggest has been a selective use of statistics[69] and a frequent, and undoubtedly emotionally powerful, use of personal anecdotes of men's suffering in the field of family justice (the 'personal tragedies' referred to above);[70]
— a conflation of the interests of fathers and children in such a way that they become, in effect, one and the same thing;[71] and
— a concern to protect or defend the (heterosexual) 'family' from the social ills of father-absence[72] and, in particular, the 'growing problem' of lone mother-hood.[73] Such accounts often rely on a negative depiction of mothers, who appear as, variously, 'alimony drones',[74] 'mendacious and vindictive',[75] 'unruly' and 'irresponsible' figures (the language varying across countries).[76]

Aspects of each of these key discursive themes are visible in the chapters that follow. However, it is becoming clear that the deployment of such rhetoric is itself shifting, contingent and, at times, explicitly strategic.[77] As such, while common themes can be discerned, the kinds of detailed contextual analyses contained in the chapters below are essential if we are to understand the importance of different FRM strategies and rhetorical devices within their specific national contexts as well as at particular historical moments.

Of all the strategies and arguments deployed in the rhetoric of the FRM, the embrace of the language of formal equality has been particularly significant in the resort to law.[78] Equality arguments form a particularly strong theme in the interviews with US FRM members that provide the basis for Crowley's contribution to this volume. They are also present, to varying degrees, in the analysis of every other chapter. Ideas of equality are particularly clear in the FRM's frequent

[67] C Smart and B Neale, '"I Hadn't Really Thought About It": New Identities/New Fatherhoods' in J Seymour and P Bagguley (eds), *Relating Intimacies: Power and Resistance* (Basingstoke, Palgrave Macmillan, 1999).
[68] Kaye and Tolmie, 'Discoursing Dads', above n 64, 172: Boyd and Young, above n 64, 56–57.
[69] Kaye and Tolmie, *ibid*, 177; http://www.fathers-4-justice.org/the_evidence/index.htm.
[70] Kaye and Tolmie, *ibid*, 175; Boyd and Young, above n 64, 59.
[71] Kaye and Tolmie, *ibid*, 178.
[72] R Collier, 'A Hard Time to be a Father?: Law, Policy and Family Practices' (2001) 28 *Journal of Law and Society* 520. Kaye and Tolmie, 'Discoursing Dads', above n 64, 181.
[73] Boyd, 'Demonizing Mothers', above n 64, 55–56. See, for example, the arguments of D Blankenhorn, *Fatherless America: Confronting Our Most Urgent Social Problem* (New York, Basic Books, 1995); N Dennis and G Erdos, *Families Without Fatherhood* (London, Institute of Economic Affairs, 1993).
[74] Kaye and Tolmie, above n 64, 185.
[75] *Ibid*, 186; Boyd and Young, above n 64, 58.
[76] Kaye and Tolmie, 'Discoursing Dads', above n 64, 188; Bertoia and Drakich, above n 8, 603.
[77] See further Rhoades and Boyd, this volume.
[78] Kaye and Tolmie, 'Discoursing Dads', above n 64, 164.

complaints that mothers are unfairly advantaged and fathers are subject to discrimination by the operation of family law systems. They also underpin their deployment of, and appeal to, formal legal rights as a way of redressing existing problems. However, the form of equality sought by the FRM is of a very particular kind. As Crowley, Boyd and Rhoades each note, it is an appeal to a 'rule-based' or formal equality, one which suggests that men and women should be treated exactly the same in judicial consideration of child support and custody/contact awards.[79] As Crowley shows, in its prescriptive extreme, this is seen as meaning that each man and each woman should shoulder exactly half of child support and caring responsibilities. Importantly, contributors to this volume suggest, what tends to be systematically effaced in such an argument are questions about the *consequences* of applying gender neutral norms to what remain, for all the arguments to the contrary advanced by the FRM, highly gendered fields of practice.

It is possible, of course, that the FRM's demand for equality should not be heard merely, or perhaps even primarily, in terms of such calls for practical change. In her chapter, Rhoades notes that the FRM submissions during the committee hearings she studied in Australia suggested that equal parenting was in many respects more of an important *symbolic* issue than a description of how children would actually be parented. The failure to accord fathers equal contact time with their children might thus be perceived to be not so much a practical problem as a psychological injury relating to men's sense of their worth as fathers; a perception of being accorded secondary importance to their children's mothers. A frequent trope in the rhetoric of the FRM is the powerful description of individual fathers' pain at being allowed to see their children only at formally sanctioned, narrowly prescribed times, while mothers as resident parents maintain seemingly unlimited access to them.[80] Even for those men who had spent little time with their children in the context of pre-separation 'intact' family life, that an external body should determine when (and sometimes even where) contact should occur may be experienced as an intolerable breaking of the bond between father and child[81]—as Collier suggests, in some sense emblematic of the violence of law itself. Yet there may also be significant problems inherent in attempting to maintain men's relationships with their children after separation, when prior to separation these relationships were often mediated through the children's mother in very significant ways.[82] This is a point that resonates across each of the jurisdictions

[79] Crowley, this volume, citing M Fineman, *The Illusion of Equality: The Rhetoric and Reality of Divorce Reform* (Chicago, University of Chicago Press, 1991).

[80] Note, for example, Bob Geldof's argument in 'The Real Love that Dare Not Speak its Name' in A Bainham, B Lindley, M Richards and L Trinder (eds), *Children and Their Families* (Oxford, Hart, 2003).

[81] *Ibid.* Oliver Phillips made this point eloquently in his remarks at the workshop that gave rise to this collection of papers. Rhoades (this volume) makes the point that this demand is for a 'rightful place' in one's children's lives, rather than requiring men to go 'cap in hand' to request time with them.

[82] Smart and Neale, above n 34.

discussed in this volume. To talk of equality in parenting in such a complex context does not begin to address the nuances of parenting practice.

What becomes apparent regarding all of the countries studied here is that there can be an important disjuncture between the equality *rhetoric* advanced by the FRM and the continuing (gendered) *realities* of parenting, both during subsisting relationships and after divorce/separation. In intact relationships, inequalities in the division of labour and parenting time may appear ambiguous and obscure, sometimes due to the active collusion of parents keen to maintain a belief in gender equality in parenting in their own family.[83] Yet the nature of judicial resolution is to set out clearly and precisely defined rights and obligations. Out of the messy and ambiguous reality of family life, law is asked to crystallise formal rules setting out residence, clearly defined contact hours and so on. It should come as no surprise if these then serve as a particularly clear target for the pain and frustration of separated fathers.

What of the FRM expectations of law itself? The limits of law in the regulation and management of intimate relationships have been well documented. In facing the 'normal chaos' of family life,[84] it has been suggested, law inevitably simplifies in order to understand and process, dealing 'in generalities ... ill-equipped to take full account of the complexities of human behaviour'.[85] Contact and residence disputes and conflicts over child support liability can be seen as normal and inevitable features of what happens when law attempts to regulate human relationships. As such, the more interesting question may be why the FRM should then 'yearn' for law.[86] Why has law assumed such a central place in their activities? This issue has at least two dimensions, which combine to result in a complex and at times contradictory relationship to law reform more generally.

First, as has already been seen, the FRM tends to see family law processes and norms as profoundly implicated in the disadvantaging of fathers. Family law is seen as 'stacked against' fathers, corrupted by legal norms which give unfair weight to mothers' interests. Further, legal norms are interpreted and applied by court personnel who are perceived as profoundly antagonistic towards fathers.[87]

---

[83] See K Backett, 'The Negotiation of Fatherhood' in C Lewis and M O'Brien (eds), *Reassessing Fatherhood: New Observations on Fathers and the Modern Family* (London, Sage, 1987) 71–90. Backett found that parents profess a belief in the equality of contemporary parental roles and develop coping mechanisms to avoid confronting the obvious mismatch between these beliefs and their own practice of child care, which remains heavily gendered. She suggests that how couples construct and sustain belief in the 'involved' father suggests, paradoxically, that this is an important factor in the maintenance of inequalities within the family group.

[84] U Beck and E Beck Gernsheim, *The Normal Chaos of Love* (Cambridge, Polity, 1995); J Dewar, above n 55.

[85] F Kaganas and SD Sclater, 'Contact Disputes: Narrative Constructions of "Good Parents"' (2004) 12(1) *Feminist Legal Studies* 1; see also SD Sclater and F Kaganas, 'Contact: Mothers, Welfare and Rights' in Bainham *et al*, above n 80.

[86] The idea of 'yearning' for law belongs to Rhoades: see this volume.

[87] See Geldof, above n 80.

Men are, in some accounts, victims of a wider 'feminisation' of government and legal institutions, including Parliament, the judiciary and the various professions that work in the courts, not least lawyers, social workers, child welfare officers and court appointed experts. As such, it is perhaps inevitable that law should emerge as a target for the FRM's frustrations and as a symbolic focus for some of their higher profile campaigns.[88]

However, secondly—and intriguingly in the light of the above—the FRM also frequently appears to place considerable faith in the ability of legal reform to solve the problems faced by their members. In this regard the FRM may appear to have succumbed to what Smart has described in an earlier, rather different context as the 'siren call of law'.[89] Here, Smart warns against the possibility that 'in worsening conditions we make the mistake of assuming that we need to apply more doses of legislation'.[90] Of course Smart's analysis, which relies in part on the problems for feminists in making use of legal norms and concepts developed in an androcentric legal order, cannot be applied in any straightforward way to the role of law in the activities of the FRM. But a clear parallel does exist in the seductive nature of law for both movements.[91]

This links to a further theme in this volume: the significance of these other social movements to the work of the FRM. As Crowley notes, earlier movements are often explicitly used for guidance: as a basis for making moral arguments based on equality claims, as a starting point for devising concrete, tactical strategies for change and as a source of motivation.[92] That FRGs have positioned themselves in a number of complex ways in relation to earlier social movements such as feminism is evident in all of the national examples discussed in this volume. How is one to make sense of this? In an early Australian study, Kaye and Tolmie tracked the parallels between FRM strategies and early legal feminist work, suggesting that such comparisons can only be taken so far.[93] Building on Naffine's taxonomy of 'waves' of feminism,[94] they argue that a problem faced by the FRM in the 1990s was an inability to progress beyond a parallel with liberal feminism in their commitment to formal (legal) equality: to progress beyond this would involve, they suggest, acknowledging that the politics of formal equality are

[88] This is perhaps most marked in the UK context: see Collier, this volume.
[89] Carol Smart, *Feminism and the Power of Law* (London, Routledge, 1989) 160.
[90] *Ibid*, 161.
[91] For example, in the language of simultaneously 'loving' and 'loathing' law used by Collier, this volume.
[92] These various aspects of the role of earlier social movements in the FRM's work are identified by Crowley, this volume.
[93] 'Discoursing Dads', above n 64, 168.
[94] For Naffine, the 'first phase' of feminism was characterised by seeing law as a male monopoly, peopled by men and therefore biased in their favour; the second phase involved attacking the male culture of law with its inherent masculine bias; and the third phase concentrated on legal rhetoric and patriarchal social order, challenging those concepts which the law invokes to defend itself: N Naffine, *Law and the Sexes* (Sydney, Allen and Unwin, 1990).

themselves unsatisfactory. Addressing such an issue would then mean coming to terms with the broader parameters of women's social and economic inequality. As has been seen above, and in line with these authors' prediction, almost ten years on from this intervention much of the FRM still appears to remain firmly enmeshed within a discourse of formal equality.

Interlinked to the above, however, it is important to recognise how during this period a significant strand of the FRM has also increasingly repositioned itself as a broadly progressive social force. Like feminist, anti-racist and lesbian, gay, bisexual and transgender (LGBT) groups before them, the FRM claims to be in favour of 'equality for all'. This begs the question, however, of the nature of the relationship between the FRM and those 'other' progressive social groups. Can the FRM fall under the umbrella of a progressive social movement? If not, why not? Does a core constituency made up of what a feminist and pro-feminist masculinity politics might well describe as an already privileged, empowered social group preclude any such positioning? Perhaps this question is itself misleading, revealing the unsustainability of thinking about such groups in terms of their being uniformly 'progressive', 'reactionary', or otherwise somehow sharing interests which can be straightforwardly politically aligned. Anti-racist groups, for example, may hold profoundly patriarchal, heteronormative views; feminist or LGBT groups may themselves be blind to racial or class inequalities, and in some instances even reinforce them. However, we would suggest that the FRM's positioning of itself as a progressive social force does raise some difficult questions for feminists. We move onto these below, before offering some concluding thoughts.

THE FRM AND LAW REFORM: QUESTIONS FOR FEMINISM?

The activities of the FRM undoubtedly excite strong emotions. This has been particularly true for feminist audiences who have abhorred the anti-mother and explicitly misogynistic strand evident in some FRM interventions. Yet we would suggest the contemporary FRM does raise a number of difficult and, at times, uncomfortable questions for feminist audiences, questions that merit further consideration of the kind advanced in this volume.

Firstly, feminist commentators have produced an extensive and compelling literature on how burdens of childcare have historically impacted disproportionately on women, with men far better positioned to opt in and out of them.[95] This

---

[95] For a taste of a huge literature, see S Boyd, *Child Custody, Law and Women's Work* (Oxford, Oxford University Press, 2003); M Fineman, *The Neutered Mother, the Sexual Family and other Twentieth Century Tragedies* (New York and London, Routledge, 1995); K Czapanskiy, 'Volunteers and Draftees: The Struggle for Parental Equality' (1991) 38 *UCLA Law Review* 415.

work has challenged the interrelated processes of the privatisation of caring and a devaluing of mothers and of motherhood. Yet this leaves open to question the extent to which this dimension of parenthood is understood or experienced by individuals as a burden or a privilege, a pleasure or a constraint; or, indeed, as both simultaneously (for social experience is, of course, rarely clear cut and without contradiction). Thinking about the pleasures of parenthood raises the question of whether there is a relationship with, or even a 'power over', children that some women may not be prepared to share with men.

Some commentators have suggested that one of the main blocks to men's greater involvement in parenting is the gender expectations of *both* parents, as well as those of the wider peer groups and networks in which they live, with some women not always willing to cede the centrality of their role as mothers in order to accommodate more involved fathers.[96] Is there any grain of truth in the suggestion made by one UK commentator that certain women may in fact not wish their male partner to look after children 'except as souped-up au pairs'?[97] In other words, how do women exercise power through and over children? And how does this relate to the nature of motherhood as one of the few positions of (relative) power that women possess?[98] Finally, what is gained, and what is lost, as such relationships develop and change over time? And how, if at all, has all this shifted in the changing political, economic and demographic contexts described above?

Secondly, it is unclear how feminists should respond to certain strands of the FRM discourse: for example the frequent criticism of some women's abilities as mothers. While it can be asserted that mothers generally make valiant efforts in difficult circumstances, the claim that 'all mothers are good mothers' would inevitably be doomed to empirical failure. Feminists have successfully drawn attention to the numerous problems with the representation of women in contact disputes, family law and in society more generally. In the former context the figure of the 'implacably hostile' mother who resists contact between her children and their father has been shown to be particularly resonant, influential and problematic.[99] While a feminist position must inevitably be alive to the danger that women will be more readily vilified for bad parenting precisely because of higher social expectations of mothers, what basis is there for a feminist analysis that concedes that some women might well act badly in some contexts?[100] What scope is

---

[96] See J Torr, *Is There a Father in the House: A Handbook for Health and Social Care Professionals* (Oxford, Radcliffe Medical Press, 2003) 35.

[97] *Sunday Times,* 1999, cited in Torr, *ibid,* 36.

[98] Custody/residence disputes provide a particularly clear example of the partial nature of this power; see eg Boyd, *Child Custody,* above n 95.

[99] This issue is discussed in detail in this volume.

[100] Didi Herman raised this issue at the workshop that preceded this volume. See further M Ashe, 'Postmodernism, Legal Ethics, and Representation of "Bad Mothers"' in M Fineman and I Karpin, *Mothers in Law: Feminist Theory and the Legal Regulation of Motherhood* (New York, Columbia University Press, 1995).

there for admitting that some women may actually be bad caregivers? And to recognise the significance of complex personal histories in a context where mothers generally are under attack and an ethic of care has itself been marginalised? Moreover, is a clear *feminist* position on the politics of contact, mediation and residence really achievable? Is it possible to separate out 'women's interests' in this context in any clear or meaningful way?[101] It is important to remember that, in many cases, women are involved on all sides in family law disputes: as mothers, as the female children of those fathers fighting for contact, and as those men's own mothers and new partners who, at times, become actively involved in the FRM themselves.[102] One feminist response may be the promotion of a politics of equality that is more nuanced and rounded than that advanced by the FRM; to offer an account which allows for the complexity of women's agency whilst contextualising such an agency within broader patterns of economic and social factors which put particular pressures on both women and men.[103] This volume might serve as one step towards developing such an agenda.

Thirdly, the relative success (or lack thereof) of the FRM also raises a range of interesting and difficult questions regarding the relationship between data, policy and interest groups at a governmental level that are particularly pressing for feminists. In an age where increasing quantities of data are ever more readily available, paradoxically, the very extent of information available may make it increasingly difficult for that data to be used in certain ways.[104] The use of 'focus groups' and 'think tanks', for example, has assumed greater importance in each of the countries discussed in this volume, and the importance of simplicity and the 'sound bite' in getting ideas heard may be more important than the more traditional academic forms of analysis presented by a book such as this.[105] Much of the 'noisy chatter' of the public debate in this area has been pitched at this level of sound bite, often making it more difficult to hear the voices of those describing the complexity of the issues involved. But feminist responses to the political interventions of the FRM also raise questions about what forms of knowledge are then seen as legitimate in reform debates—and of what happens in law to those forms of knowledge and experience which are seen as illegitimate. Feminist commentators have attacked parliamentarians' reliance on anecdote and impression, at the

---

[101] Carol Smart raised this issue at the workshop that preceded this volume.

[102] At the recent implosion of the UK group, Fathers 4 Justice, it was revealed that two women were running the group at the time. Women are also leading members and a 'public face' of the splinter group the 'Real Fathers 4 Justice': *The 5Live Report*, Julian Worricker Programme, 26 March 2006, BBC Radio 5 Live (http://www.bbc.co.uk/fivelive/programmes/worricker.shtml).

[103] For example, the processes of privatisation within neo-liberal states have themselves positioned men as assuming responsibility for the costs of childhood and ex-spouses, an issue which has put particular pressures on groups of men already disadvantaged in terms of class. We are grateful to Susan Boyd for this point.

[104] Anne Bottomley made this point at the workshop which preceded this volume.

[105] R Graycar, above n 64.

expense of careful analysis of empirical data and research.[106] Thus, for example, Kaye and Tolmie note:

> Such stories also have power because they arouse an emotional response in the reader. They speak in the moving language of loss and graphically describe situations where men have suffered genuine feelings of hurt. Their telling gives an air of authenticity to the points they illustrate. Dramatic currency is also derived from the fact that these "horror stories" do not present the *normal* case. Instead they represent the extraordinary or extreme in order to demonstrate the extent of the harm which can be caused by the family law system.[107]

Yet how does this fit with feminist assertions of the need to listen to the experiences of individual 'real' women and a critique of law for being impervious to such knowledge?[108] To what extent, and on what basis, can feminists attack the arguments of the FRM as 'anti-scientific' or unrepresentative? What is the status of such a critique and what implications does it have for feminist critiques of non-experiential knowledge in other contexts? In her chapter, Rhoades describes the problem of politicians unfamiliar with the family law system being seduced by FRM arguments that made 'intuitive sense' to them. A key issue here is the question of whose experience is likely to be heard in certain law-making contexts that, despite the protests of the FRM, continue to remain dominated by men in many respects.[109] Yet is this the case for all such contexts and for all debates relating to aspects of law reform?

Fourthly, while feminists have become alive to the dangers of essentialism in thinking about women, has this pitfall sometimes been less obvious with regard to thinking about men?[110] How, for example, can the diversity of men's lives and complex individual biographies be accommodated into accounts of men's power?[111] And do such common interests really exist across other axes of power and discrimination, such as race, class and sexuality?

One final and particularly striking aspect of the FRM's literature for feminist scholarship and politics is the perception of the power that is held by women (and specifically by feminists) who are sometimes believed to have 'colonised' important decision-making forums. Given that feminists' own sense of their position in society has historically been one of exclusion and discrimination, the temptation

---

[106] *Ibid*.

[107] Kaye and Tolmie, 'Discoursing Dads', above n 64, 176 (references omitted, emphasis in original).

[108] Didi Herman made this point at the workshop which preceded this volume.

[109] On the way in which different voices will get heard in different forums, see in particular Boyd and Rhoades, this volume; Boyd, above n 95, demonstrating the greater success of the FRM in forums which do not place heavy reliance on empirical data to support arguments.

[110] See E Spelman *Inessential Woman* (Boston, Beacon Press, 1990) for a taste of the substantial feminist literature on this issue.

[111] See further R Collier, 'Reflections on the Relationship Between Law and Masculinities: Rethinking the "Man Question"' (2003) 56 *Current Legal Problems* 345.

may be to dismiss such impressions out of hand. But a more productive response might be to ask two further questions: firstly, have feminists underestimated their own power, influence and impact to date, focusing too much on failures and not enough on successes?[112] In other words, is there in fact any basis for the FRM's impressions? And secondly, if not, should the FRM's reading of feminist success be taken as a mirror in which to examine feminists' own reading of the power of the FRM? In other words, the FRM's analysis might suggest that feminists may also have attributed too much importance to the FRM, perceiving them as enjoying much more power and influence than is really the case. If one lesson of this volume is that the FRM has had, in certain respects, very little direct impact in actually achieving concrete reforms, are feminist and liberal commentators overstating its influence?

CONCLUDING REMARKS

The general picture that emerges from the chapters below is of an often publicly visible FRM with an increasingly high media profile in many countries. Yet it would appear that the FRM's success in influencing government policy or legal reform has been muted.[113] Numerous national examples exist of legal and policy reforms that have been informed, rather, by the insights of research that has directly countered key points advanced by FRGs.[114] This can be illustrated by two of the examples referred to above: the rejection of the idea of a presumption of shared residence or custody as practically unworkable;[115] and the refutation of the assertion that any but a small minority of men are, in fact, equal carers.[116] Far-reaching concerns have been voiced about the consequences for women of the enforcement of court orders

---

[112] See S Lawrence, 'Feminism, Consequences, Accountability' (2004) 42(4) *Osgoode Hall Law Journal* 583. This raises the question, of course, of whether some women may have benefited more from feminism than others: issues of race and class, as well as broader perceptions of 'feminism' mediate impressions of any such 'success'.

[113] Although see Rhoades, this volume. This is not to deny that some key figures within the FRM and men's movement have sometimes been appointed to positions of political influence.

[114] For example, C Smart, V May, A Wade and C Furniss, *Residence and Contact Disputes in Court: Research Report 6/2003* (London, Department for Constitutional Affairs, 2003), a study of disputes over residence and contact brought to three County Courts in England in the year 2000, cited by Margaret Hodge, *Hansard*, HC Deb col 67W (5 January 2004); M Maclean, 'The Contribution of the International Research Community to UK Law Reform re Child Contact', paper presented at the Annual Meeting of the Research Committee of the Sociology of Law, ISA, Paris, 11–13 June 2005; Collier, this volume.

[115] See Boyd, Rhoades, Collier, this volume.

[116] Contrast C Grbich, 'Male Primary Caregivers and Domestic Labour: Involvement or Avoidance?' (1995) 1(2) *Journal of Family Studies* 114; and J Brannen, G Meszaros, P Moss and G Poland, *Employment and Family Life: A Review of Research in the UK (1980–1994)*, Department of Employment Research Series No 4 (University of London, 1994).

of the kind sought by FRMs and, certainly in Canada, Australia and the UK, some success has been experienced in making these objections heard.

The FRM does appear, however, to have influenced the broader culture in which decisions are made and policy is formulated. In her contribution to this volume, for example, Rhoades describes the power that fathers' rights activists can wield behind the scenes and how this may influence the direction of policy. Boyd attributes the increase in the number of joint custody awards made in Canadian courts to the fact that the general thrust of FRM arguments are having an impact on the perceptions of the public, mediators, lawyers, and judges. Likewise, Eriksson and Pringle note the FRM's successful 'meaning work' in framing fathers' rights and interests as concerned with gender equality, parental co-operation and children's interests. Their discussion of developments in Sweden provides a particularly clear example of the ways in which the FRM can have an impact in the context of debates on wide-ranging social issues. Intriguingly, as their analysis shows, the national example considered here which might be seen to have come closest to achieving the status quo desired by the international FRM is one that has been characterised by least activity on its part. Sweden is characterised by a culture of strong paternal rights to custody and care and only weak obligations in terms of economic responsibilities for child support and alimony.[117] As Eriksson and Pringle note, joint custody is ordered against the wishes of one parent in almost half of cases where there are some indications of a history of violence (generally the father against the mother) and in almost two-fifths even of those cases where the father has a criminal conviction for such violence.

This raises two more general points regarding the nature of the interaction of social movements with the law. Firstly, to succeed in being heard in policy and law-making forums is only a small part of the battle. As noted above, any social movement will find its arguments reformulated and reconstructed within the legislative processes of the political system with which it seeks to engage. Law-making forums—both judicial and parliamentary—involve complex processes of negotiation and a balancing of demands. The claims of one group will be weighed against other interests and remoulded in relation to them. The particularities of the legal process are thus profoundly important in reshaping claims in terms of its own norms and rationalities. An example of this is provided by Boyd, in this volume: the fact that the Canadian FRM's demands for the reform of child support law were not taken very seriously, she suggests, was due at least in part to the coincidence of these reforms with a neo-liberal agenda to privatise economic responsibility within the nuclear family. More generally, the family law system is faced with the task of creating legal order from 'social noise',[118] inevitably understanding

---

[117] Compare the approach of Hobson, above n 4.

[118] G Teubner, 'How the Law Thinks: Toward a Constructivist Epistemology of Law' (1989) 23 *Law & Society Review* 727; M King and C Piper, *How the Law Thinks About Children* (2nd edn, Aldershot, Arena, 1995).

claims and arguments with reference to the (legal) norms, forms and concepts already available to it. As Boyd's analysis suggests, even in receptive forums, these other processes will always mediate the impact of FRMs' interventions.

To conclude: there is considerable evidence in the chapters that follow to suggest that the fathers' rights movement is, across jurisdictions, shaping and influencing the broader cultural context in which debates about family law are taking place; that they have, in particular, created a pressure to reform the system.[119] However, as was noted above, there is less to suggest any significant measure of success in effecting the legal reforms desired or intended. A closer analysis of the limited successes of the FRM to date requires detailed, concrete analysis within specific national contexts and this is the role of the chapters that follow. Above all, what emerges from this volume is the necessity of recognising the complexity and contradictory nature of the reconfiguration of gender relations framing the present debate about fathers' rights and law. This implies engaging with wider processes of social change involving (amongst other things) shifts in the structure and experience of employment, a reappraisal of issues of identity, commitment and responsibility, and a rethinking of the relationship between men and children.

---

[119] See further chapters in this volume, particularly Boyd, Rhoades; B Neale, J Flowerdew and C Smart, 'Drifting Towards Shared Residence?' [2003] *Family Law* 904: F Gibb, 'Fathers Winning Battle to have Custody Hearing in Public' *The Times*, 10 January 2005.

2

'Robbed of their Families'? Fathers' Rights Discourses in Canadian Parenting Law Reform Processes*

SUSAN B BOYD

Like many western countries in the late 20th century, Canada witnessed a fathers' rights movement that made the legal system a particular target. Since 1985, the Canadian Divorce Act has contained a maximum contact and friendly parent principle in its custody and access provisions, in a statute that does not otherwise outline the content of the best interests of the child principle.[1] This provision resulted from early fathers' rights advocacy in Canada in combination with well-intentioned gestures towards parental equality.[2] It has been criticised for its prioritising of contact over factors such as safety, and for its unintended effect of discouraging mothers from disclosing the existence of family violence.[3] Enhancing paternal contact has represented a clear trend in Canadian courts, sometimes reflecting consensual arrangements, but sometimes in circumstances that endanger mothers and children. Joint custody awards have increased steadily since the late 1980s, diminishing sole custody awards to both mothers and fathers. In 2002, joint custody constituted almost 42 per cent of custody awards in divorce proceedings, although the extent of shared physical custody is much

* The phrase' 'Robbed of their families' is taken from a statement to the Special Joint Committee on Custody and Access by Roger Woloshyn, President of Men's Equalization Inc, 1 May 1998. This research was supported by a grant from the Social Sciences and Humanities Research Council of Canada. Thanks to Cindy Baldassi, Karey Brooks and Rachel McVean for research assistance.

[1] Section 16(10) of the Divorce Act, RSC 1985 (2nd Supp), c 3, directs judges to 'give effect to the principle that a child of the marriage should have as much contact with each spouse as is consistent with the best interests of the child and, for that purpose, [to] take into consideration the willingness of the person for whom custody is sought to facilitate such contact'.

[2] SB Boyd and CFL Young, 'Who Influences Family Law Reform? Discourses on Motherhood and Fatherhood in Legislative Reform Debates in Canada' (2002) 26 *Studies in Law, Politics & Society* 43.

[3] See, for example, J Cohen and N Gershbain, 'For the Sake of the Fathers? Child Custody Reform and the Perils of Maximum Contact' (2001) 19 *Canadian Family Law Quarterly* 121; SB Boyd, *Child Custody, Law, and Women's Work* (Oxford, Oxford University Press, 2003) ch 6.

less.[4] Moreover, law reform that further encourages shared parenting seems inevitable.

From the mid-1990s, a contentious law reform process related to post-separation parenting unfolded in Canada, during which the fathers' rights lobby had a particularly high profile. This chapter investigates the lobby's discursive strategies and its impact. It will be argued that fathers' rights advocates succeeded to a significant degree in generating the notions that mothers are favoured in family law, feminists have gained excessive control of the law reform agenda, and the government must redress this bias. However, fathers' rightists did not entirely capture Parliament's family law agenda and the influences on post-separation parenting law reform were more complex than the term 'gender wars'[5] suggests. As with many struggles over legal change in the past decade, the larger context of neo-liberalism, economic restructuring, and privatisation of responsibilities must be taken into account. This chapter's case study of fathers' rights activism in Canada offers a window onto broader trends at work in western industrialised societies and shows the complex, and often contradictory, consequences of law reform initiatives in a neo-liberal era.

Reacting to Fathers' Rights Advocacy: The Special Joint Committee (SJC)

Although the most recent wave of custody law reform has been on the federal government agenda since the early 1990s—a time when the fathers' rights movement was quiet in Canada—it has been reviewed in a particularly high profile manner since 1996. At that time, fathers' rights advocates and supporters in the Canadian Senate successfully blocked child support law reforms until the federal government agreed to review custody and access law and created the Special Joint Senate and House of Commons Committee on Custody and Access (1998). The link between money and children—that is, between the state-sponsored demand that non-custodial parents (mostly fathers) live up to their child support responsibilities and the demand by fathers for more rights in relation to their children—was patent.

The agenda for the Special Joint Committee (SJC) public consultations during 1998 was largely set by conservative fathers' rights discourse and the hearings were dominated by Committee members sensitive to the concerns of fathers and often

---

[4] Statistics Canada, *The Daily*, 4 May 2004. Custody of 49.5% of dependants was awarded to the wife, 8.5% to the husband. Joint custody diminishes when arrangements reached outside divorce are taken into account: *When Parents Separate: Further Findings from the National Longitudinal Survey of Children and Youth* (Department of Justice Canada, 2004-FC4-6E).

[5] N Bala, 'A Report from Canada's "Gender War Zone": Reforming the Child Related Provision in the Divorce Act' (1999) 16 *Canadian Journal of Family Law* 163.

hostile to female witnesses.[6] One Senator was overtly sympathetic to fathers' rights witnesses, who were often given more time to speak. Female witnesses—including those speaking on behalf of abused mothers—were sometimes heckled by men in the audience and were asked more challenging questions by committee members. The Senator often countered testimony of women's groups on the relationship between woman abuse and custody disputes by citing work suggesting that women too are violent and that domestic violence is reciprocal between women and men.[7] The media seemed broadly sympathetic to fathers' rights arguments.[8] Despite active and thoughtful engagement in the law reform process by women's groups—which emphasised mothers' caregiving responsibilities and the relevance of abuse of women and children to custody decision-making—the Committee focused on gender bias against fathers.

In their submissions, fathers' rights advocates aligned fathers' rights with children's best interests. They asserted a crucial need for the 'children of divorce' to have contact with fathers in order to ensure their psychological well-being, even though 'children of divorce' is increasingly contested as a category[9] and studies indicate that continuing contact with each parent is only one factor associated with positive outcomes in children.[10] Other key factors such as a close, sensitive relationship with a well-functioning parent and avoidance of parental conflict can compete with continuing contact in individual fact situations, particularly those involving high conflict or spousal abuse.

The discourse in child custody debates is, however, often based not on evidence in studies, but on rhetoric. It is therefore important to look at the typical arguments made by fathers' rights advocates during the reform process and examine their impact on its outcomes. Others have pointed out the many problems with fathers' rights rhetoric,[11] including its lack of correspondence with social realities.

---

[6] Boyd, above n 3; B Diamond, 'The Special Joint Committee on Custody and Access: A Threat to Women's Equality Rights' (1999) 19 *Canadian Woman Studies* 182; M Laing, 'For the Sake of the Children: Preventing Reckless New Laws' (1999) 16 *Canadian Journal of Family Law* 229.

[7] For example, Senator A Cools, questioning Carole Curtis, a witness appearing for the National Association of Women and the Law: SJC, 8 (16 March 1998), 1735. The transcripts of the hearings of the Special Joint Committee on Custody and Access are available at http://www.parl.gc.ca/common/committee.asp?Language=E&Ses=1&parl=36 (accessed 24 November 2005).

[8] See especially C Cobbs of the *Ottawa Citizen*, eg 'The Custody Fight on the Hill', 12 October 1998, A3; 'A Bill of Rights for Divorced Parents', 9 December 1998, A1.

[9] C Smart, 'Introduction: New Perspectives on Childhood and Divorce' (2003) 10(2) *Childhood* 123.

[10] MJ Bailey and M Giroux, *Relocation of Custodial Parents: Final Report* (Ottawa, Status of Women Canada, 1998) 43.

[11] SB Boyd, 'Backlash and the Construction of Legal Knowledge: The Case of Child Custody Law' (2001) 20 *Windsor Yearbook of Access to Justice* 141; C Bertoia and J Drakich, 'The Fathers' Rights Movement: Contradictions in Rhetoric and Practice' (1993) 14(4) *Journal of Family Issues* 592; M Kaye and J Tolmie, 'Discoursing Dads: The Rhetorical Devices of Fathers' Rights Groups' (1998) 22(1) *Melbourne University Law Review* 162; M Kaye and J Tolmie, 'Fathers Rights Groups in Australia and their Engagement with Issues in Family Law' (1998) 12(1) *Australian Journal of Family Law* 19.

This chapter focuses instead on identifying the rhetoric that pervaded the law reform process and the extent of its influence.

Fathers' Rights Discourse at the Special Joint Committee (1998)

Fathers' rights discourse varies in Canada, as elsewhere,[12] but little systematic research on the movement exists, other than studies of Ontario groups in the early 1990s.[13] These studies found that members of Ontario groups (which often include a few women) are a mix of professionals, white-collar workers, and blue-collar workers. Websites reveal that some groups are more clearly aligned with the men's movement whereas others such as Equal Parents of Canada purport to be focused on family justice issues faced by both men and women. However, these latter groups focus mainly on stories about the problems experienced by men. This chapter's data is drawn from one moment in time and one discursive site, the 1998 Special Joint Committee hearings. Some fathers' rights groups that appeared before that Committee appear not to exist now or do not have a web presence. As a result, this study provides a snapshot of the arguments of the groups that appeared publicly in 1998 rather than a comprehensive review of the movement.

At least 50 fathers' rights advocates appeared before the SJC, including groups and individual witnesses. Not all were men; indeed, fathers' rights positions were frequently presented by women, notably those involved in Stepfamilies of Canada, Second Spouses of Canada, Fathers Are Capable Too (FACT), New Vocal Man, Equitable Child Maintenance and Access Society, National Shared Parenting Association, and Parents Helping Parents. In a few cases, women's groups such as the right wing REAL (Real, Equal, Active, for Life) Women of Canada presented pro-family arguments similar to fathers' rights positions. Despite the differences in the fathers' rights lobby, with some focusing more on maintenance or educational support while others focused more on parental rights, overall its discourse at the SJC was socially conservative, anti-feminist, and formalistic in its approach to equality. It also reflected a negative assessment of mothering and a failure to take account of the social realities of parenting in both intact and post-divorce

---

[12] Some fathers' organisations are more progressive than others. M Flood cites Dads and Daughters in the USA and FathersDirect in the UK: 'Backlash: Angry men's movements' in SE Rossi (ed), *The Battle and Backlash Rage On: Why Feminism Cannot be Obsolete* (Philadelphia, Xlibris Press, 2004) 264. I have found little evidence of progressive fathers' groups in Canada, except Montreal Men Against Sexism, but some groups are definitely more conservative and/or anti-feminist than others.

[13] Bertoia and Drakich, above n 11; Robert A Kennedy, *Fathers For Justice: The Rise of a New Social Movement in Canada as a Case Study of Collective Identity Formation* (Ann Arbor, Caravan Books, 2004).

families. Eight themes emerge generally from fathers' rights presentations to the SJC hearings on custody and access in 1998, though not all themes appeared in all presentations.[14]

Promoting Traditional Families

Most fathers' rightists adopt a traditionalist 'pro-family' stance associated with social conservativism. The ability of single—or separated or divorced—mothers to obtain child support and raise children independently of fathers/husbands appears to threaten the ideological code of the traditional family as well as of heterosexuality.[15] Canadian fathers' rights advocates at the SJC generally promoted a traditional heterosexual form of family, asserting it as a remedy for the ills they identified and rarely discussing alternative family forms in any positive manner: 'All children have two parents, not one, not three, but two,' stated the President of Entraide pères-enfants séparés de l'Outaouais.[16] Some groups raised a passionate critique of liberalised divorce laws.[17] One suggested that introducing a joint custody norm might assist in deterring divorce because women would fear losing full care of their children.[18]

If parents must separate, fathers' rights discourse places pressure on mothers to do everything possible to recreate the family unit that has been split asunder, in the name of the best interests of children.[19] REAL Women referred explicitly to family being 'the traditional mother, father and children' regardless of whether separation or divorce had occurred.[20] The most recent catchword for this reconstituted post-divorce family form is 'shared parenting', a term that has to some extent displaced 'joint custody' in Canadian fathers' rights discourse.

The family unit that these advocates have in mind is not typically a progressive image of a symmetrical family in which fathers share childcare responsibilities with mothers. Fathers' rights rhetoric tends to obscure, and therefore reinforce the social reality of, mothers' actual caregiving responsibilities and the typically more secondary role fathers play in relation to childcare. The motto of the National Alliance for the Advance of Non-Custodial Parents is 'kids need both parents'.[21] Since the

---

[14] I analysed 34 presentations, focusing mainly on groups. Quotations are from the transcripts of the Special Joint Committee, above n 7.

[15] J Stacey, 'Dada-ism in the 1990s: Getting Past Baby Talk About Fatherlessness' in CR Daniels (ed), *Lost Fathers: The Politics of Fatherlessness in America* (New York, St Martin's Press, 1998) 55–56.

[16] 3 June 1998.

[17] Eg Alberta Federation of Women United for Families, 29 April 1998.

[18] Equitable Child Maintenance and Access Society (Edmonton), 29 April 1998.

[19] Modern child custody law may do the same: DM Bourque, '"Reconstructing" the Patriarchal Nuclear Family: Recent Developments in Child Custody and Access in Canada' (1995) 10(1) *Canadian Journal of Law and Society* 1.

[20] 1 April 1998.

[21] 3 June 1998.

parents no longer reside together, the essence of most fathers' rights arguments is that mothers should continue to do the work of primary parenting and fathers should continue to have control over the form that maternal parenting takes.[22]

The Ills of Father Absence and of Single Mothering

The second theme was the terrible consequences of father absence. Drawing often on American sources, fathers' rights advocates suggested that children suffer from paternal absence, which leads to criminality, amongst many other social ills.[23] The need for (hetero)sexual role models for children was also cited:

> [S]tatistical information backs up the high cost of fatherlessness or father absence. For girls, never feeling worthy of love from a man, it's teenage pregnancies ... For boys, it's not knowing how to be a man or how to interact with women. Often violence masks their anger in their father's absence.[24]

The corollary to the notion that children suffer from lack of contact with their fathers is that children suffer problems arising from living in single parent families, including growing up and remaining in poverty, developmental and behavioural problems, emotional difficulties, learning difficulties, delinquency, aggression, and early child-bearing: 'In the end, they will end up involved with drugs, alcohol, violence, crime and, above all, suicide.'[25] It was clear that the 'single parent' being vilified is the single mother:

> The term 'single-parent family' is used to designate the family unit consisting of the custodial parent and the children. The term 'single-parent' means that the child has only one parent. Custody of the children is granted on the basis of the parent's gender. The mother need only refuse to accept shared custody in order to immediately obtain sole custody.[26]

Taking a more extreme position, Glen Cheriton of FatherCraft Canada elaborated on the burden that single mothers impose on taxpayers, suggesting that single-father headed families were far more efficient:

> Partly it is that [fathers] are a select group; partly it is that they take it enormously seriously; and I think partly it is that their kids know, because they are not getting paid to do it. Overwhelmingly, our social policy says that fathers are not paid for fathering. The tax credits are directed towards mothers, so the kids know that the fathers are doing it out of love.[27]

---

[22] Bertoia and Drakich, above n 11; Kaye and Tolmie, 'Discoursing Dads', above n 11, 189.
[23] Equitable Child Maintenance and Access Society (Edmonton), 29 April 1998.
[24] National Shared Parenting Association, 11 March 1998.
[25] Gilles Morissette, Entraide pères-enfants séparés de l'Outaouais, 3 June 1998.
[26] Groupe d'entraide aux pères et de soutien à l'enfant, 3 April 1998.
[27] 1 June 1998.

This same group stated that mothers transfer children to fathers when the child becomes 'a problem', implying that mothers are fickle in relation to their desire to care for children. Another group suggested that under the shared custody approach 'the mother is no longer overprotected',[28] implying that single mothers are pampered by the state.

Mother Blaming

Another version of vilifying mothers was alleging that mothers actively try to keep fathers away from children. Fathers Are Capable Too (FACT) asserted:

> Fathers everywhere are desperately trying to be part of their family's life, and they are blocked by vindictiveness in most cases. ... Most of the mothers do not understand the point that the father is absolutely necessary in the life of the child.[29]

Some witnesses characterised access denial as a form of child abuse, even 'one of the most damaging forms of child abuse':[30]

> If you are going to abuse your child by refusing that child the right to maintain an ongoing relationship with both parents—so, since you're the custodial parent, you're saying, 'No, you can't see your daddy today'—that's harming the child. Then the court needs to address the fact that that is a form of child abuse.[31]

A common refrain was that mothers use dishonest tactics such as parental alienation and false allegations of sexual abuse and 'abduct and alienate children as a privilege'.[32] FACT stated that '[f]alse accusation seems to be the tool of choice in family litigation'[33] while Groupe d'entraide aux pères et de soutien à l'enfant put it this way:

> One of the problems we're facing is that, before a judge, before the bench, we absolutely have to prove that we are good fathers or that we were good fathers, whereas the mother doesn't have to prove anything at all. The mother's mere allegations are sufficient for a judge to take custody away from the father or limit his access.[34]

Mothers were also said to be financially greedy.[35] Claude Lachaine for Groupe d'entraide aux pères et de soutien à l'enfant stated that stakeholders in the system favour

---

[28] Groupe d'entraide aux pères et de soutien à l'enfant, 3 April 1998.
[29] 11 March 1998.
[30] Joe Rade, individual presentation, 1 June 1998; see also Carey Linde, Vancouver Men, 27 April 1998.
[31] National Shared Parenting Association, 11 March 1998.
[32] Men's Educational Support Association, 29 April 1998.
[33] 11 March 1998.
[34] 3 April 1998.
[35] Stepfamilies of Canada, 31 March 1998.

the single-parent approach, that is the 'single-parent mother/automatic bank teller father approach'.[36] Some fathers' rights advocates suggested that men's lack of power in relation to mothers generates desperation, including suicidal tendencies.[37]

Not only were mothers often blamed (even, quite vociferously, by other women),[38] punitive measures against mothers were often proposed. Stacy Robb for DADS Canada suggested that jail time be considered in relation to false allegations of abuse;[39] Carey Linde for Vancouver Men that '[t]here should be criminal sanctions against alienating parents'.[40]

Anti-Feminism

Closely connected to the anti-mother theme is anti-feminism.[41] Feminists are portrayed by some fathers' rightists as hostile to proper mothering within the heterosexual family, which would include ensuring that fathers are closely connected with children, preferably by staying married, but failing that, by facilitating shared parenting. Borrowing from the terminology developed by dissident feminist Christina Hoff Sommers,[42] Carey Linde for Vancouver Men suggested that:

> The organized women's movement, for all the good it has brought, gave up long ago on ideas like joint custody and shared parenting. Their silence is deafening.[43]

Some witnesses complained that feminists have sought equality (for women) in the workplace but not (for men) in the home.[44] Moreover, some said that the legal system has responded to the former initiative but not the latter, and that judicial education (presumably over-influenced by feminists) has favoured mothers:

> In the last decade this sexism has markedly increased, after judges were taught that women seeking custody were at a disadvantage in the courtroom. Fathers who wish to

---

[36] 3 April 1998.

[37] Victoria Men's Centre, 27 April 1998; Fathers for Equality, 19 May 1998.

[38] Notably those in Stepfamilies of Canada and Second Spouses of Canada, 31 March 1998.

[39] 30 March 1998.

[40] 27 April 1998. This discourse ignores the less than positive conduct that some fathers who feel alienated from their families and children have shown towards their spouse and children. M Gordon, 'No Anti-Male Bias in the Tragic White Family Case' *Edmonton Journal,* 7 April 2000, A15; R Matas, 'The Pain Behind a Suicide' *The Globe and Mail,* 8 April 2000, A3. On Kirby Inwood, spokesman for Coalition of Canadian Men's Organizations (31 March 1998), see *R v Inwood* [1989] OJ No 248 (Ont CA); *Inwood v Sidorova* [1990] OJ No 1140 (Ont HCJ); *Inwood v Sidorova* [1991] OJ No 1417 (Ont Ct GD).

[41] For detail, see SB Boyd, 'Backlash Against Feminism: Canadian Custody and Access Reform Debates of the Late Twentieth Century' (2004) 16(2) *Canadian Journal of Women and the Law* 255.

[42] CH Sommers, *Who Stole Feminism? How Women Have Betrayed Women* (New York, Simon and Schuster, 1994).

[43] 27 April 1998.

[44] FACT, 11 March 1998.

parent their children post-divorce today have a situation even more pronounced than women entering the workforce only a few decades ago.[45]

Fathers' rightists also advanced a conspiracy theory, that feminists hold excessive power in relation to institutions such as women's shelters, psychotherapy, and hospitals, which inappropriately influence mothers against fathers. For example, Parents Helping Parents stated:

> The feminist orientation of women's shelters and other support services for women have permeated the justice system to establish an ideology which suggests that women are incapable of violence or deceit, and men are all potential violent, sexual predators.[46]

The BC Men's Resource Centre asserted:

> In the area of child abuse allegations, the Salem witch-hunts have taken their toll, as extremists have attempted to hang everyone in their path. The Children's Hospital has recently been advised of several self-admitted, gender-feminist medical staff practicing their witchcraft in this hospital, using children as both the bait and the weapon with which they have extracted the penalty for being the wrong gender.[47]

In an increasingly familiar challenge to feminist analysis of male violence against women and to statistics on male violence against women,[48] William Taylor Hnidan for the BC Men's Resource Centre stated that violence is not a gender-specific phenomenon,[49] a theme echoed by several others. Harvey Maser for the Victoria Men's Centre said that 'violence and domestic violence is, if not equal, slightly predominant by the mother or the woman in the family' and that 'violence is very often translated into animosity toward the other partner in divorce'.[50]

Suggesting that women's groups are inappropriately funded by the state, some fathers' rights advocates argued for greater resources for men's groups,[51] such as '[a] legal action fund ... to enable fathers to legally challenge their longstanding historical disadvantages in family law'.[52]

Bias of the Legal System Against Fathers and For Mothers

Many fathers' rightists also argued that an enormous gender bias in the legal system was complicit in excluding fathers from the lives of their children[53] and

---

[45] Men's Educational Support Association, 29 April 1998.
[46] 1 May 1998.
[47] 27 April 1998.
[48] W DeKeseredy, 'Tactics of the Antifeminist Backlash Against Canadian National Woman Abuse Surveys' (1999) 5(11) *Violence Against Women* 1258.
[49] 27 April 1998.
[50] 27 April 1998.
[51] Eg Fathers for Equality, 19 May 1998.
[52] Men's Educational Support Association, 29 April 1998.
[53] FatherCraft Canada, 1 June 1998.

empowering women to take actions without fear of consequences.[54] Government was not exempt from criticism, with the Men's Educational Support Association arguing that government 'removed gender bias against women only to replace it and make a gender bias against men'.[55] The judicial system was, however, the key target, with many witnesses stating that mothers almost automatically receive custody of children and are always believed in court. For example:

> There's a definite gender bias [against fathers] ... I find if you go into family court as a father, you have to prove your worth to visit your child. As a mother, you're deemed intrinsically better just by being.[56]

Fathers' rights advocates invoked the language of sexual and systemic discrimination developed within feminist equality analysis, often citing statistics on custody and suggesting that anything other than a fifty-fifty sharing of custody would be discriminatory.[57] A key argument was that primary caregiving was inappropriately emphasised, which in turn disempowered fathers.[58] Fathers' rightists equated judicial emphasis on caregiving with a maternal presumption.[59] Taking a different tack, some witnesses claimed that primary caregiver fathers lost to mothers because of bias in a large number of cases.[60] Not only were custody and access orders criticised, but also failure to enforce orders giving fathers rights.[61]

Finally, governmental efforts to address domestic violence were said to make men guilty until they find a way to prove themselves, thus criminalising men who 'just want to be fathers'.[62] Men's Equalization Inc suggested that men arrested under zero tolerance policies in Manitoba 'have been robbed of their families'.[63]

Unfair/Excessive Child Support Orders Against Fathers

As mentioned at the outset, the 1998 custody reform debates emerged as a result of governmental efforts to enhance and enforce child support obligations, which incited the ire of fathers' rights advocates. At the SJC, groups complained

---

[54] New Vocal Man Inc, 1 May 1998; Parents Helping Parents, 1 May 1998.

[55] 29 April 1998. See also Kirby Inwood for the Coalition of Canadian Men's Organizations, 31 March 1998.

[56] FACT—National Association, 11 March 1998.

[57] Groupe d'entraide aux pères et de soutien à l'enfant, 3 April 1998; Entraide pères-enfants séparés de l'Outaouais, 3 June 1998.

[58] National Alliance for the Advance of Non-Custodial Parents, 2 June 1998.

[59] Equitable Child Maintenance and Access Society (Edmonton), 29 April 1998; Vancouver Men, 27 April 1998.

[60] FatherCraft Canada, 1 June 1998; National Shared Parenting Association (Saskatchewan), 30 April 1998.

[61] FACT, 11 March 1998; Jay Charland, Men's Education Network, 29 April 1998.

[62] Parents Helping Parents, 1 May 1998.

[63] 1 May 1998.

that fathers were suffering as a result of the new child support system, and if they could only see their children more, they would pay more.[64] One group alleged:

The existing system culminates in the refusal of men to support their children, from who they are unjustifiably separated and their access excommunicated.[65]

In general it was implied that mothers did not contribute to children's expenses: 'Dump the kids on mom. Stick dad with the bill.'[66] Glen Cheriton suggested that child support orders were not enforced against mothers in the same way as they were against fathers.[67]

In addition to arguing for enhanced paternal rights, several groups pushed for stepped-up maternal financial obligations.[68] For some, equal treatment of fathers and mothers meant not only equal rights in relation to children but also that child support awards should be paid in the same amount by female and male non-custodial parents (regardless of the fact that women tend to earn less).[69] Stepfamilies of Canada took a more punitive approach, suggesting that if mothers are going to get custody, they should assume full financial responsibility:

If women want the kids, give them kids. They'll have to be truly feminist and accept both financial ... and emotional responsibility for the children.[70]

Treat Fathers Equally: The Formal Equality Model

The method proposed by fathers' rightists to redress the alleged bias in favour of mothers was equal legal treatment of fathers, a formalistic vision of equality that tended to prioritise parental rights over children's interests:

Basically, both parents' right to be equal and to parent their children equally must be respected.[71]

A program of affirmative action should be created within the judicial system to encourage awarding of children to fathers. ... A section should be added to the Divorce Act that overtly states that both sexes have equal ability to parent their children post-divorce.[72]

[64] BC Men's Resource Centre, 28 April 1998.
[65] Men's Educational Support Association, 29 April 1998.
[66] William Levy for FED-UP, 3 April 1998.
[67] FatherCraft Canada, 1 June 1998.
[68] Eg Equitable Child Maintenance and Access Society, Calgary Chapter, 29 April 1998.
[69] New Vocal Man Inc, 1 May 1998.
[70] 31 March 1998.
[71] Entraide pères-enfants séparés de l'Outaouais, 3 June 1998; see also Victoria Men's Centre, 27 April 1998.
[72] Men's Educational Support Association, 29 April 1998.

One group suggested that fathers should have rights based on biology alone, asserting an essentialist vision of parenthood that obviates the significance of social parenting, for which mothers tend to take more responsibility:[73]

> I believe when a child is born, the child should have equal access to both parents ... I think it should be a law that both parents are on the birth certificate. I believe if the mother does not tell who the father is but if a man does come forward at any time, even if it's 10 years later, and says 'I am that child's father', that due diligence is done. ... A simple test will prove if that man is the father, and then that man will have the opportunity to enter into that child's life in a productive role.[74]

Several groups took a troubling, formulaic approach, proposing, for instance, that no divorce should occur without automatic joint custody and that no parent is only 51 per cent parent.[75] One group wanted presumptive shared custody to kick in automatically immediately upon marital breakdown, with the child's physical and social environment remaining intact. Each parent would have an equal share of the child's time and upkeep. The kicker was that a parent who refused to comply with this formula would concede custody to the other.[76] In other words, a mother who raised an issue about this formula or its impact on a child would lose custody.

Arguments for equal treatment usually implied that fathers should have equal rights in relation to decisions regarding children, regardless of caregiving patterns. This notion has been much criticised by those who have shown that joint (legal) custody gives fathers rights—including the right to control women and children—without responsibilities.[77] It leaves mothers with responsibility not only for childcare, but also for consulting with the other parent. Some witnesses explicitly endorsed this unequal division of labour:

> The mother may be the primary caretaker, but the father should have equal involvement with regard to medical concerns, education, health.[78]

Others invoked a parenting model that reinforced traditional, gender-based, asymmetrical models of mothering and fathering.[79]

---

[73] H Lessard, 'Mothers, Fathers, and Naming: Reflections on the *Law* Equality Framework and *Trociuk v British Columbia (Attorney General)*' (2004) 16(1) *Canadian Journal of Women and the Law* 165.

[74] Family Forum, 19 May 1998.

[75] Eg FED-UP, 3 April 1998.

[76] Entraide pères-enfants séparés de l'Outaouais, 3 June 1998.

[77] Eg Boyd, above n 3, 123; AM Delorey, 'Joint Legal Custody: A Reversion to Patriarchal Power' (1989) 3(1) *Canadian Journal of Women and the Law* 33; Bertoia and Drakich, above n 11.

[78] REAL Women, 1 April 1998.

[79] FatherCraft Canada, 1 June 1998.

Ken Wiebe for the Dick Freeman Society used language that suggested that parental (paternal?) authority over the family was a key concern in the claim for equality:

> The responsibility of the legislature and the courts in this issue is to ensure that there is a post-divorce situation that respects the equality, the parental authority, the integrity and the sanctity of the family ...[80]

Adopting an anti-state approach, he added that he was not interested in having the legislature or courts define his parental responsibilities, whether they be financial or time-related. Overall, the equality approach asserted by fathers' rightists implied a desire for paternal (patriarchal) authority over children and, thus, over mothers, rooted in a biogenetic definition of paternity.

Remedies: Shared Parenting, Joint Custody, or Paternal Custody

Although some fathers' rights recommendations focused on child support, the most popular remedy was a norm or presumption of shared parenting or joint custody. Danny Guspie, of the National Shared Parenting Association, even said that children have a 'God-given right' to shared parenting.[81] This remedy was typically based on an argument that such a norm would end discrimination against fathers (and benefit children):

> The first thing [the Committee] needs to do is to eliminate the parental inequity that is flagrant today, to set things straight, to clearly establish that parental equity is the norm today and that shared custody must be presumptive.[82]

Several groups referred explicitly to equal parenting time in addition to equal decision-making.[83] However, the equal rights embodied by the concept of joint custody would be granted presumptively, generally regardless of the history of care or uneven assumption of responsibilities. Moreover, references made to 'equality' of parenting prior to separation reinforced a notion of formal rights without responsibilities, favouring paternal authority and maternal responsibility.[84]

Arguments for shared parenting were sometimes linked to arguments for diminished child support obligations, suggesting a financial rationale. The Equitable Child Maintenance and Access Society (Calgary) proposed that 'child support guidelines be based on a sliding scale for time spent with the child'.[85] Mothers who shared custody with fathers might lose financial support even though their own expenses remained constant.

[80] 27 April 1998.
[81] 11 March 1998.
[82] 11 March 1998.
[83] Eg Men's Equal Access Society, 20 May 1998.
[84] Ken Wiebe, Dick Freeman Society, 27 April 1998.
[85] 29 April 1998.

A few groups advocated paternal sole custody as a better, cheaper remedy, because single mothers need more (state) money than single fathers. The ostensible reason for fathers' more effective parenting was 'because [fathers] are not getting paid to do it'.[86] When asked whether single-father headed families were more successful because fathers had more help, Cheriton agreed, but still attributed the success of the father to having extra (female) help. Overall, however, joint custody was the primary remedy sought.

Uneven Influence: Fathers' Rights Discourse and Law Reform

Fathers' rights advocacy at the SJC brought the above issues clearly to the forefront of the Canadian imagination, with considerable media coverage and many stories about fathers' grievances. Most key themes identified above were carried into the House of Commons by various Members of Parliament from the mid-1990s through 2003.[87] Yet fathers' rightists did not influence law reform outcomes in a straightforward manner. The remainder of this chapter identifies both the extent of, and the factors that mediate, the influence of fathers' rights discourse, by examining the SJC Report (1998) and government responses to it.

Special Joint Committee Report

As we have seen, the immediate catalyst for Canada's re-consideration of its custody laws was a political move by the fathers' rights movement. However, this process occurred after countries such as Australia and England radically changed their laws on post-separation parenting and when empirical studies on the sometimes unanticipated impact of these changes were emerging.[88] The SJC did not conduct a comprehensive search of those studies, some of which were not complete. However, it did hear from researchers conducting studies in Australia and Washington State.[89] These experts signalled problems such as those experienced

---

[86] FatherCraft, 1 June 1998.

[87] SB Boyd and CFL Young, 'Feminism, Fathers' Rights, and Family Catastrophes: Parliamentary Discourses on Post-Separation Parenting, 1966–2003' in DE Chunn, SB Boyd and H Lessard (eds), *Feminism, Law, and Social Change: (Re)Action and Resistance* (forthcoming).

[88] Eg H Rhoades, R Graycar and M Harrison, *The Family Law Reform Act 1995: The First Three Years* (Final Report, University of Sydney/Family Court of Australia, 2000); C Smart and B Neale, *Family Fragments* (Cambridge MA, Polity, 1999); R Bailey-Harris, J Barron and J Pearce, 'From Utility to Rights? The Presumption of Contact in Practice' (1999) 13 *International Journal of Law, Policy and the Family* 111.

[89] R Graycar and J Dunne: SJC, 35 (4 June 1998); 19 (27 April 1998). Rhoades, Graycar and Harrison, *ibid*; JE Dunne, EW Hudgins and J Babcock, 'Can Changing the Divorce Law Affect Post-Divorce Adjustment?' (2000) 33 *Journal of Divorce and Remarriage* 35.

under the Australian regime: shared parental responsibility for child care had not increased, the population who used the law tended to be in high conflict, and the notion of shared parental responsibility promoted the possibility of harassment rather than meaningful sharing of responsibility. The SJC Report observed that the Washington State Parenting Act had not achieved its objectives[90] but seemed less clear about the impact of reforms in England and Australia.

Overall, the SJC Report evinced clear sympathy for the arguments of fathers' rights advocates and was endorsed by them. It did not recommend a shared parenting presumption, but came close by recommending replacement of the terms 'custody' and 'access' by 'shared parenting'. It also recommended a Preamble be added to the Divorce Act affirming the right of the child to contact with both parents. The Committee frequently referred to research supporting fathers' rights arguments that divorce is harmful to children, loss of contact with fathers compromises children's well-being, and that children benefit from the involvement of both parents.[91] However, it also referred to research that tempered suggestions that family law is biased against fathers.[92]

Fathers' rights discourse clearly influenced the SJC regarding violence against women. The impact of studies showing that violence against women is a serious problem in Canadian society was tempered by the Committee's characterisation of the groups that raised these issues as 'representing the interests of the *adult* members of divorcing families', as opposed to children's interests.[93] The SJC recommended against a definition of family violence that would emphasise violence against women, because violence against men also exists.[94] This gender-neutral approach to domestic violence, which in turn downplays its negative impact on children, influenced subsequent government initiatives. Overall, the SJC dismissed the insights of women's groups who testified on violence, even when their evidence was grounded in research about the relevance of abuse to custody disputes. In turn, this research was not taken as seriously as it might have been and questions of abuse and safety were neutralised.

The SJC set the scene for increasing gender-neutrality in government responses to child custody law reform. This compromise approach, which accords much discretion to the judiciary and gives little guidance to separating parents, may have been the key legacy of the fathers' rights interventions. For example, the SJC recommended against employing legislative presumptions, whether in favour of primary caregivers or against abusers (as proposed by many women's groups) or for joint

---

[90] Canada, Special Joint Committee on Child Custody and Access, *For the Sake of the Children*, (Ottawa, Parliament of Canada, 1998), 40 (hereinafter 'SJC Report').

[91] See, for example, SJC Report, 10–12, 14, 29, 30.

[92] For instance, it cited statistics showing that in the vast majority of post-divorce arrangements, children are placed in maternal custody, acknowledging that this usually occurs by agreement: SJC Report, 4.

[93] See, for example, SJC Report, 12 (emphasis added). Testimony about women's responsibility for caregiving of children was similarly characterised.

[94] *Ibid*, 81.

custody (as proposed by fathers' rights advocates). This caution set the stage for the 'one size does not fit all' approach that ultimately dominated government initiatives.

Government Response

The Government of Canada was cautious in its initial responses to the SJC Report, echoing that there should be no presumptions in relation to post-separation parenting, thus distancing itself from both fathers' rights and women's groups.[95] But removal of the win-lose language of custody and access was mentioned frequently, as was contact as a key concern, both points being consistent with fathers' rights. The government took the time to conduct further consultations and to commission research and statistical reports, generating the wrath of fathers' rightists seeking more immediate implementation of SJC recommendations.

The government-initiated research studies were in fact influenced by fathers' rightists, ensuing partly pursuant to the SJC's own call for more research, which reflected its preoccupations with issues most commonly raised by fathers' rights advocates, such as false allegations and the impact of losing contact.[96] As we have seen, fathers' rights witnesses suggested frequently before the SJC, mostly without citing research, that there was a systemic bias against fathers. The research commissioned by the government can be construed as reacting mainly to these concerns. None of the studies dealt specifically with violence against women, the impact on children of witnessing violence, gender bias in family law, or the relationship between law reform and shifting actual caregiving responsibility. Nor did the federal government comply with its obligation to conduct a specifically gender-based analysis of the impact of a proposed legal change.[97] To that extent, the studies responded more to fathers' rights claims than to concerns raised by women's groups. Nevertheless, the studies offered some valuable insights—for instance that factors other than frequency of contact with a non-resident parent (such as payment of child support) are more important for a child's well-being.[98] The 'one size does not fit all' theme also emanated from some studies.[99]

[95] Canada, Department of Justice, *Response to the Report of the Special Joint Committee on Child Custody and Access: Strategy for Reform* (Ottawa, Department of Justice Canada, 1999) 10, 12, http://canada.justice.gc.ca/en/ps/pad/reports/sjcarp02.html (visited 28 November 2005).
[96] SJC Report, 78.
[97] Status of Women Canada, *Setting the Stage for the Next Century: The Federal Plan for Gender Equality* (Ottawa, Status of Women Canada, 1995) para 35, http://www.swc-cfc.gc.ca/pubs/066261951X/199508_066261951X_e.pdf (visited 28 November 2005).
[98] Canada, Department of Justice, *An Overview of the Risks and Protectors for Children of Separation and Divorce* by SC Bernardini and JM Jenkins (2002, prepared for Family, Children and Youth Section) iii, http://canada.justice.gc.ca/en/ps/pad/reports/2002-fcy-2e.pdf (visited 28 November 2005).
[99] Eg Canada, Department of Justice, *Post-Separation Visitation Disputes: Differential Interventions* by R Birnbaum and W McTavish (2001, paper prepared for the Family, Children and Youth Section) 18 http://canada.justice.gc.ca/en/ps/pad/reports/2001FCY6.pdf (visited 28 November 2005).

The commissioned research, as well as reports on family law in other countries, clearly informed the 2002 *Final Federal-Provincial-Territorial Report on Custody and Access and Child Support* (Final Report),[100] which was quite 'academic' and balanced in tone. It noted key findings from Washington State, England, and Australia, that the new legal regimes have neither reduced conflict or litigation in family matters, nor changed caregiving patterns.[101] It observed that 'changing legal terminology cannot alter attitudes or force parties to abandon confrontation'[102] and that the Australian studies found that the child's right to contact appeared to be given more weight than any other principle, including provisions trying to protect family members from violence.[103] Moreover, imposition of shared decision-making on parents not able to deal with one another without conflict can engender more conflict, to children's detriment.[104] These findings mediated the impact of fathers' rights discourse.

The Final Report also incorporated some suggestions made by women's groups before the SJC, especially concerning violence, and used few recommendations of men's groups for punitive measures against custodial mothers or joint custody presumptions. It noted that while considerable attention had been paid to wrongful denial of access, much complained about by fathers' rightists, problems of failure to *exercise* access and difficulties respecting enforcement of a right of custody also arose.[105] Moreover, serious problems with access are far more likely to occur when a history of abuse or high conflict exists between the parents, and a review of the current legislation had not revealed gender bias in favour of mothers.[106] The Final Report thus manifested some sensitivity to the conditions under which shared parenting does and does not work. Recommendation Six emphasised that parental arrangements should be based on the best interests of the child in the context of that child's circumstances, with no legal presumptions that one parenting arrangement is preferable. Other significant recommendations included no legislative presumptions regarding the degree of contact, and that legislative criteria defining best interests include 'any history of family violence and the potential for family violence' and 'facilitating contact with both parents *when it is safe and positive to do so*'.[107]

---

[100] Canada, Department of Justice, *Final Federal-Provincial-Territorial Report on Custody and Access and Child Support: Putting Children First* (2002, Custody and Access Project of the Federal-Provincial-Territorial Family Law Committee) (hereinafter 'Final Report'), http://canada.justice.gc.ca/en/ps/pad/reports/flc2002e.pdf (visited 28 November 2005).

[101] *Ibid*, 9 and Appendix B, 75–77.

[102] *Ibid*, 13.

[103] *Ibid*, 76–77.

[104] *Ibid*, 15.

[105] *Ibid*, 24. This Report also pointed out that the level of false allegations of child abuse (a huge issue during the Special Joint Committee consultations) seemed relatively low: *ibid*, 19.

[106] *Ibid*, 41, 16.

[107] *Ibid*, 19, Recommendation Eight (emphasis added).

These aspects of the Final Report diluted the impact of fathers' rights discourse. That said, its language was on the whole problematically gender-neutral, including when it discussed highly gendered social phenomena such as violence and caregiving. The aversion to using presumptions that had evolved during the Canadian process also dictated against any presumption against custody or unsupervised access for an abusive spouse[108]—a key recommendation of women's groups. Overall, the Final Report trod cautiously, emphasising diversity of family arrangements and the need for a flexible legal framework. It thereby avoided the positions most commonly associated with either fathers' rights or women's groups.

One Size Does Not Fit All (Bill C-22) ... Canadian Compromise

Ostensibly reflecting this philosophy, An Act to Amend the Divorce Act[109] was introduced to Parliament on 10 December 2002. Although it was shelved following a change in government, it will likely inform subsequent bills. Bill C-22 embodied several reform objectives, including promotion of parental co-operation and reduction of conflict, enhancement of parental responsibilities, and elimination of the 'proprietorial' terms custody and access.[110] Unlike England and Australia, however, these terms were not replaced with the language of residence and contact, which have been perceived as replicating the results of the earlier custody (mothers) and access (fathers) orders. Instead, parenting orders would have allocated parental responsibilities (parenting time and decision-making responsibilities) in whatever way parents negotiated or was deemed appropriate by judges. Possibly this decision reflected a desire to empower non-custodial fathers.

Bill C-22 would have introduced a best interests checklist into the Divorce Act, requiring judges to take into account twelve needs and circumstances of the child. Several points diverged from a clear move towards shared parenting, generating protests from fathers' rightists. Of note was the absence of any right of contact principle—or right to parenting time—and the listing of history of care as a factor. In addition, an effort was made to accord greater significance to evidence of 'any family violence' in custody determinations.[111] However, the recommendation

---

[108] Even though a commissioned research paper pointed out a significant distinction between the reasoning behind presumptions such as joint custody or primary caregiver, and presumptions regarding violence: Canada, Department of Justice, *An Analysis of Options for Changes in the Legal Regulation of Child Custody and Access* by B. Cossman (2001) 65 http://canada.justice.gc.ca/en/ps/pad/reports/2001-FCY-2E.pdf (visited 28 November 2005).

[109] 2nd Sess 37th Parl 2002.

[110] *House of Commons Debates* 052 (4 February 2003) 1010 and 1030 (hereinafter *Hansard*).

[111] But see LC Neilson, 'Putting Revisions to the Divorce Act Through a Family Violence Filter: The Good, the Bad and the Ugly' (2003) 20(1) *Canadian Journal of Family Law* 11, regarding the Bill's failure to consider the complex impact of family violence.

of the Final Report that contact with both parents should be facilitated only when it is safe and positive to do so was not introduced.

Although no right to contact was inscribed in Bill C-22, detracting from a fathers' rights focus, judges were required to consider the benefit to the child of developing and maintaining meaningful relationships with both spouses, and each spouse's willingness to support the development and maintenance of the child's relationship with the other spouse. This factor was a watered down version of the much-criticised maximum contact/friendly parent principle currently in the Divorce Act. In moving it to a list of several factors under the best interests checklist, the government intended that the importance of the relationship between a parent and a child be weighed along with other factors.[112] On its face, then, the Bill did not clearly endorse a fathers' rights standpoint, nor establish any particular model of post-separation parenting as normative.

Fathers' rightists, however, were not the least bit pleased about the Bill's lack of preference for shared parenting. Women's groups too were critical of the Bill's failure to recognise the highly gendered nature of childcare responsibilities and women's ongoing inequality. The Bill took a formal equality approach to post-separation parenting—one that ignores realities in the same way that fathers' rights discourse does—and put faith in gender-neutral legal principles, and interpretation thereof by professionals such as lawyers, mediators and judges, to achieve fair outcomes. Both women's groups and fathers' rights advocates thus criticised Bill C-22, the latter continuing to call for the introduction of a joint custody norm and the former insisting on the need to take into account women's inequality and its repercussions for childcare and custody disputes.

The House of Commons

When Canada's former Minister of Justice introduced Bill C-22, he emphasised the government's desire to focus on children, not parents' rights, thereby trying to avoid criticism by those advocating joint custody or other presumptions.[113] At second reading, he similarly adopted the 'one size does not fit all' concept that rejected presumptions, and also endorsed the promotion of non-adversarial methods of dispute resolution,[114] which tend to be favoured by fathers' rightists.[115]

The Minister's effort to avoid heated debate failed. Fathers' rights discourse had already penetrated the House of Commons, particularly from the mid-1990s when child support law reform was introduced. All themes canvassed earlier were

[112] *Hansard* 052 (4 February 2003) 3102–29.
[113] *Ibid.*
[114] *Ibid,* 3102 (Martin Cauchon, Lib Minister of Justice).
[115] C Bertoia, 'An Interpretative Analysis of the Mediation Rhetoric of Fathers' Rightists: Privatization Versus Personalization' (1998) 16(1) *Mediation Quarterly* 15.

manifested, including dramatic references to 'the awful tragedy that is imposed upon fatherless homes where there is only one parent'[116] and to men being driven to suicide or other desperate acts after being denied visitation by vindictive spouses.[117] In 2001, a Canadian Alliance (CA) MP eloquently invoked fathers' rights arguments in support of a private member's bill on joint custody.[118]

Fathers' rights discourse in the Commons crystallised around the government's introduction and second reading of Bill C-22. Several MPs raised fathers' rights positions explicitly and reference was made to:

> fathers' groups set up all across the country that have been crying out for a little equity within the Divorce Act.[119]

Some MPs supporting shared parenting referred to 'both parents' in a gender-neutral manner when arguing for shared parenting and access or discussing suicide (of men) due to excessive financial support obligations.[120] Others referred very explicitly to fathers and mothers in a discourse that pitted women against men, and blamed women for harms to men. Val Meredith (CA) alluded to:

> the biases of the courts toward females in any kind of child custody decisions and biases of courts towards females against the males in a lot of situations that come out of a breakdown of a marriage.[121]

Other MPs referred to fathers effectively becoming 'divorced from [their] own children'.[122] One MP said that he had gathered 'data on males, the fathers, who have committed suicide one after the other', linking this overstatement with 'perceptions that courts have been biased toward females'.[123]

Reference was made to mothers alienating children from fathers[124] and lack of access was cited as an excuse for fathers' failure to pay child support.[125] Both the adversarial system and mothers were held responsible for this problem.[126] Women were said to be as abusive as men:

> [I]ncidents of domestic violence or violence was *[sic]* perpetrated equally by men against women and women against men. I believe this tells us that the issue of family violence or domestic violence should not have a gender with respect to our discussions.[127]

---

[116] *Hansard* 052 (4 February 2003) 3123; see also *Hansard* 064 (20 February 2003) 3798; 047 (28 January 2003) 2772.

[117] Eg *Hansard* 176 (25 April 2002) 10862; 061 (14 May 2001) 3972–3; 020 (23 Feb 2001) 1126–7.

[118] *Hansard* 020 (23 February 2001) 1127–8.

[119] *Hansard* 052 (4 February 2003) 3127.

[120] *Hansard* 064 (20 February 2003) 3792–9.

[121] *Hansard* 052 (4 February 2003) 3149.

[122] *Hansard* 098 (9 May 2003) 6001.

[123] *Hansard* 064 (20 February 2003) 3792.

[124] *Hansard* 052 (4 February 2003) 3120–1, 3127.

[125] *Ibid*, 3153.

[126] *Ibid*, 3153, 3125.

[127] *Ibid*, 3116, 3126.

In addition, the differences between men and women were de-emphasised: 'There are no more deadbeat dads out there than there are deadbeat moms.'[128]

Interestingly, some conservative MPs criticised the shift to the language of parental *responsibility* due to its focus away from parental *rights*. They urged that parental *rights* also be given ample consideration so that decisions did not 'exclude one parent from the desired contact', leading to 'terrible ramifications which can lead to situations ... where children are abducted, where parents react violently'.[129] Despite the gender neutrality, they clearly were referring to their concern that an emphasis on responsibility might result in fathers receiving fewer rights, not more, in relation to custody or decision-making.

Similarly, several MPs asserted that 'parental arrangements before divorce should have no relevance on the care a child will receive after a separation between parents'.[130] In other words, they felt that a mother's primary responsibility for childcare before separation should not be relevant to subsequent custody determinations. Indeed, Peter MacKay (PC) complained that in Bill C-22, the history of care carried the same weight as the nature, strength and stability of the relationship between the child and each spouse. He suggested that equal weighting of these factors 'may afford an unfair advantage to the parent providing the most day to day, hands-on care'.[131] Similarly, Val Meredith asserted a traditional view of the difference between female and male parenting, arguing that shared parenting could imply various scenarios, not necessarily shared care.[132]

Debate also revealed pointed discussion about both 'the gender wars' and the notion that feminists had undue influence. Some MPs appeared to believe that the government had adopted the position of women's groups, even though many had criticised the Bill and the process leading to it. Possibly the MPs influenced by fathers' rights discourse felt that any reform short of joint custody or shared parenting reflected a reform proposed by women's groups. Paul Forseth (CA) alleged that the Minister of Justice had 'made a serious mistake by succumbing to the *special interests* and twisted Liberal ideology' (emphasis added).[133] Val Meredith (CA) suggested even more openly that the government had bowed to women's groups.[134]

Two female MPs pointed out the false assumptions underlying many of the fathers' rights positions, countering them by reference to women's realities.[135] These rather solitary interventions had little impact other than to generate a response from MPs influenced by fathers' rights, who argued that domestic

---

[128] *Ibid*, 3155.
[129] *Ibid*, 3120.
[130] *Ibid*, 3108.
[131] *Ibid*, 3119.
[132] *Ibid*, 3150, 3153; *Hansard* 052 (4 February 2003) 3106.
[133] *Hansard* 080 (28 March 2003) 4860.
[134] *Hansard* 052 (4 February 2003) 3151.
[135] *Ibid*, 3114–16; 3144–6.

violence did not have a gender,[136] an emphasis on violence should not unduly shape the debate,[137] the change in the roles that men and women play should indicate a need to look at shared custody,[138] and many fathers shared parenting of children.[139]

The government continued to adhere to its gender-neutral endorsement of 'parental responsibilities' as well as 'one size does not fit all'. Moreover, the Minister of Justice distinguished the parental responsibilities approach in Bill C-22 from a shared parenting approach,[140] missing the slippage between the two concepts.[141] No doubt this government position fuelled fathers' rights groups' suspicion that the government was bending to feminist pressure.

Fathers' rights recommendations for a presumption of joint custody were thus not endorsed *per se* by the government; indeed, the government emphasised that it was not introducing shared parenting. The concerns that were registered about the *lack of rights* for parents during the debates on Bill C-22 indicate that MPs operating from a fathers' rights perspective feared that the Bill might in practice favour mothers, due, for instance, to its reference to history of care. Thus, Bill C-22 simultaneously worried feminists for its formal equality failure to address gendered realities and angered fathers' rightists for its failure to introduce the quintessential formal equality custody norm: joint legal custody.

False Adversaries and Canadian Compromise: Listening to 'The Professionals'

Overall, Canada's law reform process was influenced by the perceived political need for the government to negotiate the demands of groups representing the 'consumers' of the system, in particular those advocating for fathers and for mothers. Despite the extent to which the reform process has been characterised as 'the gender wars', law reform documents have become surprisingly gender-neutral over the same period. Governmental bodies have walked a careful line in order to present an appearance of not bowing to either women's groups or fathers' rightists.[142] Ironically, in so doing, reform may nevertheless have been influenced by

---

[136] *Ibid*, 3116.
[137] *Ibid*, 3117.
[138] *Ibid*, 3145–6.
[139] *Ibid*, 3146.
[140] *Hansard* 080 (28 March 2003) 4860.
[141] Australia's parental responsibilities model was often interpreted as pointing towards a presumption of shared parenting: H Rhoades, 'The Rise and Rise of Shared Parenting Laws: A Critical Reflection' (2002) 19(1) *Canadian Journal of Family Law* 75.
[142] See SB Boyd, 'Walking the Line: Canada's Response to Child Custody Law Reform Discourses' (2003) 21 (3) *Canadian Family Law Quarterly* 397–423.

the demands of lobby groups, particularly fathers' rightists representing extreme positions. Characterising fathers' rights and women's groups as adversaries falsely implies that all advocacy groups offer equally valid analyses and recommendations grounded in research.

The way that government bodies invoked research was influenced by the perceived need to 'walk the line' between women's groups and fathers' rightists. As a result, research on the incidence of violence against women and the impact on children of witnessing violence between their parents,[143] presented by witnesses from battered women's shelters, helplines, and counselling services, as well as from organised women's groups, may not have been taken as seriously as it ought. The more fathers' rights advocates bombarded the government with rhetoric and anecdotal tragic tales, even threatening to sue the government,[144] the less likely government was to address the concerns of women's groups, no matter how rooted in reality and research.

More influential, perhaps, was the support for avoiding presumptions in favour of shared parenting or otherwise, found in the testimony of SJC witnesses who offered a social work or mediation perspective.[145] These witnesses may have been perceived as taking a more 'objective' stance than women's groups, which often argued for the use of presumptions, for instance against unsupervised contact with abusers. Two male academics also pointed in their presentations to the need to avoid being formulaic (especially in terms of gender issues)[146] and to the notion that 'one size does not fit all'.[147] Moreover, the Report summarising nationwide consultations held in spring 2001 supported this compromise position. It concluded that while many men's organisations supported implementing the SJC recommendations, and many women's organisations argued that a gender analysis should take place before proceeding, many *professionals* (for example, lawyers and service providers) felt that the term *parental responsibility* had merit as a flexible option that could address many of the concerns raised by other respondents.[148] Thus, the 'one size does not fit all' approach, attached to the language of

---

[143] See, for example, SJC, 13 (31 March 1998) 1005–15 (Beth Bennet, Program Director, Assaulted Women's Helpline, and E Morrow, Lobby Coordinator, Ontario Association of Interval and Transition Houses); SJC, 19 (27 April 1998) 1955–2000 (J Lothien, Representative, Family Services of Greater Vancouver); SJC, 20 (29 April 1998) 1630 (J Black, Coordinator, Calgary Status of Women Action Committee).

[144] S Alberts, 'Class-Action Suit Threatened over Suffering by Children of Divorce' *National Post*, 20 July 1999, A7. The suit was threatened by Dannie Guspie of the National Shared Parenting Association.

[145] For instance, C Guilmaine noted that abuses of automatic presumptions could occur, such as the former shared custody presumption in California: SJC, 16 (3 April 1998) 955 (Social Worker and Family Mediator, Ordre professionel des travailleurs sociaux du Québec).

[146] SJC, 27 (19 May 1998) 1445 (Professor D Dutton, Department of Psychology, University of British Columbia).

[147] *Ibid*, 2040 (Professor B Beyerstein, Psychologist, Simon Fraser University).

[148] Canada, Department of Justice, *Custody, Access and Child Support in Canada: Report on Federal-Provincial-Territorial Consultations* (Ottawa, IER Planning, Research and Mgmt Services, presented to Federal-Provincial-Territorial Family Law Committee, 2001) 8.

parental responsibility, emerged as a middle ground endorsed by professionals with their cloak of objectivity.

Conclusion

This chapter has shown that fathers' rights discourse increasingly permeated Canada's most recent law reform process from the mid-1990s, yet did not fully determine its outcome. The greatest reception for fathers' rights arguments was in the 1998 Special Joint Committee public consultations and the 'theatre' of the House of Commons. The impact of these receptive forums for fathers' rights arguments was mediated by the governmental processes discussed in the previous section, in addition to factors such as the rising influence of neo-liberalism on family policy, which I will now address.

RW Connell argues that although explicit backlash movements such as fathers' rightists have not generally had a great deal of influence, neo-liberalism has been very important in defending gender inequality.[149] Family law reform took place in a period that witnessed the rise of neo-liberalism and privatisation, accompanied by a renewed emphasis on the rational liberal individual, choice, contract, and individual responsibility. This neo-liberal individual ostensibly has no gender and, as a result, social justice initiatives for women are generally not pursued. What this really means is that men's still more dominant positions are empowered to some degree while women's interests are rendered further invisible.

Responsibility and responsibilisation are key watchwords of neo-liberalism, appearing in family law as 'parental responsibility'. And yet, at a social level, responsibility for children remains highly gendered. As a result, 'divorcing responsibly'[150] and assuming parental responsibilities are gendered phenomena too. Ostensibly, the language of parental responsibility (now used extensively in Canada even though legislation does not use this term) is invoked to encourage parents to act selflessly in their children's best interests and avoid parental rights discourse. Whether this can be achieved is another question. As numerous authors have pointed out, a heavier onus rests on mothers to act responsibly in relation to children. In particular, it is a mother's responsibility not only to place the children's interests first, but also to ensure that the children develop good relationships with their father after separation or divorce, whether or not they had good relationships before and whether or not this is good or bad for the children or their caregivers. Moreover, in the modern state, women are hit with a double

---

[149] RW Connell, 'Change Among the Gatekeepers: Men, Masculinities, and Gender Equality in the Global Arena' (2005) 30(3) *Signs: Journal of Women in Culture and Society* 1801, 1815.
[150] H Reece, *Divorcing Responsibly* (Oxford, Hart, 2003).

whammy: they are expected to be (genderless) workers and mothers, and yet social welfare measures that previously went some way towards enabling them to 'balance' work/family responsibilities have been eroded.

Yet fathers too are negatively affected by neo-liberalism, in that they are expected to take responsibility as payors, regardless of their working conditions in an economy that increasingly privatises, downsizes, and renders their employment ever more uncertain.[151] Notably, fathers' rights protests about the amounts and enforcement of child support were not taken very seriously by the Canadian government, arguably due to the coincidence between these reforms and the neo-liberal agenda to privatise economic responsibility within the nuclear family.[152]

Fathers' rights arguments had more success in relation to child custody law reform, with Bill C-22 introducing changes mirroring those in other countries intended to promote paternal contact, which might in turn increase the likelihood of fathers being fiscally responsible in relation to payment of child support. That said, the force of fathers' rights discourse was mediated by research and by the government's wish to avoid 'the gender wars' and, possibly, the extreme nature of some fathers' rights discourse.[153] As with the 1985 Divorce Act reforms, the government avoided an explicit presumption in favour of joint custody.[154] This time, it promoted a package of reforms that gestured towards the ideal of shared parental responsibilities but left flexibility in the system to deviate from that ideal. At the same time, it neither introduced measures to generate the conditions necessary to facilitate shared responsibilities nor provided safeguards against the risks of promoting contact.

Meanwhile, as the increase in joint custody awards illustrates, the general thrust of the fathers' rights arguments has had a wider cultural influence on the public, mediators, lawyers and judges. Whether the legislative product of law reform determines the climate within which parents resolve custody disputes is in question in Canada: many of the problematic results seen in jurisdictions that have introduced reforms following fathers' rights pressure arise in Canada despite its old-fashioned legislation. Paradoxically, perhaps, the fathers' rights movement, in combination with neo-liberalism, has influenced family law policy to adopt a gender-neutral position that cannot possibly comprehend, or address, the complex gendered reality that underpins modern families—both intact and separated. Fathers' rights discourse has not, perhaps, won the day, but it has enhanced the power of fathers in relation to post-separation parenting.

[151] See K Robson, *Wrapped in the Flag of the Child: Post-Divorce Parenting Experiences in an Era of Guidelines and Privatization* (PhD thesis, Department of Sociology, Queen's University, defended 11 November 2005).

[152] B Cossman, 'Family Feuds: Neo-Liberal and Neo-Conservative Visions of the Reprivatization Project' in B Cossman and J Fudge (eds), *Privatization, Law and the Challenge to Feminism* (Toronto, University of Toronto Press, 2002).

[153] Connell, above n 149, suggests that one reason for the relative lack of influence of fathers' rightists is their tendency to inflate the extent of women's power.

[154] Boyd and Young, above n 2.

3

'The Outlaw Fathers Fight Back': Fathers' Rights Groups, Fathers 4 Justice and the Politics of Family Law Reform— Reflections on the UK Experience

RICHARD COLLIER*

The press have described F4J as 'The Outlaw Fathers' and 'The New Militant Men's Movement.' Whatever you think of these labels, for the first time they are now writing about the fathers who are fighting back. And if we won't fight for our kids, just what will we fight for?[1]

Introduction

The development of the fathers' rights movement in the UK[2] can be located in the context of a range of struggles and debates around the question of how law responds (or does not respond) to the 'transformations of intimacy'[3] which frame contemporary family practices.[4] In the UK, as in the other countries discussed in this volume, the nature of these contestations has changed considerably over the past three decades. Recent events suggest not simply a heightening of concern about the relationship between law and fatherhood[5] but a growing *politicisation*

---

* I would like to acknowledge the support of an AHRB Research Leave Scheme award (AN 8065/APN 16739) in funding the leave period during which research for this paper was conducted. Some material appeared previously in R Collier, 'Fathers 4 Justice, Law and the New Politics of Fatherhood' (2005) 17(4) *Child and Family Law Quarterly* 1. I am grateful to the publishers for permission to reprint this here.

[1] http://www.fathers-4-justice.org/our_pledge/index.htm

[2] On the notion of a 'movement' in this context see further Collier and Sheldon, this volume.

[3] A Giddens, *The Transformations of Intimacy* (Cambridge, Polity, 1992). See also U Beck and E Beck Gernsheim, *The Normal Chaos of Love* (Cambridge, Polity, 1995).

[4] D Morgan, *Family Connections: An Introduction to Family Studies* (Cambridge, Polity, 1996).

[5] There has been, more generally, a significant growth in the study of fatherhood. See, for just a flavour of this work: D Lupton and L Barclay, *Constructing Fatherhood: Discourses and Experiences*

of these debates, notably (although by no means exclusively) in relation to the area of post-divorce/separation contact law.

This chapter seeks to address the arguments presented by, and the possible impact of, fathers' rights organisations in the UK in seeking to set a reform agenda in the area of contact law. An increasingly vocal, visible and organised fathers' rights movement (henceforth FRM) has been credited with influencing perceptions of the politics of family justice internationally. Fathers, for some, have become the 'new victims' of a range of laws relating to the family which have moved 'too far' in favour of mothers. This chapter will explore these claims in the context of the emergence of a 'new militant' direct action fathers' rights agenda, one which has appeared across different countries and which is best illustrated in the UK by the pressure group 'Fathers 4 Justice' (henceforth F4J).[6] Having set out a brief history of the development of fathers' rights groups in the UK, the chapter proceeds to locate the emergence of F4J in relation to wider policy debates around divorce law reform. It will be suggested that, in order to make sense of what has been happening in this area, it is necessary to rethink the politics of fathers' rights in the context of recent research into post-separation life, parenthood and, importantly, childhood.

Contexts: F4J, Fathers' Rights and Law Reform

Fathers' Rights Groups in the UK

There is no one fathers' rights perspective in the UK and, within what is at best a loosely based coalition, there exists a diversity of approaches and political views.[7]

(London, Sage, 1997); B Hobson (ed), *Making Men into Fathers: Men, Masculinities and the Social Politics of Fatherhood* (Cambridge, Cambridge University Press, 2002); B Featherstone, 'Taking Fathers Seriously' (2003) 33 (2) *British Journal of Social Work* 239; N Dowd, *Redefining Fatherhood* (New York, New York University Press, 2000); R Larossa, *The Modernization of Fatherhood: A Social and Political History* (Chicago, University of Chicago Press, 1997); R Parke, *Fatherhood* (Cambridge, MA, Harvard University Press, 1996); R Collier, 'A Hard Time to Be a Father?: Law, Policy and Family Practices' (2001) 28 *Journal of Law and Society* 520; W Marsiglio (ed), *Fatherhood: Contemporary Theory, Research and Social Policy* (London, Sage, 1995); C Lewis, *A Man's Place in the Home: Fathers and Families in the UK* (York, Joseph Rowntree Foundation, 2000).

    [6] See further http://www.fathers-4-justice.org.
    [7] It is important to differentiate the views of fathers' rights groups from those of 'fathers' in any more general sense. See further A Gavanas, 'The Fatherhood Responsibility Movement: The Centrality of Marriage, Work and Male Sexuality in Reconstructions of Masculinity and Fatherhood' in B Hobson (ed), above n 5: WF Horn, D Blankenhorn and MB Pearlstein, *The Fatherhood Movement: A Call to Action* (Lexington, MD, Lexington Books, 1999): MA Messner, *Politics of Masculinities: Men in Movements* (Thousand Oaks, CA, Sage, 1997); M Flood, 'Men's Movements' (1998) 46 *Community Quarterly* 62; R Collier, '"Coming Together?": Post-Heterosexuality, Masculine Crisis and the New Men's Movement' (1996) 4(1) *Feminist Legal Studies* 3. In the UK essentially pressure group organisations, as above, are distinct from government-funded bodies such as *Fathers Direct—The National Information Centre on Fatherhood* (http://www.fathersdirect.com).

It would be misleading, moreover, to see the emergence of fathers' rights groups and political agendas based on the promotion of their legal rights as a recent phenomenon. Concerns about fathers' legal rights have been addressed in relation to diverse issues and across a range of debates which have framed the history of family law reform in England and Wales.[8] The 1969 Divorce Reform Act, the Matrimonial Causes Act 1973 (hereafter MCA 1973), the Matrimonial and Family Proceedings Act 1984, the Child Support Act 1991 (subsequently amended), the Children Act 1989 and the 1996 Family Law Act (FLA) each, for example, prompted discussion about 'what is happening to' the legal rights and responsibilities of fathers, as well as the relationship between law and parenthood in a more general sense.

In the period since the MCA 1973 diverse organisations[9] have emerged and sought to campaign on a range of issues relating to fathers' rights. The pressure group and registered charity Families Need Fathers[10] (henceforth FNF), formed in 1974, is of especial significance in terms of having secured a public profile during this period. FNF has, in contrast to F4J, been described as the 'respectable' face of fathers' rights. Other groups, such as the Campaign For Justice on Divorce (CJD),[11] founded in 1978, have often tended to focus on specific issues. In some cases these groups have had a fairly limited life-span, certainly far shorter than that of FNF, reflecting the role of key individuals in their establishment and day to day running. At the time of writing, and notwithstanding the recent developments regarding F4J which are discussed below, groups such as the Equal Parenting Council[12] have had more influence than F4J in terms of direct impact on policy debates, perhaps because the form of the latter's protests has made it unlikely that politicians will accord them a place at the table. Nonetheless, and in terms of their general aims, if not the methods they adopt, F4J exemplifies the broader objectives of many fathers' rights activists within and beyond the UK.

The perceived failures and limitations of these other groups provide a context within which F4J has come into existence. There has been a growing sense of frustration on the part of some fathers with the more traditional routes of law reform and campaigning, deemed to have proved inadequate to date in representing fathers' interests. 'Something stronger'—a strategy that will make politicians and policy makers 'sit up and take notice'—has become necessary if real change is ever to be achieved. By consciously turning to the tactics and methods of other protest

---

[8] R Collier, *Masculinity, Law and the Family* (London, Routledge, 1995).

[9] In addition to FNF, F4J and the Equal Parenting Network and Council, other groups addressing a range of related issues and agendas (by no means fathers' rights groups *per se*) include: Child Rescue, Family and Youth Concern, the UK Men's Movement, The Cheltenham Group, National Society for Children and Family Contact, National Association for Child Support Action, Family Rights Group, Association of Shared Parenting, and the False Allegation Support Organisation.

[10] http://www.fnf.org.uk

[11] http://homepages.force9.net/tradeck/cjd/cjdleaf.htm

[12] http://www.equalparenting.org

movements,[13] it is hoped that the form of direct action politics embraced by F4J will draw attention to the plight of fathers in a way that the previous campaigns of groups such as FNF signally failed to achieve.

The transition that has occurred in the profile of fathers' rights groups over the past thirty years reflects something more, however, than simply a change in tactics around law reform campaigning. Each of the major pieces of legislation noted above resulted from political, religious and public reassessments of procedural laws and substantive concerns pertaining to transitions in legal status. Yet, on closer examination, it is possible to detect over this period a number of interrelated shifts in *how* fathers' rights has been constituted as a particular kind of social problem and object of concern. A complex convergence of developments has, not least in the context of post-divorce/separation parenting, served to reposition men in the popular consciousness as the *new victims* of family law reform.

There are three strands to this transition. First, as noted above, there has been a growing disillusionment with the traditional processes of law reform in relation to which FNF, in particular, have failed to 'get the message across' to policy makers and politicians. Second, there has been a shift in how ideas about fatherhood more generally relate to the morality arguments which frame debates about family law policy.[14] This transition has involved a complex amalgam of issues; a convergence of ideas about crises in the (heterosexual) family and paternal masculinity;[15] a rethinking of men's role in the family resulting from demographic, economic, technological and cultural changes;[16] and a reappraisal of

---

[13] 'A designer, marketing and public relations man by trade, Matt [O'Connor] was able to use the valuable experience gained in campaigning in the Anti-Apartheid movement, CND and Amnesty International when he was younger and weave this knowledge together with that gained working on numerous international multi-million pound food and drinks brands.' http://www.fathers-4-justice.org/introducing%20f4j/index.htm.

[14] The DRA 1969 and MCA 1973, above, have been interpreted as part of a broader 'emancipatory moment' marked by a concern to protect women from the consequences of new liberalised divorce laws. In the parliamentary debates that preceded these reforms, the combination of men's economic power relative to women, alongside the making of assumptions about men's 'natural' proclivities towards 'sexual (mis)adventuring', served to constitute the (innocent) wife as the potential victim of divorce reform (albeit that this was a victim status mediated by assumptions about class and sexual propriety). A recurring image in the debates of the late 1960s and early 1970s was of the husband as a (potentially) adulterous man, a man who would, given the opportunity, discard his 'faithful' middle-aged wife for a younger and more sexually attractive woman. This idea underscored the perception at the time of the DRA and MCA reforms as a 'Casanova's Charter' which would result in 'blameless' wives being repudiated by their husbands and left in economic difficulties: K O'Donovan, *Family Law Matters* (London, Pluto, 1993) 77–79.

[15] R Collier, 'Men, Heterosexuality and the Changing Family: (Re)constructing Fatherhood in Law and Social Policy' in C Wright and G Jaggar (eds), *Changing Family Values* (London, Routledge, 1999).

[16] By the early 1980s increasing numbers of divorced men appeared to feel aggrieved with the reformed law and, in particular, the financial and property settlements being made under the legislation. The financial protection for divorced women which the MCA 1973 had sought to secure (above n 14) had been premised on the belief that the primarily financial obligation entailed by marriage was that of a husband's duty 'to maintain' his wife. The law had thus sought to ensure that a man should

men's contribution to practices of care and caring prompted, in part at least, by the impact of the women's movement, feminism and women's increased participation in paid employment.

Thirdly, and importantly, this period has seen a subtle shift in the *ways in which* a distinctive fathers' rights discourse has sought to engage with law reform. A change has occurred in the kinds of argument that have been made to support the view that fathers have become the victims of injustice in the field of family law. By the early to mid-1980s a combination of women's increased employment and other cultural and sexual-political realignments were widely seen as having undermined the economic and social basis of previous law reforms. At this moment arguments of equity and justice relating to both men[17] and women[18] were widely deployed, albeit in different ways, in calls for law reform to take place. Whilst such equity arguments remain strong, however (see below), by the mid-1990s other influences were increasingly beginning to frame the construction of the divorced father as victim of family justice. These include: a heightened and, by the 1990s, increasingly culturally pervasive (if ill-defined) notion of 'crisis of masculinity', in which the father had become a central element; the emergence, and growing profile, of a broader 'new men's movement', strands of which are marked by an increasingly virulent antifeminism; and, of particular significance, a shift in the degree of visibility and level of organisation of fathers' rights groups themselves, not least as a result of the arrival and development of the Internet. It is difficult to overstate in this regard the growing sophistication of the ways in which men's grievances have been politically mobilised and expressed during this period, or the importance of the Internet in facilitating the sharing of experiences amongst communities of men.

It is against this background that F4J has emerged as the most high-profile and, in terms of how they have produced a 'step change' in the wider agenda about fathers' rights, politically effective fathers' rights group.

F4J and the 'New Militancy'

Who *are* those guys? What does it all mean—the Marvel Comics costumes, the orchestrated gantry stunts, the banners, the Santa outfits, the nooses, the desperate measures?[19]

---

not be 'freed' from such an obligation. Implicit was a construction of marriage as something which the husband 'escapes' and of the husband himself as a man who must pay a 'price for his freedom'. The contrast with the father in recent debates is marked here.

[17] For whom it was increasingly 'unfair' to have to 'support' a former wife frequently capable of supporting herself and who would also, in many cases, have access to a second partner's finances.

[18] For whom such a situation not only promoted a circle of economic dependence on husbands; it was also economically and psychologically damaging to the 'emancipation' of women by encouraging, in the widely used term imported from North America, 'alimony drones'.

[19] J Walsh, 'Revenge of the Angry Fathers' *The Independent (Review)*, 5 February 2004.

F4J, as noted above, is a relatively new organisation in the field, one which has attracted considerable media attention[20] as a result of demonstrations involving fathers and their supporters.[21] At the time of writing the future of F4J as an organisation is uncertain. The founder of F4J, Matt O'Connor, announced in January 2006 that the group would be disbanding following the reporting in the British media of a 'plot' to kidnap the five-year-old son of the Prime Minister Tony Blair.[22] It remains to be seen if the emergence of a splinter group, termed the 'Real Fathers 4 Justice',[23] will continue the campaign of F4J (or whether, indeed, there will be intensification in their activities).[24] What is clear is that the protests of F4J have, since their formation, been diverse in form, organisation/planning and public visibility. They have encompassed the traditional civil rights march;[25] physical attacks on government offices (in particular those of the Children and Family Court Advisory and Support Service (CAFCASS)); protests outside the homes of solicitors, barristers and judges[26] (as well as, in September 2004, the British Royal Family); and a series of confrontations with senior government figures including, in May 2004, an incident which involved the throwing of a condom containing purple flour at the Prime Minister.[27] F4J have become most well known, however, for a series of protests involving men dressed as comic book characters scaling a succession of cranes, bridges, courthouses and other public structures and buildings around the country.

Activists from F4J have, to date, staged numerous protests in cities across Britain, with fathers 'dressed as Batman, Robin, Superman and Spiderman'[28]

---

[20] See further the data analysis produced by Reputation Intelligence, *F4J Heralds a New Era in Political Campaigning: Media Report* (London, Reputation Intelligence, 2004).

[21] 'The group comprises Fathers, Mothers, Grandparents, Teachers, Doctors, Company Directors, Policemen, Barristers—a complete cross section of society': http://www.fathers-4-justice.org/introducing%20f4j/index.htm. Some F4J activists (for example, Matt O'Connor, Jason Birch and David Chick) have become public figures in the UK as a result of their involvement in the protests. Chick, who held a vigil in a crane over Tower Bridge in London in November 2003, was subsequently voted second in a BBC Radio 4 Poll for 'Man of the Year 2003' (reported in the *Independent on Sunday,* 8 February 2004). See also 'Who's The Daddy?' *Independent on Sunday,* 16 April 2006.

[22] 'Father of All Plots: The Kidnap that Wasn't and the End of a Protest Group' *The Independent,* 19 January 2006: 'Fathers 4 Justice is disbanded over "plot" to kidnap Leo Blair' *The Times,* 19 January 2006: 'Father Xmas 4 Justice' *The Sun,* 19 January 2006: 'Fathers Give Up Campaign' *The Daily Telegraph,* 19 January 2006. See further the statement at http://www.fathers-4-justice.org. 'Forgotten Fathers?' *The 5Live Report,* Julian Warwicker Programme, Sunday 26 March 2006, BBC Radio 5 Live, http://www.bbc.co.uk/fivelive/programmes/worricker.shtml (accessed 27 March 2006).

[23] A conscious and disturbing echo of the 'Real IRA'.

[24] Subsequent to its disbanding and the emergence of the Real F4J protests have continued: 'Egg Thrown at Kelly Outside Court' http://news.bbc.co.uk/1/hi/england/manchester/4685496.stm.

[25] *The Rising: Outlaw Fathers Fight Back* (October 2003); *The McDad Day Demo* (planned for June 2005, subsequently cancelled; see Laville, n 29 below).

[26] 'We are going to target solicitors, members of the judiciary and barristers and we have a list of the people we are looking at': Peter Molly, activist, reported in *The Guardian,* 3 February 2004.

[27] 'Blair Hit During Commons Protest' *BBC News,* 19 May 2004. This attack prompted MPs to evacuate the chamber and resulted in the arrest of two activists.

[28] Above n 19.

becoming an increasingly common sight across bridges, gantries and other public buildings. Controversies during 2005 surrounding aspects of the membership and practices of the organisation had already, prior to the events of January 2006, prompted a degree of realignment within the group,[29] as well as a revision of the public profile they sought to present. Nonetheless, and notwithstanding recent developments, F4J remain, at the time of writing, the most visible and high-profile fathers' rights group in the UK.[30]

The development of case-law and detail of the policy agendas which have informed the rapidly shifting debate around contact law reform in England and Wales are beyond the scope of this chapter.[31] The extensive media coverage of the F4J campaign, backed by the public support of Bob Geldof,[32] has been highly critical as well as broadly supportive of both the means and ends of the organisation.[33] There is little doubt however, that politicians and policy makers have taken notice of the growing profile of fathers' rights which has resulted from the campaign.[34] The wider debate at the time of writing is focused on the introduction of early intervention schemes and parenting plans, revision of the available court sanctions and the promotion of further reforms aimed at shifting the attitudes and behaviour of parents towards separation and 'divorcing responsibly'.[35]

Whilst many have broadly welcomed attempts on the part of government to seek an end to the much criticised adversarial system in contact disputes, such proposals have been considered by F4J to be 'too little, too late'.[36] Why is this so? The F4J campaign, like that of the FRM generally, addresses a broad range of

---

[29] During 2005 a number of personal and political tensions within F4J surfaced, culminating in a peak-time television 'exposé' of the activities and membership of the organisation (ITV, *Tonight With Trevor MacDonald*, 14 November 2005); S Laville, 'Batman and Robin Quit Protest Group' *The Guardian*, 9 June 2005: 'You've Heard of the Real IRA. Now Meet Real Fathers4Justice, the caped crusaders who refuse to give up the fight.'

[30] In a curious twist to the history of F4J, 'the 'heroes' of direct-action group Fathers 4 Justice are to be immortalised in *F4J: The Movie*, with filming due to commence in early 2007: 'Men in Tights: movie debut for Fathers 4 Justice' *The Independent*, 2 February 2006. Discussed further in 'Forgotten Fathers?' *The 5Live Report*, above n 22.

[31] Although F4J have been active throughout the UK, the discussion which follows relates primarily to law reform debates in England and Wales.

[32] B Geldof, 'The Real Love that Dare Not Speak its Name' in A Bainham, B Lindley, M Richards and L Trinder (eds), *Children and Their Families* (Oxford, Hart, 2003). Interestingly, government reforms (below) were announced during a Ministerial interview with Bob Geldof on BBC Radio 4: *Media Monitoring Unit: Transcript The Today Programme*, 3 April 2004 (GICS, 2004). See also 'Bob's Message to Families Need Fathers' at: http://www.fnf.org.uk/bobg.htm.

[33] Much discussion has focused on the ethics and efficacy of the protests as a form of 'gesture politics': A Phillips, 'Most Fathers Get Justice' *The Guardian*, 13 October 2004.

[34] *Parental Separation: Children's Needs and Parents' Responsibilities*, Cm 6273 (London, HMSO, 2004); *Parental Separation: Children's Needs and Parents' Responsibilities, Next Steps*, Cm 6452 (London, HMSO, 2005). There has been considerable agreement, across diverse perspectives, that F4J have indeed influenced the debate in this area: see eg 'Forgotten Fathers?' *The 5Live Report*, above n 22.

[35] *Putting Children First: Parenting Plans, a Planner for Separating Parents* (London, DCA, 2005).

[36] 'Fathers Spurn Plan to Save Parents from Court Battles' *The Guardian*, 20 March 2004.

concerns. There is one core issue, however, in relation to which the government has steadfastly refused to move: the call by F4J for the institution of a legal presumption of contact and shared equal parenting, whereby non-resident parents will, it is proposed, have a legal *right* to see their children.[37]

How is one to make sense of these events? For all their activities and public visibility the success of F4J in influencing government policy would appear to be limited.[38] Shared equal parenting has been explicitly and unequivocally rejected.[39] The government's position has been informed, rather, by the insights of a body of research, including that of socio-legal scholarship,[40] much of which has directly countered key points advanced by F4J: the assumption, for example, that the vast majority of men are, in fact, equal carers; the belief that the '50/50' shared parenting split is, in the vast majority of cases at least, workable in material and practical terms.[41] Critics have noted the conceptual ambiguity of the 'meaningful relationship' with children sought by fathers' rights activists.[42] Concern has been expressed over the consequences for women of the enforcement of court orders of the kind sought and related issues around post-separation financial arrangements. The central claim that fathers are now the 'victims' of family law has been described as profoundly wrong (see further below). And, importantly, the assumption that contact is what children themselves want, and that it is always in their best interests, has been revealed as problematic. Research suggests, rather, that what many children want is flexibility in post-separation arrangements and, in particular, to have a voice which is heard in establishing what such arrangements will be.

In the remainder of this chapter I wish to chart a way through what appears to be this apparent disjuncture between, on the one hand, official discourse, research studies and policy goals; and, on the other, what is presented by the FRM and groups such as F4J as the lived realities of many men's lives—a social experience of divorce which has led to a perception, on the part of apparently growing numbers of men, that family law is unjust, oppressive and corrupt in how it treats

[37] Although the Children Act 1989 states that the welfare of the child is best served by maintaining a relationship with both parents as far as possible, there is no statutory 'right' to contact in the legislation.

[38] There is an overlap in this regard with developments in other countries such as Canada and Australia (see Boyd and Rhoades, this volume).

[39] 'Some fathers' groups have come to believe that the courts and the law are biased against them. *We do not accept this view*': C Falconer, C Clarke and P Hewitt, 'Ministerial Forward' in *Parental Separation: Children's Needs and Parents' Responsibilities*, Cm 6273 (London, HMSO, 2004) 1, emphasis added.

[40] For example, C Smart, V May, A Wade and C Furniss, *Residence and Contact Disputes in Court: Research Report 6/2003* (London, DCA, 2003), a study of disputes over residence and contact brought to three county courts in England in the year 2000, cited by Margaret Hodge, *Hansard, HC Debates*, col 67W (5 January 2004).

[41] See further F Kaganas and C Piper, 'Shared Parenting—A 70% Solution?' [2002] 14 (4) *Child and Family Law Quarterly* 365.

[42] Note generally, for example: A Bainham, 'Contact as a Fundamental Right' (1995) 54 *Cambridge Law Journal* 255.

men who are fathers. It is necessary, first, to consider how divorce has been conceptualised within this growing debate about contact.

The 'Co-Parenting Turn', the New Fatherhood and the Good Divorce

Divorce, Kaganas and Day Sclater have argued,[43] is a process which obliges parents to 'position themselves in relation to a range of often competing discourses (legal, welfare, therapeutic and, more recently, human rights) and to find ways of living alongside them'.[44] Divorce is 'framed at the intersections of legal practice, social policy, welfare ideology, relationship breakdown and personal pain'.[45] This kind of conceptualisation of divorce has proved influential within a range of studies in recent years which seek to unpack the emergence of what has been described as a now dominant welfare discourse in the field of family policy. Within the 'co-parenting turn', it is argued, children have been conceptualised as vulnerable, and divorce and separation have been seen as particularly damaging—for the individuals concerned, for children and for society.[46]

Locating this development within the context of a refocusing on ideas of the 'civilising process' and responsibility[47] within a broader frame of neo-liberal governmentality, Smart and Neale describe[48] nothing less than a clear and determined attempt to effect 'social engineering' in the area of the family by 'changing the very nature of post-divorce family life'.[49] Importantly, a repositioning of fatherhood has been widely seen as a key element within this process. Ideas of 'good' fatherhood have been 'reconstructed', 'reconstituted', 'remade' (the terms vary in the literature) in the legal regulation of post-divorce family life.[50] This

---

[43] F Kaganas and S Day Sclater, 'Contact Disputes: Narrative Constructions of "Good Parents"' (2004) 12(1) *Feminist Legal Studies* 1; see also, S Day Sclater and F Kaganas, 'Contact: Mothers, Welfare and Rights' in Bainham, Lindley, Richards and Trinder, above n 32.

[44] Kaganas and Day Sclater, *ibid*, 2–3.

[45] *Ibid.*

[46] C Piper, 'Divorce Reform and the Image of the Child' (1996) 23(3) *Journal of Law and Society* 364; B Neale and C Smart, 'In Whose Best Interests? Theorising Family Life following Parental Separation or Divorce' in SD Sclater and C Piper (eds), *Undercurrents of Divorce* (Aldershot, Ashgate, 1999).

[47] See further H Reece, *Divorcing Responsibly* (Oxford, Hart, 2003); also C Piper, *The Responsible Parent* (Hemel Hempstead, Harvester Wheatsheaf, 1993).

[48] See C Smart and B Neale, *Family Fragments?* (Cambridge, MA, Polity, 1999); B Neale and C Smart, 'Experiments with Parenthood?' (1997) 31(2) *Sociology* 201; C Smart and B Neale, 'Good Enough Morality? Divorce and Postmodernity' (1997) 17 (4) *Critical Social Policy* 3.

[49] C Smart, 'Wishful Thinking and Harmful Tinkering? Sociological Reflections on Family Policy' (1997) 26(3) *Journal of Social Policy* 1.

[50] C Smart, 'The "New" Parenthood: Fathers and Mothers After Divorce' in E Silva and C Smart (eds), *The New Family?* (London, Sage, 1999); C Smart and B Neale, '"I Hadn't Really Thought About It": New Identities/New Fatherhoods' in J Seymour and P Bagguley (eds), *Relating Intimacies: Power and Resistance* (Basingstoke, Palgrave Macmillan, 1999).

wider context around divorce, however, raises three important issues pertaining to an analysis of fathers' rights.

First, what constitutes 'good enough' post-divorce parenting is not, and has never been, universally agreed. It is about struggles over meaning and desired norms, and the complex interrelationships between social and legal knowledge(s) and power.[51] Secondly, the welfare discourse, as above, has involved a model of child welfare that 'places cooperative parenting and contact with the non-resident parent at the centre of children's well-being'; a non-resident parent who is, in the majority of cases, the father. Thirdly, the 'new paradigm' of divorce law has positioned men and women in different ways as, variously, good, responsible (or irresponsible) subjects of divorce (see below).

When seen against this backdrop the arguments advanced by F4J would, on the surface at least, appear to chime in a number of respects with the dominant welfare discourse. They each evoke, for example, the idea of the vulnerable child in need of contact with their father; of the responsible parent who should, in turn, facilitate or seek such contact. There has emerged a powerful and, arguably, culturally hegemonic representation of a form of good, benign fatherhood in law; a father figure, and an approach to co-parenting, which is itself not dissimilar to that evoked by fathers' rights groups in their critique of the law. How accurate, in such a context, is the argument that fathers have become the new victims of law?

Are Fathers Really the 'New Victims' of Contact Law?

F4J make use of a variety of rhetorical devices in advancing their argument. In contrast to more established groups such as FNF, they have been particularly associated with a depiction of women,[52] and a blaming of 'lone mothers',[53] which has been seen as distinctly negative in tone. Fathers are routinely depicted as respectable and socially 'safe'[54] subjects, as 'sharer[s] of responsibilities',[55] active

---

[51] See further S Boyd, 'Backlash and the Construction of Legal Knowledge: The Case of Child Custody Law' (2001) 20 *Windsor Yearbook of Access to Justice* 141. Generally, S Boyd, *Child Custody, Law and Women's Work* (Oxford, Oxford University Press, 2003); K Kurki-Suonio, 'Joint Custody as an Interpretation of the Best Interests of the Child in Critical and Comparative Perspective' (2000) 14(3) *International Journal of Law, Policy and the Family* 183; M King, 'Foreword' in Day Sclater and Piper, above n 46, 49; M Fineman, 'Dominant Discourse, Professional Language, and Legal Change in Child Custody Decision Making' (1988) 101 *Harvard Law Review* 727.

[52] M Kaye and J Tolmie, 'Discoursing Dads: The Rhetorical Devices of Fathers' Rights Groups' (1998) 22 *Melbourne University Law Review* 162, 184.

[53] S Boyd, 'Demonizing Mothers: Fathers' Rights Discourses in Child Custody Law Reform Processes' (2004) 6(1) *Journal of the Association for Research in Mothering* 52, 60. Note, for example, the accusations of misogyny which have surfaced in debates about the political direction of F4J during 2005: nn 22, 29.

[54] See further Collier, above n 8.

[55] Smart and Neale, above n 50.

participants in paid employment, child care and domestic labour.[56] Fathers are 'carriers of rights',[57] individuals whose full citizenship is embodied, or denied, by a formal legal recognition of their equal status. Such an appeal to 'treat fathers equally' is aligned with earlier feminist campaigns: fathers' rights activists are 'suffra*gents*', men engaged in a campaign itself branded via use of the suffragettes' traditional purple.

Arguments, Myths and Realities: 'Motherhood Descending'?[58]

This depiction, I have suggested, maps in a number of respects to the model of fatherhood associated with the welfare discourse. What, however, has it meant in practice—for fathers, mothers and children? A growing theoretical and empirical research base has questioned the consequences of these developments for parents who divorce—and, in particular, it has raised concerns about the impact of the new contact culture on mothers. A rich body of research has emerged which suggests that the new fatherhood has impacted on the practices of the courts, lawyers, family welfare professionals and parents in a number of complex ways; and the picture being painted is very different from that suggested by F4J.[59]

Research has identified, for example, the emergence in case-law during the 1990s of the figure of the 'implacably hostile', bad, selfish mother.[60] Men, it is argued, have tended to be absented from the obligations arising from the co-parenting project based on co-operation; there is no such figure as the 'implacably *irresponsible*' father.[61] Within the fathers' rights discourse it is assumed that fatherhood is only revealed as problematic for law at the point of divorce or separation. Yet, Smart and Neale suggest,[62] there exists a disjuncture between the equality *rhetoric* advanced by groups such as F4J and the continuing (gendered) *realities* of parenting, both during subsisting relationships and after divorce/separation. Rhoades and Boyd, writing of recent developments in Australia and Canada respectively, note further consequences of a new ideology

---

[56] See further Lewis, above n 5; J Warin, Y Solomon, C Lewis and W Langford, *Fathers, Work and Family Life* (York, Joseph Rowntree Foundation/Family Policy Studies Centre, 1999).

[57] Smart and Neale, above n 50.

[58] M Fineman, *The Neutered Mother, The Sexual Family and Other Twentieth Century Tragedies* (London, Routledge, 1995).

[59] R Bailey-Harris, J Barron and J Pearce, 'From Utility to Rights? The Presumption of Contact in Practice' (1999) 13 *International Journal of Law, Policy and the Family* 111; C Smart and B Neale, 'Arguments Against Virtue: Must Contact Be Enforced?' [1997] *Family Law* 332.

[60] C Bruch, 'Parental Alienation Syndrome and Alienated Children—Getting it Wrong in Child Custody Cases' [2002] 14 (4) *Child and Family Law Quarterly* 381; C Williams, 'Parental Alienation Syndrome' [2002] *Family Law* 410; J Masson, 'Parental Alienation Syndrome' [2002] *Family Law* 568.

[61] See further Smart and Neale, above n 50.

[62] *Ibid*, 118. Contrast J Warin *et al*, above n 56; J Bernard, 'The Good-Provider Role: Its Rise and Fall' (1981) 36 *American Psychologist* 1.

of motherhood in family law, in the constitution of stories about selfish
mothers which, they suggest, can have far-reaching implications for women
who do wish to raise concerns about the capacity of some fathers to care for
their children.[63]

   This research suggests that the reasons for the breakdown of contact arrangements may themselves be more complex than the image of women 'refusing'
access would seem to suggest.[64] Leaving aside the questionable empirical reality
of large numbers of mendacious mothers acting in such a way, and far from
women deploying a form of uni-directional power, others suggest that some
mothers may be experiencing a form of 'debilitative power' on the part of fathers;
a constraining of their own drive to independence, autonomy and self-develop-
ment in the period after separation.[65] This issue assumes particular importance
in relation to questions of domestic violence. Non-resident fathers, it has been
argued, may have been empowered by the new contact order culture (an
'enabling context' for violence) in such a way that new pressures have then been
placed on women to agree to contact arrangements, notwithstanding concerns
that might be held about violence. Issues of violence, others argue, have been
marginalised within much divorce mediation practice.[66] The depiction of violence as 'exceptional', and of the hostile mother/aggrieved father dualism as a
somehow typical scenario, is one which itself does not reflect the reality of what
is known about the presence of violence within many marriages (and, in particular, in the period following separation).[67] As Kaganas[68] puts it, in her analysis of
the development of case-law on parental responsibility in England and Wales, it
is 'almost impossible to conceive of a father who is harmful to children unless he
inflicts direct violence on them'.[69] In a more recent review Kaganas and Day
Sclater put the point starkly:

> ... the dominant welfare discourse [has been] interpreted so as to create so strong an
> association between contact and welfare that neither risks to mothers' health nor, until

[63] In addition to work cited above, H Rhoades, 'The "Non Contact Mother": Reconstructions of Motherhood in the Era of the New Father' (2002) 16 *International Journal of Law, Policy and the Family* 72; H Rhoades, 'The Rise and Rise of Shared Parenting Laws—A Critical Reflection' (2002) 19 *Canadian Journal of Family Law* 75.

[64] See, for example, the work of Smart and Neale, *Family Fragments*; 'Experiments'; and 'Good Enough Morality?', above n 48.

[65] See further S Day Sclater, *Divorce: A Psycho-Social Study* (Aldershot, Ashgate, 1999). A theme which emerges in some media reporting of F4J activists: 'Jason [Birch] is so busy fighting to see his other kids he spends no time with ours' reported in *The Sun*, 15 September 2004.

[66] D Greatbatch and R Dingwall, 'The Marginalization of Domestic Violence in Divorce Mediation' (1999) 13(2) *International Journal of Law, Policy and the Family* 174; F Kaganas, 'Contact, Conflict and Risk' in Day Sclater and Piper, above n 46.

[67] Rhoades, 'Non Contact Mother', above n 63.

[68] Kaganas, 'Contact, Conflict and Risk', above n 66.

[69] F Kaganas and C Piper, 'Contact and Domestic Violence: The Winds of Change?' [2000] *Family Law* 630.

recently, serious violence on the part of the non-resident father were regarded as sufficient reason to deny an order.[70]

These arguments would seem to undermine the position of F4J. A body of academic research, policy and professional literature has charted what appears to be,
if anything, an empowering of fathers as a result of the emergence, embedding
and consolidation of the new welfare discourse. Research suggests that fathers *are*
accorded considerable significance; indeed, they may have become so central to
the new contact culture that, if anything, it is the interests of mothers that have
been downgraded or, to use Fineman's term, writing of developments in the
United States, 'neutered'.[71] Smart has suggested in the UK context that there has
been an 'erasure' of a moral discourse of care in relation to motherhood.[72]

Does this mean, however, that F4J and other fathers' rights organisations such
as FNF are simply 'wrong'? Do they exemplify an anti-feminist 'backlash' in family law and in society? Why is it felt—so strongly, and with such force—that law *is*
systematically discriminating against men, given the presence of a body of
research which would seem to suggest that, if anything, the opposite is the case?
Or are we dealing here, at its crudest, with a matter of 'false consciousness' on the
part of these men? Men who are in reality truly empowered, if only they could
realise it?

There is, of course, no 'one' divorce. Individual life-history and biography, as
well as specific economic, cultural and legal contexts, mediate social experience.
The question of why some men turn to fathers' rights groups, albeit for one
moment in their lives, and may invest in the subject position of 'fathers' rights
activist' (whilst others do not), is beyond the scope of this chapter.[73] We cannot
ascertain from an analysis of the rhetorical devices of the FRM a knowledge of the
cultural, economic and psychological investments individual men make in adapt-
ing to (or, indeed, resisting) practices, attitudes and values commonly associated
with participation in fathers' rights groups. By looking more closely at recent
research concerned with the changing nature of post-divorce/separation family
life, however, it is possible to find some tentative answers to these questions.
Something *is* happening in this area which, I want to suggest, is of considerable
significance—developments which it would be misleading to characterise as a
'reactionary' anti-feminist backlash on the part of men.

---

[70] Kaganas and Day Sclater, above n 43, 6–7, footnotes omitted.

[71] Fineman, above n 58.

[72] C Smart, 'Losing the Struggle for Another Voice—The Case of Family Law' (1995) 18 *Dalhousie
Law Journal* 173; S Coltrane and N Hickman, 'The Rhetoric of Rights and Needs: Moral Discourse in
the Reform of Child Custody and Support Laws' (1992) 39 *Social Problems* 400. For an excellent discussion of the broader issues engaged here see Boyd, 'Child Custody', above n 51.

[73] See further R Collier, 'Reflections on the Relationship Between Law and Masculinities: Rethinking
the "Man Question" in Legal Studies' (2003) 56 *Current Legal Problems* 345.

Rethinking Fathers' Rights

Post-Separation Life: Gendered Rationalities, Gendered Lives?

Empirical research into post-separation life[74] over the past decade suggests that relationships formed during marriage and cohabitation can be reshaped, often in far reaching ways, following separation; and that in this process, different models and understandings of what constitutes 'good' fathering practice can emerge from those which prevailed during subsisting relationships. Research suggests, moreover, that the prescriptions for good parenting to be found in law, along with related assumptions about what is best for children, may have 'entered parents' vocabularies ... [and are] routinely used by parents as a framework for understanding and talking about their experience'.[75] Although this might be accepted in the abstract, however, both women *and* men 'actively interpret it according to their own criteria'. Law's prescriptions for the 'responsible divorce', in short, are not passively accepted. They are matters for 'active, often critical'[76] negotiation.

This point is of considerable significance in seeking to understand the changing status of fathers' rights agendas within reform debates. Drawing on a growing body of research concerned with the 'fluid, evolutionary' nature of post-separation life, it is possible to make two points in this regard. First, research suggests, as above, fathers are not alone in framing 'the meaning of the dispute in terms of a battle of the sexes'.[77] That this should be so is unsurprising for, as Kaganas and Day Sclater observe, parenting remains a profoundly gendered activity. While law may thus be *ascribing* equal value to fathering and mothering, for many women the recognition accorded to motherhood within the new contact culture does not reflect the reality of their greater responsibilities for day-to-day caring practices within their post-separation households.

Secondly, if it is the case that women and men frame their grievances via reference to the welfare of children, they nonetheless appear to do so in ways which reflect their own distinctive 'gendered lives' and what have been termed 'gendered rationalities'. Issues of gender frame and mediate many aspects of social experience, not least perhaps in relation to ideas of family life and normative parenting practices.[78] The way in which an emphasis on contact can clash with women's drive to

---

[74] Eg C Lewis, A Papacosta and J Warin, *Cohabitation, Separation and Fatherhood* (York, YPS/Joseph Rowntree Foundation, 2002); C Smart and P Stephens, *Cohabitation Breakdown* (York, Family Policy Studies Centre/Joseph Rowntree Foundation, 2000).

[75] Kaganas and Day Sclater, above n 43, 15.

[76] *Ibid*, 16.

[77] *Ibid*.

[78] S Duncan and R Edwards, *Lone Mothers, Paid Work and Gendered Moral Rationalities* (Basingstoke, Palgrave Macmillan, 1999); S Duncan, A Carling and R Edwards (eds), *Analysing Families: Morality and Rationality in Policy and Practice* (London, Routledge, 2002).

'independency'[79] within the post-separation context has been noted above. What is also becoming clear, however, is that the emergence of the new fatherhood might be reshaping *men's* interpretations and experiences of separation.

The rhetorical devices and arguments deployed by the FRM, as detailed elsewhere in this volume, would appear to resonate strongly with the discursive strategies at play within men's own negotiations and experiences of divorce and separation. Both, for example, are marked by such features as the denial, minimising and normalising of conduct which, it is felt, might be subject to criticism;[80] by a distinguishing of the 'good father' from 'other' men, deemed the 'bad', 'feckless' or 'deadbeat' father;[81] by a belief that the good father would and should 'fight for' his children, given the messages conveyed within the new contact culture;[82] and, as noted above, by a deployment of the 'bad mother' as a figure who, in failing her children, will further necessitate the presence of the father in their lives.

In making these arguments it is unsurprising that the narrative of the good father as a responsible and caring parent should be drawn upon, given the dominant discourse around co-operation. However, alongside a repositioning of discourses around maternal care, as noted above, it would also appear that a reframing of what is considered to be acceptable behaviour on the part of men (whether it be within or beyond the home) is an issue which is linked to the apparent tendency for men, in particular, to display a greater propensity to evoke a rights discourse within the process of separation; and, in turn, to engage in what has been termed a 'masculinised discourse' of divorce.[83] Aspects of the new fatherhood—what it involves, what it calls into being—appear to correlate with this tendency for men to relate to, and appeal in their engagement with law in terms of, a rights-based framework. It is, after all, what a 'good father' would do.[84] Law's prescriptions towards consensus, however, on closer examination, clash in other respects with the *emotional* imperatives that drive this engagement, not least in relation to the complex issue of conflict—an issue which, I wish to suggest,

---

[79] See further Day Sclater, above n 65.

[80] A theme noted in recent work concerned with interventions in the field of domestic violence: D Gadd, 'Masculinities, Violence and Defended Psycho-Social Subjects' (2000) 4 *Theoretical Criminology* 429.

[81] Compare G Furstenberg, 'Good Dads—Bad Dads: Two Faces of Fatherhood' in AJ Cherline (ed), *The Changing American Family and Public Policy* (Washington, DC, The Urban Institute Press, 1988).

[82] J Dewar, 'The Normal Chaos of Family Law' (1998) 61 *Modern Law Review* 467 suggests, for example, that the concerns about justice expressed by fathers' rights groups appear to be shared by many men who have expressed a growing dissatisfaction with the perceived limits of a broad discretionary system in the family law field.

[83] See, for example: T Arendell, *Fathers and Divorce* (Thousand Oaks, CA, Sage, 1995); T Arendell, 'The Social Self as Gendered: A Masculinist Discourse of Divorce' (1992) 15 *Symbolic Interactionism* 151. The form of the protests of groups such as F4J can themselves be seen to be masculine in nature in this regard; public displays of physical endeavour, outward projects of an inner anger.

[84] As F4J put it: 'We are driven by a sense of duty, responsibility and the need to create change and bring about justice': http://www.fathers-4-justice.org/our_pledge/index.htm.

informs the ultimately contradictory nature of aspects of the fathers' rights lobby's engagement with law.

Fatherhood, Divorce and the Negation of Conflict

I have argued that there appears to be a series of mutual resonances between the new welfare discourse and the arguments of groups such as F4J. Conflating the interests of fathers and children, in particular, would appear to be an effective strategy in raising the profile of fathers' rights organisations in engaging with policy makers. Yet if we look closer, the arguments of F4J, as well as those of the FRM more generally, seem to stand in a more ambivalent relationship to the welfare discourse than might at first appear to be the case. This is particularly evident in relation to the issue of emotion, the negation of conflict and the assumption that contact and consensus between the parties is itself an *a priori* social good.[85]

Why is this so? The public protests of F4J and the emotional imperatives that drive them—the profound sense, for example, of injustice, anger, betrayal and loss[86]—clash starkly, indeed violently at times, with an official discourse which suggests that contemporary divorce has evolved into an arena 'beyond politics' (a view present not just in the UK but across the jurisdictions discussed in this volume). There is in this regard, curiously, a shared acceptance between fathers' rights organisations and their diverse critics that questions of equity, morality and politics *cannot*, in fact, be effaced from debates around contact and divorce. For F4J the dominant interpretation of the terms 'children's welfare' and 'best interests of the children' by judges, lawyers, mediators and welfare officers conceals a powerful moral agenda; one never explicitly acknowledged but which is seen as unjust to men in the way in which it fails to recognise the new realities of men's lives as fathers. What law also fails to 'see', however, and to adequately recognise, is the force, nature and consequences of these emotional conflicts around separation on individual men—and, in particular, their psychological impacts on men whose experiences of and commitments to fatherhood are felt to be very different from those of previous generations.

It is precisely these psychological ambivalences of loss accompanying the end of human relationships which, Day Sclater argues, jar in a more general sense—for both women and men—with the powerful rhetoric of the harmonious divorce central to the welfare discourse.[87] The dominant discourse functions in

---

[85] This is not to deny the desirability of establishing, or to underestimate the complex problems that can revolve around, maintaining contact.

[86] See below.

[87] See further Day Sclater, above n 65; S Day Sclater, *The Psychology of Divorce: A Research Report to the ESRC* (London, University of East London, 1998); S Day Sclater, 'Divorce—Coping Strategies, Conflict and Dispute Resolution' [1998] *Family Law* 150; S Day Sclater and C Yates, 'The Psycho-Politics of Post Divorce Parenting' in A Bainham, S Day Sclater and M Richards (eds), *What is a Parent? A Socio-Legal Analysis* (Oxford, Hart, 1999); J Brown and S Day Sclater, 'Divorce: A Psychodynamic Perspective' in Sclater and Piper, above n 46.

such a way as to negate the legitimacy of, and to deny the space to articulate, these conflictual feelings of loss, guilt and anger; emotions which, for Brown and Day Sclater,[88] almost inevitably accompany the process of divorce and the break-up of family relationships. The psychological processes of separation, in other words, are enmeshed with the gendered rationalities discussed above in ways which mediate how men and women experience divorce and their engagements with law. This is evident, as above, in ways that appear to foster a view on the part of men that it is the legal system that is to blame for what they are experiencing, that law is somehow 'at fault'. Yet the rise of fathers' rights agendas, not least around the question of how men psychologically respond to divorce and separation, is an issue bound up with something else—a shift not only in social relationships between women and men but also, importantly, between men and children.

Childhood, Individualisation and the Responsible Father

The growing interest of fathers in issues of contact law reform has been linked with two interrelated processes: a rise of individualisation across western societies,[89] and an interconnected refiguring of understandings of children and the idea of childhood. The figure of the child has long been seen, across a range of literatures, as the symbolic focus for questions of social stability and integration. Debates about childhood have encompassed (and cannot be confined to) questions about the changing nature of adult interdependencies and, increasingly, issues of risk, anxiety and security associated with the physical safety and psychological well-being of children.[90] Shifts in the nature of adult investments in and relationships to the child and childhood are of considerable significance when seeking to understand the changing profile of fathers' rights agendas.[91] The relationship between men and children has, generally, become problematic in several respects over the past three decades. Hitherto normative ideas of masculinity, not least in relation to men's status in the family and paid employment, are widely perceived to have been fractured and reformed, contested and politicised, notably (although not exclusively) as a result of shifts in women's paid employment.[92]

---

[88] Ibid.

[89] U Beck and EA Beck Gernsheim, Individualisation (London, Sage, 2002); J Lewis, The End of Marriage? Individualism and Intimate Relations (Cheltenham, Edward Elgar, 2001).

[90] Cf U Beck, The Risk Society (London, Sage, 1992); F Furedi, Paranoid Parenting (London, Allen Lane, 2002).

[91] C Jenks, Childhood (London, Routledge, 1996) 20–21.

[92] J Lewis, 'The Decline of the Male Breadwinner Model Family' (2001) 8 Social Politics 152; K Gerson, No Man's Land: Men's Changing Commitments to Family and Work (New York, Basic Books, 1993).

If the extent of change in men's participation in domestic work and child care remains contested, however, research on fatherhood does suggest that childhood has assumed a different significance and duration within the life experience of many men; and, as children demand a labour (cognitive, affective and manual) that stands in marked contrast to the practices associated with ideas of 'good fatherhood' prevailing at earlier historical moments,[93] men's relationships to children both during and after marriage would also appear to have shifted. In such a context the figure of the child (indeed, the very body of the child—to be 'owned', to be split 50/50 by law?) would appear to assume a powerful experiential significance in providing meaning to many men's lives at a time such as divorce or separation. This is a moment of life transition, it is important to remember, often marked by feelings of disorientating change and uncertainty, not least in relation to questions about men's role and status in the family—the very concerns, of course, central to the fathers' rights discourse. In such a context it is important to recall that much of the FRM does not just hold out the offer of a sense of belonging and community (see below); it affords an opportunity to benefit from a range of services that might otherwise be unavailable to many men, such as counselling and support meetings, information provision, discussion of men's health issues and so forth. It also offers, in some contexts, a return to what may perhaps be a reassuring and appealing, albeit anachronistic, image of the father as authority-figure and breadwinner; a father, that is, who remains an unambiguous stable masculine identity in what can otherwise appear an increasingly uncertain world.

It is in the light of shifting adult investments, in short, that the sense of loss of the child experienced in the process of divorce and separation might appear to be so keenly felt. This does not explain, however, why the consequences of this should be projected with such force onto the perceived failings of the legal system. In this regard that the dominant welfarist principle of care discussed above would itself appear to inform the development of a sense of grievance and injustice on the part of fathers. The problematic positioning of the vulnerable child within the welfare discourse has been subject to extensive and critical commentary.[94] Critics have noted how children's voices have been interpreted, understood and processed in questionable ways.[95] The 'irrebuttable presumption' in favour of contact, as

---

[93] Although it is important to recognise that such practices are informed by ideals which are mediated by class, race and ethnicity: W Hatten, L Vinter and R Williams, *Dads on Dads: Needs and Expectations at Work and Home* (Manchester, Equal Opportunities Commission, 2002).

[94] See F Kaganas and A Diduck, 'Incomplete Citizens: Changing Images of Post-Separation Children' (2004) 67(6) *Modern Law Review* 959, who suggest a recent 'blending' of paradigms in which the child is increasingly seen as *both* an autonomous social actor and a vulnerable object of concern.

[95] A Wade, B Neale and C Smart, *The Changing Experience of Childhood: Families and Divorce* (Cambridge, Polity, 2001); C Piper, 'Assumptions About Children's Best Interests' (2000) 22 *Journal of Social Welfare and Family Law* 261.

noted, can itself run counter to the views and feelings of children.[96] Yet it would appear that the very ideal of co-parenting supported by law might itself serve to fuel conflicts between divorcing parents in certain circumstances, notably where it is perceived to be the product, not of a shared ideology, but of legal or financial coercion or other unresolved tensions; tensions and psychological conflicts which, in the case of the men participating in fathers' rights organisations, there is clearly reason to believe might well remain unresolved.

Far from reducing conflict, the legislative interventions discussed above have been linked to an increase in the frequency of disputes,[97] an issue that can be related to the (gendered) psychological dimensions of separation referred to above. The way in which the divorce process is negotiated and experienced has been seen as part of the development of a broader 'project of the self' within the social conditions of late modernity.[98] The welfare discourse exemplifies a new mode of neo-liberal 'governmentality', one marked by a growing pressure to behave in standardised ways and to normative prescriptions. This phenomenon is particularly clear in the UK context, where polices of the New Labour government, across a range of areas, have sought to promote the idea of 'responsible' citizenship. This is also a context, moreover, in which the 'good citizen' is positioned across a range of contexts (not just in family law)[99] as an *information-seeking* subject, an individual who will, given appropriate information/education, act (or in this case divorce) 'responsibly'.[100] The problem with this in the family law context, though, is that such pressure for private decisions to run on 'standard biography' lines can run counter to the psychological and emotional realities of separation discussed above. Men, like women, for understandable psychological as well as practical/material reasons, may be focusing on the 'I' at a time when law is exhorting them to focus on the 'we'. And, like women, men appear then to be reinterpreting the neutral language of welfarism in terms of the lived realities of family life as it is experienced by them *as men*.[101]

A further problem lies in the fact that the ideal of the new fatherhood bound up with the co-parenting contact culture is itself pervaded by some contradictory assumptions. Firstly, men are understood as both economic providers/breadwinners

[96] C Smart and B Neale, '"It's My Life Too"—Children's Perspectives on Post-Divorce Parenting' [2000] *Family Law* 163; C Smart, 'From Children's Shoes to Children's Voices' (2002) 40 *Family Court Review* 305; A Wade and C Smart, *Facing Family Change: Children's Circumstances, Strategies and Resources* (York, YPS/Joseph Rowntree Foundation, 2002); J Dunn, 'Contact and Children's Perspectives on Parental Relationships' in Bainham, Lindley, Richards and Trinder, above n 32.
[97] *Ibid.*
[98] Giddens, above n 3.
[99] Compare, for example, S Day Sclater and C Piper, 'Re-Moralising the Family? Family Policy, Family Law and Youth' [2000] 12 (3) *Child and Family Law Quarterly* 135.
[100] See, for example, Reece, above n 47, who identifies shifts in political and legal ideas of responsibility as evidence of broader shifts towards a form of 'post-liberalism' and neo-liberal governance.
[101] See further the argument of Day Sclater, above n 65.

and nurturers, as simultaneously committed to their work, home and children and trapped between ideas of the father as primary *resource* and the father as *carer*.[102] Secondly, fathers are caught between a denial of emotion which runs alongside a cultural and legal acceptance that men should deal with feelings of loss and vulnerability by recourse to rights. And, thirdly and finally, in the case of F4J, there is a tension between ideas of fathers as 'humorous' playful figures of fun, 'superheroes' to their children who dress as comic-book characters; and at the same time, men who are the 'foot-soldiers' in a new sex-war 'battle', men destroyed and banished to a 'Siberia of the broken'; men who, in spectacular displays of grief, can declare their pain by putting a noose around their heads, 'risking everything' for the children they feel they have lost.[103]

It is no wonder, in such a context, that these contradictions and confusions would appear to pervade the FRM. Many men, recent theoretical and empirical research on fatherhood suggests, do appear to be caught in a double-bind between powerful discourses of provider/breadwinner and carer/nurturer; and, in turn, deal with feelings of loss and vulnerability by appealing to equity, justice and rights. In the wider context presented in this chapter it becomes easier to see, perhaps, why the appeal to a sense of belonging and community projected by F4J and other fathers' rights organisations, as well as the opportunity to express and discuss conflictual emotions, should appear so powerful and to speak so forcefully to the lived experience of significant numbers of men. To downplay the reasons why this appeal exists would be to misread the social significance of the FRM as well as the diversity of the voices and viewpoints that it now contains.

Concluding Remarks

The limits of law in the regulation and management of intimate relationships have been well documented within family law scholarship. In facing the 'normal chaos'[104] of family life, it is argued, law inevitably simplifies, reducing the insights of other disciplines to its own ends.[105] Law 'deals in generalities and is ill-equipped to take full account of the complexities of human behaviour'.[106] The open-ended,

---

[102] Featherstone, above n 5.

[103] A representation of suicide has played a particularly significant part within the F4J campaign. For example, in December 2003 a man dressed as Santa Claus tied himself to the gantry above the A40 in London with a rope and put a noose around this neck; he unfurled a banner that read 'Children Need Both Parents This Christmas'. 'Try and arrest me,' he was reported as telling police, 'and I'll hang myself'. *The Independent*, 5 February 2004.

[104] U Beck and E Beck Gernsheim, above n 3; Dewar, above n 82.

[105] M King and C Piper, *How the Law Thinks About Children* (2nd edn, Aldershot, Arena, 1995).

[106] Kaganas and Day Sclater, above n 43.

contradictory and double-edged nature of family law reform has been widely noted within legal scholarship.[107] There is much evidence that the present court system in England and Wales for dealing with contact disputes does have serious faults; that it is, in particular, ill-adapted to deal with the difficult human dilemmas involved in the enforcement of its orders. The conflicts around fathers' rights and law described in this paper may, on one level, appear to be normal and inevitable features of what happens when law attempts to regulate human relationships.

Yet what is at stake in these debates around law and fatherhood is, as Dewar[108] suggests, something more than simply a balancing exercise between questions of individual rights and social utility. What we are dealing with are a number of different and incompatible ways of approaching decision making in the family law field itself. As Dewar argues, transferring inescapably political issues about principles, philosophy and the meaning of 'family values' to the field of law and administration makes it unsurprising that the legal arena should be marked by these unresolved (and, perhaps, unresolvable) tensions. Following Dewar's analysis, it is unremarkable that some potentially unworkable contradictions should run through the conceptualisation of fatherhood contained within the fathers' rights discourse.

There is considerable force to the argument that elements within the FRM in the UK have at times embraced and advocated a distinctive anti-feminist politics. The 'sex war' rhetoric common to much of the media reporting of the contact debate itself strongly echoes the language of groups such as F4J. Importantly, the fathers' rights discourse appears to efface complex questions about the *consequences* of applying gender-neutral norms to what can remain, for all the arguments advanced to the contrary, highly gender*ed* fields of practice. This discourse would appear to be unable to move conceptually beyond a core commitment to formal legal equality. In marked contrast to recent feminist scholarship,[109] it also betrays a failure to engage with the conceptual basis of the private family itself, as well as broader questions about the changing nature of law, legal regulation and governmentality. 'Fatherhood' tends to be understood largely within psychologistic, personal and individualised terms, devoid of any appreciation of the complex social and economic developments reshaping family practices. Meanwhile the

---

[107] See, for example, C Smart, 'Feminism and Law: Some Problems of Analysis and Strategy' (1986) 14 *International Journal of the Sociology of Law* 109; also J Dewar, 'Family Law and its Discontents' (2000) 14 *International Journal of Law, Policy and Family* 59.

[108] Above n 82.

[109] S Sevenhuijsen, *Citizenship and the Ethics of Care: Feminist Considerations about Justice, Morality and Politics* (London, Routledge, 1998); JC Tronto, *Moral Boundaries: A Political Argument for an Ethic of Care* (London, Routledge, 1993); JC Tronto, 'Women and Caring: What Can Feminists Learn about Morality from Caring?' in A Jaggar and S Bordo (eds), *Gender, Body, Knowledge* (Newark, NJ, Rutgers University Press, 1989).

issue of care and the unequal division of unpaid work in the 'intact' family has not been a primary issue for the FRM, just as it has not been for policy makers.

Yet it would be misleading to conceptualise what is taking place in this area as illustrating, or as simply symptomatic of, an anti-feminist 'backlash' in the field of family law. Such an argument curiously mirrors the thinking of the fathers' rights lobby in the way in which it tends to evoke a uni-directional form of power (and, indeed, a central binary of the powerful/powerless mother/father).[110] The contact debate, Rhoades has suggested, might more accurately be seen as exemplifying a new *kind* of political conflict in late modernity, one based around questions of how perceived inequalities are distributed and experienced.[111] In seeking to make sense of recent developments, this chapter has sought to draw out some of the complexities of this debate. I have explored, in particular, why fatherhood should have become such a contested issue in this area of law.

What may well be taking place in law at the present moment is something akin to the emergence of a paradigm marked by a *reconstruction* of the rhetoric of liberal legality. This is not simply a matter of conceptualising law as sufficiently malleable to accommodate the claims of fathers' rights agendas. This paradigm has, in a sense, constituted and *brought into being* the very claims to equality now advanced by the FRM. That is, as the debate on fatherhood enters the legal arena and engages with the language of law reform, so law calls into being precisely the kinds of protest strategies now being deployed by much of the FRM. This is a form of engagement rooted in the history of law reform struggles. And just as the suffering of men who are fathers is revealed and made visible, other hitherto (good) 'family men' are repositioned within this discourse as the (potential) victims of the injustice(s) of law. As has been recognised in other contexts, it is unsurprising that the 'end point' of social movements as distinctive moral enterprises should be the achievement of legal reform. The well-documented paradox, of course, noted within a rich feminist literature, is that legal success carries with it its own dangers. The frequent evocation of parallels with earlier movements is thus revealing in that it displays an acute awareness of the political force of such equality claims; yet, at the same time, it exposes a failure to engage with the limitations and contradictions of law reform itself.

It is, I have argued, necessary to recognise the complex and contradictory nature of the reconfiguration of gender relations framing these debates about fathers and contact law reform; and, following Smart,[112] to acknowledge the

---

[110] On the 'zero-sum' conception of power implicit in this kind of argument see R Collier, 'From "Women's Emancipation" to "Sex War"? Beyond the "Masculinized Discourse" of Divorce' in Day Sclater and Piper, above n 46.

[111] Rhoades, 'The "Non Contact Mother"', above n 63, citing Z Bauman *Intimations of Postmodernity* (London, Routledge, 1992).

[112] C Smart, 'The Ethic of Justice Fights Back: Family Law and the Rise of the New Paternity', paper presented at the Canadian Law and Society Association Annual Meeting, 'Law's Empire', 26–29 June 2005.

significance of the 'different registers' of fathers' voices which appear to be emerging around discourses of welfare, justice and, increasingly, care. In charting the limits of formal legal equality in this arena, it is possible to detect a 'fragmentation' of fatherhood itself;[113] a process which involves (among other things) processes of social change encompassing shifts in the structure and experience of employment; a reappraisal of issues of identity, commitment and responsibility; an appreciation of the limits of formal equality (as above); and, in particular, a rethinking of the relationship between men and children. It also necessitates rethinking 'what happens to' emotion and conflict (not least to feelings of pain and loss) in the legal arena.

The language of pain pervades much of the fathers' rights discourse. In one sense it is inseparable from the idea of reciprocity, of 'getting even' through recourse to law. Yet it is also entwined with what might be termed the *embodiment* of perceived injustice and inequality, something particularly evident in the protests of F4J. What is spectacularly visible in the F4J campaigning is the (gendered) body. The protests of the 'good father' are—indeed, they must be—viewed, judged and performed in public; on the bridges, gantries and rooftops of what are, in many cases, the structures which embody the authority of law itself (the courthouse, the parliament, the homes of judges: sites which, from one perspective, somewhat ironically, bespeak 'the law of the father'). It is not a private grief but pain and suffering *made visible*. The negation of emotion discussed in this chapter echoes the more general assumption, noted within a growing body of law and society scholarship, that law is a phenomenon and social practice in which emotion is deemed to have little or no place.[114] The FRM's engagement with law powerfully counters any such assumption for it is, in essence, about emotion.

In the experiences of men dealing with the family courts and lawyers, and in the form and content of the campaigns and the protests of F4J themselves, a range of conflictual emotions are the 'very stuff' of fathers' rights politics; emotions such as anxiety, anger, compassion, disgust, enmity, fear, guilt, hate, humour, love, pleasure, remorse, resentment, sadness, shame,[115] each as powerful as they can be contradictory in how they relate to understandings of the place and purpose of

---

[113] See, for example, in the context of developments in reproductive technologies, S Sheldon, 'Fragmenting Fatherhood: The Regulation of Reproductive Technologies' (2005) 68(4) *Modern Law Review* 523; R Collier and S Sheldon, *Fatherhood: A Socio-Legal Study* (Oxford, Hart, forthcoming).

[114] See, for an alternative view: SA Bandes (ed), *The Passions of Law* (New York, New York University Press, 1999); L Bently and L Flynn (eds), *Law and the Senses* (London, Pluto, 1996); M Douglas, 'Emotion and Culture in Theories of Justice' (1993) 22(4) *Economy and Society* 501; M Nussbaum, *Hiding from Humanity: Disgust, Shame and the Law* (Princeton, NJ, Princeton University Press, 2004).

[115] 'For years fathers have been struggling [with] ... what we call a bereavement ... a Siberia of the broken': http://www.fathers-4-justice.org/our_pledge/index.htm. At the same time 'the costume reflects the fact that every father is a superhero to his children, yet, in some cases, the only time the children will see their father is when he's on the telly or in the papers, dressed as Superman': Matt O'Connor, quoted in *The Independent*, 5 February 2004.

law and legal regulation. Law is simultaneously 'loved and loathed', desired and rejected. It is inadequate. Legal agents are decried for their failures in 'emotional management'. Yet, at the same time, more law is called upon. Law does not simply embody violence[116] (in some accounts, the violence of a 'feminised' state), law *does* violence in the way it 'tears asunder' the 'sacred bond' between father and child. Yet, simultaneously, more coercion, more violence from law is called for.

Whilst the study of emotions has been explored in some detail in other legal contexts,[117] the contradictory and ambivalent relation between law and emotion in the field of family law is a less developed terrain. Such an engagement might, however, shed further light on the shifting narratives deployed by the FRM and help us to understand the passion and anger driving recent campaigns—emotions around the developmental stages and experience of loss which can run counter to the appeals to 'rationality' and 'reasonableness' emanating from elsewhere; the calls of politicians for these (foolish?) men dressed as comic book 'superheroes' to reconsider their actions and to act in more rational and responsible (ironically, more masculine?) ways. Put bluntly, in this respect the fathers' rights discourse ill-fits, and speaks in a different register to, the dominant nomos and narrative[118] of contemporary family law policy.

There is considerable evidence to suggest that the UK FRM has, to degrees, shaped and influenced the broader cultural context in which a range of debates about family law reform are now taking place; that they have, in particular, created a pressure to reform the system.[119] Their direct impact and influence, however, appears to have been limited. More research is needed on whether the re-articulation of the narratives of justice, care and welfare advanced by fathers might be reflecting the emergence of a different consciousness on the part of men in a more general sense; or, in contrast to such a (pro-feminist?) 'embrace of responsibility' on the part of men, whether what might actually be happening in this area is a more familiar articulation of an essentially self-interested form of power.[120] Yet ultimately, as Day Sclater argues, perhaps real change will require that parents 'of whatever gender' engage with these questions of emotion and:

> find better ways of dealing with the vulnerabilities that separation throws up. We must
> learn to grieve our losses without acting out or dumping on the children. We can't go

---

[116] R Cover, 'Violence and the Word' (1986) 95 *Yale Law Review* 1601.

[117] For example: W de Haan and I Loader, 'On the Emotions of Crime and Punishment and Social Control' (2002) 6(3) *Theoretical Criminology* 243; K Laster and P O'Malley, 'Sensitive New-Age Laws: the Reassertion of Emotionality in Law' (1996) 24 *International Journal of the Sociology of Law* 21.

[118] R Cover, 'Nomos and Narrative' (1983) 97 *Harvard Law Review* 4.

[119] Evident, for example, in the contributions to 'Forgotten Fathers?' *The 5Live Report*, above n 22. See further work cited above: also B Neale, J Flowerdew and C Smart, 'Drifting Towards Shared Residence?' [2003] *Family Law* 904.

[120] Smart, above n 112; also C Smart, 'Equal Shares: Rights for Fathers or Recognition for Children?' (2004) 24(4) *Critical Social Policy* 484.

on disowning our feelings, imagining that our children, not us, are the vulnerable ones ... These are the displaced emotions that fuel legal battles. That's why changing the law won't solve the real problems that fathers face. Solving those is much more difficult, because it means confronting ourselves.[121]

This chapter broadly supports the claims of those who have suggested that the new fatherhood ideology has led in practice to a devaluing of the social importance of mothers and mothering. Importantly, however, and whatever the fate of a specific group such as F4J might be, it is unlikely that the wider issues raised by fathers' rights agendas will 'go away' in the UK. In the light of the arguments presented here it is possible that these concerns will be with us for some time and may well, indeed, intensify in years to come. This chapter has presented an attempt to advance understanding of these debates; to question what they can tell us—and what they do not tell us—about the changing nature of family practices; about love, pain, loss and desire.

---

[121] SD Sclater, 'Families Reunited' (2003) *FQ: The Magazine For Modern Dads* (Winter) 56.

4

Adopting 'Equality Tools' from the Toolboxes of their Predecessors: The Fathers' Rights Movement in the United States

JOCELYN ELISE CROWLEY

Over the past several decades, the United States has witnessed a massive increase in the number of children growing up in single-parent families.[1] In 1970, approximately 8.4 per cent of all children lived with only one parent. By 2003, that number had escalated to 27.5 per cent.[2] These statistics have been propelled by two simultaneous trends: a rising divorce rate, as well as a surge in the number of children born out of wedlock. Given this dramatic change in the socio-demographic landscape, the central question facing policymakers has been how to care physically and financially for these children. During the early 1970s, prevailing social mores dictated that the division of responsibilities between the sexes would be fairly clear-cut: mothers would be the primary physical caretakers, while fathers would be the primary financial caretakers. These distinct roles hardened over time as judges continued predominantly to award residential custody to mothers, while federal and state legislators added stricter enforcement teeth to the then-evolving child support system in pursuing monetary assistance from fathers.

By the early 1990s, however, these rigid boundaries of responsibility were under increasing attack from fathers' rights groups who demanded expanded opportunities to parent.[3] The 'helping professions', including psychologists, mediators and

---

[1] CR Daniels, 'Introduction' in CR Daniels (ed), *Lost Fathers* (New York, St Martin's Press, 1998).

[2] US Census Bureau, *America's Families and Living Arrangements: 2003*, Annual Social and Economic Supplement, Current Population Series, Current Population Reports, P20-553 and earlier reports (2003). The most recent statistics from the Census Bureau demonstrate the intransigence of these early decisions. By 2002, approximately 84% of all custodial parents were mothers, while only 16% were fathers; see T Grall, *Custodial Mothers and Fathers and their Child Support: 2001* (2003) Current Population Reports, US Census Bureau, P60-225. In this chapter, therefore, I will use the terms 'custodial parent', 'woman' and 'mother' interchangeably, and 'non-custodial parent', 'man' and 'father' interchangeably.

[3] JE Crowley, *The Politics of Child Support in America* (New York, Cambridge University Press, 2003).

social workers, reinforced this perspective by pointing out that there were both legal and emotional consequences to a familial breakdown.[4] While lawyers could settle the legal questions, both parents had to be equally responsible for promoting personal recovery and ultimately proper developmental growth for all involved children. Armed with this new world view, and backed by these professional opinions, fathers' rights groups quickly moved into the public policy arena in order to transform what they characterised as outdated and potentially damaging practices of restricting children's access to one parent.

How did this revolution in public debate take place? More specifically, how have fathers' rights groups used the historical experience of previous social movements in building their case for reform? This analysis begins to answer these questions by first providing a brief history of fathers' rights groups in the United States, along with a presentation of their most commonly-held views on child support and child custody reform. Second, this chapter will review the methodology involved in the data collection effort completed here, which included conducting 158 in-depth interviews of fathers' rights activists located across the United States in 2003. Researchers have recently expended considerable effort in mapping out the lives of divorced fathers and poor, unmarried fathers in great detail.[5] However, beyond sketching out their child support and child custody views, no scholar has focused on securing a large, primary data set from the highly motivated and highly politicised men involved in America's fathers' rights groups. In addition, no scholar has asked these men to situate their campaign for equal rights in the context of other social movements that have come before them, a 'learning framework' which is only starting to be developed in the social movement literature overall. This study thus fills these voids. Third, this chapter will present the results of the study, which illustrate what fathers' rights groups have learned from the equality-based civil rights movements undertaken by gays/lesbians, Black Americans, and women that have come before them. Finally, this analysis concludes by discussing the policy implications of fathers' rights groups' claims in the years to come.

Fathers' Rights Groups in the United States: An Introduction

Modern fathers' rights groups in the United States resulted from the convergence of three previous threads of male-based activism. The first thread was the divorce

---

[4] MA Fineman, *The Illusion of Equality: The Rhetoric and Reality of Divorce Reform* (Chicago, University of Chicago Press, 1991).

[5] T Arendell, *Fathers and Divorce* (Thousand Oaks, CA, Sage, 1995); M Waller, *My Baby's Father: Unmarried Parents and Paternal Responsibility* (Ithaca, NY, Cornell University Press, 2002).

reform movement, which began in the 1960s.[6] Participants in these groups, such as the Divorce Racket Busters, drew attention to what they viewed as discriminatory treatment in the court system after a family breakdown, which frequently resulted in men's financial and emotional devastation. They advocated for the institution of a much more humane system of resolving family disputes, such as mediation. The second thread behind the fathers' rights movement began with those involved in men's rights activism in the 1970s and beyond. Groups such as the Coalition of Free Men and MEN International argued that 'men have a right to be men' and cautioned against what they perceived as the emasculating excesses of the feminist movement.[7] The final contributory thread involved the rise of religious groups, such as the Christian Promise Keepers and participants in the Million Man March. These groups emerged in the 1990s to promote male responsibility consistent with what their members perceived to be God's plan for an appropriate and proper family order.[8]

While each thread focused most specifically on its own priorities as outlined above, they each shared a common belief in the capacity of all men to renew their commitment to the moral and legal enterprise of fatherhood. These unifying beliefs provided a common ideological foundation as well as the beginnings of a membership base to modern fathers' rights groups in the United States, which really intensified in terms of grassroots mobilisation during the 1990s.[9] Because these groups emerged from the bottom-up without a centralised, co-ordinated master plan, they have come to assume a variety of organisational forms. Some, such as the American Coalition for Fathers and Children (ACFC), are strictly national in scope and work as umbrella structures to bring both local groups and individuals together to strive towards one unified, pro-fatherhood agenda.[10] Others, such as the Children's Rights Council (CRC), have a national office along with state-level chapters.[11] In this way, they hope to reshape policy in Washington, DC as well as at lower levels of government. The most common structure, however,

---

[6] Crowley, above n 3.

[7] For examples of writing in this tradition, see H Goldberg, *The Hazards of Being Male: Surviving the Myth of Masculine Privilege* (New York, Signet, 1976); F Baumli (ed), *Men Freeing Men: Exploding the Myth of the Traditional Male* (Jersey City, NJ, New Atlantis, 1985); W Farrell, *The Myth of Male Power: Why Men are the Disposable Sex* (New York, Simon & Schuster, 1993).

[8] S Coltrane, 'Marketing the Marriage Solution: Misplaced Simplicity in the Politics of Fatherhood' (2001) 44 *Sociological Perspectives* 387; A Quicke and K Robinson, 'Keeping the Promise of the Moral Majority: A Historical Critical Comparison of the Promise Keepers and the Christian Coalition, 1989–1998' in DS Claussen (ed), *The Promise Keepers: Essays on Masculinity and Christianity* (Jefferson, NJ, McFarland and Company, 2000); SD Johnson, 'Who Supports the Promise Keepers?' (2001) 61 *Sociology of Religion* 93; GK Baker-Fletcher (ed), *Black Religion after the Million Man March* (Maryknoll, NY, Orbis, 1998).

[9] D Blankenhorn, *Fatherless America: Confronting our Most Urgent Social Problem* (New York, Basic Books 1995); W Horn, 'Did You Say "Movement"?' in W Horn, D Blankenhorn and MB Pearlstein (eds), *The Fatherhood Movement: A Call to Action* (Lanham, MD, Lexington Books, 1999).

[10] See http://www.acfc.org.

[11] See http://www.gocrc.com.

is simply a state-level organisation with local chapters, such as Louisiana Dads, Parents and Children for Equality (PACE) in Ohio, and Fathers Are Parents, Too (FAPT) in Georgia.[12] This organisational form enables members to pool all of their resources to influence state legislatures and state courts, the primary arenas for family policymaking in the United States.[13]

Given these structures, how do these groups operate on a day-to-day basis, and what are their primary goals? Local chapters, the workhorses of these organisations, generally meet monthly in donated church spaces, public libraries, private residences, or local places of business.[14] Their meetings usually last from one to two hours in length, during which a group leader along with group members discuss a variety of topics. Personal case management, whereby members ask other attendees for advice regarding court processes, constitutes a substantial part of each meeting. Also important is the emotional support that the members provide to one another regarding their interactions with their former partners and with their children. Of course, the groups also use a significant amount of their meeting time to devise legislative as well as judicial strategies which aim to affect public policy. Their efforts have not gone unnoticed. In the areas of child support and child custody, fathers' rights groups have carved out detailed policy positions which are becoming increasingly influential in American politics. Indeed, while their support bases may come from different parts of the country, fathers' rights groups show a remarkable degree of homogeneity in their views on these two topics, which they hope will make them even more successful in pressing forward with their claims.

Issue 1: Child Support Reform

One of the most significant areas of reform for fathers' rights groups in the United States is child support law. Currently, the states and the federal government work in conjunction in all aspects of enforcing support, from parental location to paternity establishment (which has gradually moved from the courts to administrative processing), to the creation of awards and, finally, to collections.[15] In its totality, the child support programme served close to 16 million families and collected $21.2 billion in support in the fiscal year 2003.[16]

---

[12] See http://www.ladads.org, http://www.pacegroup.org, and http://www.fapt.org.

[13] JE Crowley, 'Organizational Responses to the Fatherhood Crisis: The Case of Fathers' Rights Groups in the United States' (2006) 39 *Marriage and Family Review* 99.

[14] This description of the group meetings is from JE Crowley, book manuscript entitled More than a Paycheck: Fathers' Rights Groups in America, in preparation.

[15] JE Crowley, 'Supervised Devolution: The Case of Child Support Enforcement' (2000) 30 *Publius: The Journal of Federalism* 99; JE Crowley, 'Who Institutionalizes Institutions? The Case of Paternity Establishment in the United States' (2001) 82 *Social Science Quarterly* 312; JE Crowley, 'The Rise and Fall of Court Prerogatives in Paternity Establishment' (2002) 23 *Justice System Journal* 363.

[16] Office of Child Support Enforcement (OCSE), *Child Support Enforcement FY 2003 Preliminary Data Report* (2004).

The legal expansiveness of the programme, however, did not emerge overnight; instead, the growth in its capacity and reach has been incremental in nature. Prior to the Social Security Amendments of 1975, decisions on whether, when, and how much child support to award to single-parent families—most often mothers—were made by individual judges.[17] As a result of this decentralised system, judges held an enormous amount of power over the lives of families falling within their jurisdiction. By passing the 1975 law, Congress attempted to institute more uniformity in the treatment of these cases. In brief, this law created the first Federal Office of Child Support Enforcement in Washington, DC, and instructed the fifty states to form their own partnering agencies.[18] While the original intent of lawmakers was to pursue fathers of children receiving welfare, or Aid to Families with Dependent Children (AFDC), in order to recoup these public expenditures, the programme became so popular that working, middle and upper class women wished to be included as programme beneficiaries as well.[19] They achieved this victory with the Child Support Enforcement Amendments of 1984, which mandated that the states provide equal paternity establishment, order creation and enforcement vehicles for all women, regardless of class.[20]

The Family Support Act of 1988 went even further in promoting uniformity by requiring automatic wage withholding in all new cases, so that single-parent families would be less likely to miss any payments.[21] Perhaps even more importantly, the Family Support Act of 1988 mandated that the states develop and utilise new child support award guidelines for their clientele across the board. In response to this law, the states gradually converged upon four guideline models: the percentage-of-income standard, the income shares model, the Melson formula, and a hybrid formula.[22] The percentage-of-income standard is the most straightforward, in that fathers simply pay a set percentage of their earnings to their children. As the number of children increases, so the percentage increases as well. Slightly more complex is the income shares model, which is based on the idea that a child should receive the same proportion of a parent's income that would have resulted if the family had remained intact. By this method, the parents' earnings are added

---

[17] See Public Law 93-647.

[18] I Garfinkel, DR Meyer, and SS McLanahan, 'A Brief History of Child Support Policies in the United States' in I Garfinkel, SS McLanahan, DR Meyer and JA Seltzer (eds), *Fathers Under Fire: The Revolution in Child Support Enforcement* (New York, Russell Sage, 1998).

[19] JE Crowley, 'The Gentrification of Child Support Enforcement Services, 1950–1984' (2003) 77 *Social Services Review* 585.

[20] See Public Law 98-378.

[21] See Public Law 100-485.

[22] J Venohr and RG Williams, 'The Implementation and Periodic Review of State Child Support Guidelines' (1999) 33 *Family Law Quarterly* 7; See also the National Conference of State Legislatures for tables that categorise each state by guideline adopted at http://www.ncsl.org/programs/cyf/models.htm.

together to create a clearly specified childrearing sum, and then each parent's share is pro-rated based on his/her income. The Melson formula acknowledges that after a family dissolves, each parent must be able to afford to live independently. Once this 'self-reserve' is taken into account, the formula calculates an award based on a child's needs and a standard of living adjustment. Finally, some states rely on a hybrid system, using the percentage-of-income standard when fathers fall below a certain level of income, and the income shares model when they earn above that level.

Once these guidelines were in place, Congress continued to pass major legislation throughout the following years to strengthen the enforcement system further.[23] For example, the Child Support Recovery Act of 1992 imposed a federal criminal penalty on those guilty of the nonpayment of interstate support, and the Ted Weiss Child Support Enforcement Act of 1992 amended existing law to require that all consumer credit agencies report child support delinquencies on their official statements.[24] The Full Faith and Debt for Child Support Orders Act of 1994 clarified interstate issues of support jurisdiction, and the Bankruptcy Reform Act of 1994 prevented individuals from discharging their child support obligations in bankruptcy proceedings.[25] Finally, the Personal Responsibility and Work Opportunity Reconciliation Act of 1996 required all states to report new hires to state employment agencies in order to expedite seamless wage withholding; the Deadbeat Parents Punishment Act of 1998 imposed a maximum two-year imprisonment penalty on parents willfully avoiding at least $5,000 in interstate support; and the Child Support Performance and Incentive Act of 1998 created new financial incentives to encourage efficiency among the state child support agencies.[26]

Not unexpectedly, as the penalties for noncompliance have toughened over the years, fathers' rights groups in the United States have become increasingly vocal about their dissatisfaction with the child support system.[27] In setting the stage for their claims, these groups maintain that men and women have equal opportunities to thrive in the economic sphere. Child support is thus an anachronistic holdover from an era when many women chose to be homemakers, or when they faced severe discrimination in the labour market. Disregarding research that demonstrates that women continue to face barriers to upward mobility, pay inequality, and occupational segregation both before and after familial disruption, fathers' rights groups assert that child support policy must recognise the

---

[23] *The Green Book: Background Material and Data on the Programs within the Jurisdiction of the Committee on Ways and Means* (Washington, DC, US Government Printing Office, 2004).

[24] See Public Laws 102-521 and 102-537, respectively.

[25] See Public Laws 103-383 and 103-394, respectively.

[26] See Public Laws 104-193, 105-187, and 105-200, respectively.

[27] S Coltrane and N Hickman, 'The Rhetoric of Rights and Needs: Moral Discourse in the Reform of Child Custody and Child Support Laws' (1992) 39 *Social Problems* 400.

level economic playing field between the sexes that they argue is now in existence.[28]

How should this transformation in policy be accomplished? While some desire the complete abolition of the child support programme, the majority of fathers' rights activists make what they view as two more moderate suggestions for reform.[29] First, they maintain that the child support system discriminates against them in favour of mothers in both the mathematical formulas that are used to calculate awards and in the tax codes. In terms of setting awards, most states treat children as adding a per capita cost to maintaining the custodial parent's household, rather than a marginal cost to the expenses of a household. By using the per capita method, states are continuously and inequitably overcharging well-meaning fathers in order to benefit mothers. In addition, most states calculate child support obligations based on a father's gross income rather than net income. This practice again creates a substantial financial burden for all fathers, as their gross income can be radically different from their net, take-home pay. Finally, custodial parents receive the majority of tax breaks related to having children in their homes in the United States, such as the favourable head of household status, child care tax credits, earned income tax credits, and other types of exemptions. In fact, by law, non-custodial parents can make none of these claims.[30] Through all of these practices, fathers' rights groups argue, the child support system continues unfairly to deplete the monetary resources of men across the country, some of whom will never recover their previous financial independence.

Second, fathers' rights activists argue that child support is simply alimony, or exorbitant and unnecessary spousal support, in disguise.[31] In other words, women use this money to benefit themselves, not their children. This issue, they assert, should trouble all those concerned with protecting individual liberty and freedom from the government's pernicious inclination to redistribute wealth. To guarantee that child support monies are spent only on children, rather than on their ex-partners, several fathers' rights groups have advocated for the creation of accountability systems. These systems would take the form of a special type of credit/debit card or receipt system that would guarantee that all money sent as 'child support' could only be spent on child-related activities. In this way, men would no longer be discriminated against and forced inappropriately to transfer money to women.

---

[28] *Women in the Labor Force: A Databook* (Washington, DC, Bureau of Labor Statistics, United States Department of Labor, 2004); KC Holden and PJ Smock, 'The Economic Costs of Marital Dissolution: Why Do Women Bear a Disproportionate Cost?' (1991) 17 *Annual Review of Sociology* 51; PJ Smock, 'Gender and the Short-Run Economic Consequences of Marital Disruption' (1994) 73 *Social Forces* 243; SM Bianchi, L Subaiya and J Kahn, 'The Gender Gap in the Economic Well-Being of Nonresident Fathers and Custodial Mothers' (1999) 36 *Demography* 195.

[29] Crowley, above n 3.

[30] S Braver and D O'Connell, *Divorced Dads: Shattering the Myths* (New York, Tarcher-Putnam, 1998).

[31] MA Fineman, *The Neutered Mother, the Sexual Family, and Other Twentieth Century Tragedies* (New York, Routledge, 1995).

Issue 2: Child Custody Reform

In addition to child support reform, fathers' rights groups have also become increasingly active on child custody issues.[32] There are two types of joint custody in existence in the United States today: joint legal and joint physical.[33] Joint legal custody pertains to shared parental authority over the major decisions affecting the child's life, and joint physical custody refers to a child spending relatively equal amounts of time in each parent's household. Currently, thirty-eight states have some type of joint custody legislation in place, although the strictness of how these standards are written varies.[34] For example, some states promote maximally feasible joint physical custody, while others only promote such a standard if both parents agree.

Joint custody laws in the United States have taken many decades to evolve into their present form. During the early 20th century, the tender years doctrine prevailed, which argued that young children had special needs that could only be satisfied by their mothers.[35] By the 1960s, however, state legislators became uncomfortable with this doctrine as it relied on the increasingly suspect 'innate' traits of women as better nurturers and caregivers. By the beginning of the 1980s, legislators moved to the 'best interest of the child' standard. Under this model, the parent who could provide the home that was most suitable for the child would be awarded custody.[36] A whole host of factors would define this 'best interest', such as each parent's capacity to contribute to the child's physical and mental health, emotional and spiritual well-being, and intellectual growth.[37]

While these changes in standards moved custody decisions to more neutral territory on paper, day-to-day judgments issued by the courts continued overwhelmingly to place children with the mother. In response, fathers' rights groups once again started to formulate their objections to this state of affairs.[38] In their view, mothers still predominantly received custody because judges have refused to treat fathers equally in the courtroom. There remains, in a very real sense for these groups, a strong sense of bias against men who wish to pursue joint or sole custody arrangements with their former partners. As in the case of child support

---

[32] Crowley, above n 3.

[33] See generally LD Elrod, *Child Custody, Practice and Procedure* (Clark Boardman Callaghan, 1993 and Supp 2002).

[34] See the Children's Rights Council's data on joint custody laws in the states at http://www.gocrc.com.

[35] E Ellis, *Divorce Wars: Interventions with Families in Conflict* (Washington, DC, American Psychological Association, 2000); DA Luepnitz, *Child Custody* (Lexington, MD, DC Heath and Company, 1982).

[36] S Brown, 'Changes in Laws Governing Divorce: An Evaluation of Joint Custody Presumptions' (1984) 5 *Journal of Family Issues* 200; MA Mason, *The Custody Wars: Why Children are Losing the Legal Battle and What We Can Do About It* (New York, Basic Books, 1999).

[37] S May, 'Child Custody and Visitation' (2001) 2 *Georgetown Journal of Gender and the Law* 382.

[38] GI Williams and RH Williams, 'All We Want is Equality: Rhetorical Framing in the Fathers' Rights Movement' in J Best (ed), *Images of Issues: Typifying Contemporary Social Problems* (New York, Aldine de Gruyter, 1995); MA Messner, *Politics of Masculinities: Men in Movements* (Thousand Oaks, CA, Sage, 1997); Arendell, above n 5.

enforcement, where fathers' rights groups argue that men and women are already equal in the economic sphere, in the custody arena, fathers' rights groups maintain that men and women are already equal in the childrearing arena. Contrary to much academic evidence that suggests that women still do the majority of work in raising children when families are intact, fathers' rights activists testify to their complete parental engagement—past, present, and future—that should not be breached by the legislative and judicial branches of government.[39]

In order to ensure greater equality between the sexes in custody matters, fathers' rights activists make two concrete policy recommendations. As a starting point, they insist that unless one parent is proven unfit, there should be a standard presumption of 50-50 joint custody—both legal and physical—in all of the states.[40] In the American court system, judges have wide-ranging authority over matters such as child placement. Therefore, even when the law changed to the seemingly gender-neutral 'best interest' standard, fathers' rights groups point out, judges did not have to alter their behaviour. The reasons behind this intransigence were manifold, including the personal preferences of parents and child, competing work-related commitments of mother and father, traditionalism, and most importantly according to fathers' rights activists, simple bias. Activists declare that they are just as skilled as women in raising children, and that the only way this aptitude will be recognised across the country is if the legislatures pass and judges uphold strong joint custody legislation.

The second policy recommendation in this area revolves around the concept of shared parenting.[41] For many couples, co-ordinating living arrangements for their children may be challenging. Parents may reside geographically far apart or work odd hours. To accommodate these parents, fathers' rights activists argue, judges need to be much more flexible in allocating children's time. In the past, judges have awarded most fathers a standard visitation schedule with their children; in general, this has meant that fathers tend to spend every Wednesday night and every other weekend with their children. Shared parenting implies much more fatherly involvement, ranging from 20 to 49 per cent of the child's time (with under 20 per cent, or 73 overnights, defined as traditional or uncompensated visitation). Of course, since children are spending more time with their fathers, activists argue that these men's child support obligations should be reduced as well.

In fact, with the exception of Minnesota, the states have already moved in this direction.[42] Some states rely on a 'deviation' system, whereby judges agree to consider claims related to a downward support modification if requested by one parent. The remaining states that consider these types of adjustments use a variety of

---

[39] JF Sandberg and SL Hofferth, 'Changes in Children's Time with Parents: United States, 1981–1997' (2001) 38 *Demography* 423; LC Sayer, SM Bianchi and JP Robinson, 'Are Parents Investing Less Time in Children?' (2004) 110 *American Journal of Sociology* 1; Coltrane and Hickman, above n 27.

[40] Crowley, above n 14.

[41] MS Melli, 'Guideline Review: Child Support and Time-sharing by Parents' (1999) 33 *Family Law Quarterly* 219.

[42] See the National Conference of State Legislatures for tables that list these formulas by state at http://www.ncsl.org/programs/cyf/shared.htm.

formulas that can be applied systematically across cases. The cross-credit approach, used in states such as Oklahoma and New Mexico, establishes a support order based on each parent's income and then allocates financial credits to each parent based on the amount of actual time spent with the children. Alternatively, states such as Hawaii and Montana compensate non-custodial parents based on the number of overnights the children spend with them. Still other states allow some categories of costs to be compensated when the children spend substantial time with the non-custodial parent, or employ another type of mathematical equation to transfer support dollars from mothers back to fathers when the children are in their care. While not guaranteeing 50-50 physical placement, these changes, according to fathers' rights groups, represent real progress towards the goal of equality with women in all childrearing responsibilities.

Methodology: Casting a Deep Net Through In-Depth Interviews

From this background of understanding their policy positions in general, this study then sought to speak with actual members of fathers' rights groups to understand how they use discourse from previous American social movements to frame their current activism. There were four central steps in collecting data on this population: selecting a target set of groups to study, accessing members within these groups, conducting the actual interviews, and analysing the results. First, in selecting groups to study, I searched the Internet and non-profit directories for groups currently in operation. This task was complicated by several factors. Groups label themselves in unique ways that tend to obfuscate their agendas; some choose to be called 'fathers' rights' groups, while others prefer the term 'children's rights' group. Another challenge was that some of these groups meet only in the cyber-world rather than the 'real world'; this was a cause for concern as I was also interested in understanding interpersonal, organisational dynamics for my larger project on fathers' rights.[43] To overcome these problems, I decided to examine only organisations interested primarily in child support and child custody reform, rather than similarly named groups that focus on related issues, such as domestic violence legal reform and paternity fraud. In addition, I sought to focus only on groups with a 'real world' membership. In other words, members had to meet in person on a consistent basis in order to qualify for this study. At the end of this process, I had a sampling pool of 50 groups to investigate.

The second task was accessing the members within these groups. I accomplished this by contacting the leader of each organisation via e-mail, letter and/or telephone

---

[43] Crowley, above n 14.

with information about the research project. Negative responses and non-contacts reduced my final sample to 26 groups located across the United States. After interviewing each leader, I typically placed an announcement on the group's website or sent an e-mail message regarding my request for respondents to the group's listserv. However, in the case of eight groups which I observed as part of my larger project on fathers' rights in the United States, I simply passed around a sign-up sheet requesting participants. This 'snowball sampling' technique produced a total of 158 respondents who each agreed to a one-hour, tape-recorded, telephone-based interview. The sample overall reflects the relatively privileged nature of these members, with the majority of respondents identifying themselves as white, possessing some college education, and holding a white-collar job (see Table 1).

Table 1: Sociodemographic Characteristics of Fathers' Rights Members Included in this Study

Mean Age	46
Mean Number of Biological Children	2
Gender	
Male	85%
Female	15%
Current Marital Status	
Married	41%
Divorced/Separated	51%
Widowed/Single	8%
Race	
Caucasian	87%
Black	8%
Hispanic	2%
Asian	1%
Multiple/Unspecified	1%
Refuse	1%
Education	
High School Diploma/GED	9%
Associate's Degree/Some College/Vocational Training	31%
Bachelor's Degree	30%
Graduate Degree (Master's, Doctorate, or Professional)	30%
Employment	
White Collar	78%
Blue Collar	13%
Retired	6%
Unemployed/Student/Volunteer	3%
Sample Size	158

Third, I asked all of my respondents questions on either five or six topical areas, of which their attitudes towards other social movements emerged in our discussion of the fifth category, 'Political Behaviour': (1) Demographics, (2) Group Patterns of Recruitment and Goals, (3) Relationships with Past Partners, (4) Relationships with Children, (5) Political Behaviour, and (6) Challenges Related to Leadership (asked of leaders only). The specific question within Category 5 that elicited the largest percentage of responses asked participants whether or not they believed that fathers' rights groups constituted a ground-breaking social movement in the United States. Participants used this opportunity to compare their activities with other social movements in American history.

Fourth, all of these taped interviews were professionally transcribed. I then used grounded theory methods to analyse all of the data relating to how these respondents conceptualised their activities in the context of the social movements that have come before them.[44] The software program Atlas.ti helped in aggregating the most important themes that emerged across the interviews. Finally, all respondent names as well as other key identifying characteristics were changed to protect their confidentiality.[45]

Results: Fathers' Rights Activists as Standing on the Shoulders of Giants?

In crafting their views about public policy, fathers' rights activists draw heavily on the legacies of gay/lesbian, Black Civil Rights, and women's movements in the United States.[46] At the most macro-level, social movement scholars have noted that any type of rights-based political activity can have strong reverberations beyond the singular issue domain which is presently being contested. In one dominant view, protests by one collectivity create opportunities for other aggrieved groups by signaling that the current political order is unstable and ripe for challenge.[47] In other words, mobilisation by previous activists provides information to future activists that political transformation in a variety of issue arenas is, in fact, possible.

---

[44] A Strauss and J Corbin, *Basics of Grounded Theory: Grounded Theory Procedures and Techniques* (Newbury Park, CA, Sage, 1990).

[45] Note that the groups that were cited at the beginning of the article in describing the policy positions of fathers' rights groups more generally are not necessarily those sampled in the interviews reported here.

[46] Arendell, above n 5, briefly describes some of these views in her work on divorced men more generally.

[47] S Tarrow, *Power in Movement: Social Movements, Collective Action and Politics* (New York, Cambridge University Press, 1994); C Conell and S Cohn, 'Learning from Other People's Actions: Environmental Variation and Diffusion in French Coal Mine Strikes, 1890–1935' (1995) 101 *American Journal of Sociology* 366.

But prior cycles of movement activity do much more than simply plant the seed of potential change among emerging groups; older movements can also offer their younger counterparts insights into the precise philosophical and action-based repertoires that can prove necessary in achieving legitimacy and reform.[47a] More specifically, social movement theorists have described the process of collective action 'framing' to encompass the entire evolutionary trajectory whereby a set of individuals within society come to see a particularised system of citizenry relations as unjust and then attempt to do something about it.[48] Not all of this work, however, must be innovative. Frames may become 'modular' or available for adoption, modification and reinterpretation across time and space.[49] In the case of fathers' rights groups, modular framing is definitely apparent in that the gay/lesbian, Black Civil Rights and women's movements have each provided fathers' rights groups with the foundation for their equality-based mobilisation campaigns in the areas of child support and child custody in three primary ways: (1) the construction of morality arguments; (2) the formulation of strategic options; and (3) the motivation to protect themselves against their political foes.

Prior Movements Help Fathers' Rights Activists to Make their Own Morality Arguments

The first way in which fathers' rights activists depend on the historical precedent of other American social movements is by drawing a parallel claim as to the moral rectitude of their cause. As one activist named Daniel points out, both women and Black Americans have stood up for a similar cause of freedom at different times over the past two hundred years.

> Men and women don't want to see people taken advantage of—they want to go with what the truth is. And when the truth is being distorted and corruption exists, I think these people rally behind what is right ... I took an interest in the tragedy of the Civil War ... Of course, that was a springboard for the women's movement which was [inspired by] Clara Barton and several other women and [the Civil Rights Movement which was inspired by] several Blacks like Frederick Douglass ... The more I pressed into it, the more you see how they overcame [injustice] ... People [were] just outraged by [by these past injustices]. The American dream is what we all want.

[47a] M Berbrier, 'Making Minorities: Cultural Space, Stigma Tranformation Frames, and the Categorical Status Claims of Deaf, Gay, and White Supremacist Activists in late Twentieth Century America' (2002) 17 *Sociological Forum* 553.

[48] R Benford and D Snow, 'Framing Processes and Social Movements: An Overview and Assessment' (2000) 26 *Annual Review of Sociology* 611.

[49] D McAdam and D Rucht, 'Cross National Diffusion of Social Movement Ideas' (1993) 528 *The Annals of The American Academy of Political and Social Science* 56; DS Meyer and N Whittier, 'Social Movement Spillover' (1994) 41 *Social Problems* 277; S Tarrow, 'Modular Collective Action and the Rise of the Social Movement: Why the French Revolution was Not Enough' (1993) 21 *Politics and Society* 69.

While Daniel casts his claim for fathers' rights in the context of the 'American dream', another respondent named Jordan situates his rights-based assertions in the context of what he believes to be universal human capacities; that is, that all individuals, regardless of sex, have the ability to care for and love their children. Here he points out that what fathers are going through today is similar to the women's movement of the early 20th century; both are movements to secure additional liberty for their members.

> [In] the US, it is so unfair that men, most of the time, are not given equal [time with their children]. I [compare] it to the women's rights [movement] of 100 years ago and voting rights. Females weren't allowed to vote, but now today good fathers and men are not even given 50 per cent [time with] their children ... [That] is exactly why I think that there is a [fathers' rights] movement today. We are equal today and we love [our children] just as much as [women do].

To Jordan, denying women the right to vote was an egregious moral error of the past, just as denying fathers the right to parent is an egregious moral error in the present. In a similar way, Marco, another fathers' rights activist, compares his support for the cause in relation to the quest for gay/lesbian rights in America. In his view, both causes are moral and just, but have tended to be hidden from public discussion. The major difference between the movements now is that while the gay/lesbian community has begun successfully to air and address its main concerns, fathers have remained conspicuously silent. He concludes that without an extensive debate about fathers' concerns, families will continue to suffer from the devastating effects of inappropriate governmental intervention in the areas of child support and child custody.

> Back in 1994, I made a vow that I would tell two people [about fathers' rights] a day. I said, I'm going to tell two people every day about the horror that our social infrastructure is doing to the American family. And I don't always do that, but you're the second person I talked to today ... It's almost like the gays from 8 years ago or 9 years ago; until you come out of the closet and until people have a social dialogue about it, [things are] not going to change ... Until the dialogue gets out there and until [our cause] becomes a social dialogue, it's not going to change.

Like many of his counterparts in these organisations, Marco reflects a willingness to do his part to achieve his vision of a just society. And in all of the above cases, fathers claim that they have an equivalent moral right to equality within the family as Blacks, women, and gays/lesbians have earned within contemporary American society.

Other activists go even further, however, by insisting that fathers experience *worse* social circumstances than other groups who ultimately formed social movements in America. Ignorant or uninformed about the historical evidence that documents in detail how Black slave children were ripped apart from their families prior to the Civil War, a respondent named Harvey argues that current social policy in the

United States represents the most horrific form of governmental abuse possible. According to Harvey, family policy today inexcusably tears children from their fathers, which is more devastating than any discrimination Black Americans may have faced in their own lives. To pursue their own moral cause, Harvey asserts that fathers everywhere must unite in solidarity behind their own civil rights campaign.

> [The] parents' rights movement is the civil rights movement of this century ... Because we're seeing abuses that are even worse than racial [discrimination]. We transcend race on this issue. The Blacks were never stripped of their children to steal money from them. It's worse in a lot of ways than the original [Black] Civil Rights Movement ... Slowly but surely, though, [things will change]. Once we win some major lawsuits, [our movement] will pick up. I think you probably notice when you look at this movement compared to the Civil Rights Movement, we're as organised as they were in the early 1950s. We're kind of fractured; there is [disagreement] amongst other organizations as to what the primary objective and methods should be. At heart, [though], [fathers' rights groups] all have equality in mind.

Harvey claims that through disciplined action, fathers can turn their current circumstances around and correct this moral injustice. Another activist named Nolan echoes this theme that other social movements had an 'easy' task before them as compared with those facing contemporary fathers.

> I am Southern man. I live in the South. The Black people and the white people get along wonderfully. I have cousins that are Black; they have cousins who are white. Now there are Asians, Mexicans, and Arabs [here in the South]. The South is now inundated with the whole world ... I live in a small city ... Back during segregation, all I know is what the old people tell me. The Black people rode in the back of the bus and drank from Black fountains. It was segregation, it was evil, and it was wrong. [Then] they stood up: the white people, the Black people. [Black people] are human beings, and they are children of God, too; they have a shot at [making it] and Darwin will take care of it. He has. There are basketball players making millions of dollars who are Black. The cream has risen to the top. [Being a father] is a new form of segregation. God decided to make me a man. I am being punished for God's decision. Because I am a man, I am stripped of my children; I've lost my children for over 10 years and have paid over $50,000 because I am a man—because God decided to make me a father. That is just like God made you Black; you [must get to] the back of the bus. There is no justice to that. Not only do I pay, but also my children pay. You need your mom and dad; God made that. That wasn't my decision.

In this statement, Nolan argues that what happened to Black Americans in the form of segregation was inherently wrong and evil. But now, Black Americans have expansive opportunities according to Nolan's not-so-subtle racist views; they can make millions of dollars playing basketball. Fathers, however, continue to confront societal barriers because of 'God's decision' to make them into men. They are thus currently in a worse position than Black Americans, and only through a strong moral crusade will they be able to change their lot.

Prior Movements Help Fathers' Rights Activists to Formulate their Own Strategic Mobilisation Options

In addition to helping them to craft morality arguments on behalf of their cause, prior social movements also offer fathers' rights activists strategic blueprints for actually carrying out their equal rights campaigns. To a respondent named Brent, the current fathers' rights movement is in disarray and could benefit from studying the methods used by prior groups seeking social change. Here he describes the activities surrounding the Million Dads March, an annual event (since 2002) held in the nation's capitol that attempts to bring disengaged fathers from all over the country together to press policymakers for family law reform.

> I do know that in the states here they need to get a lot more organized. I was at the Million Dads March in DC on Father's Day and it was very chaotic … It wasn't well organized. A lot of the speakers were really shell-shocked guys. My heart went out to them. There were a lot of these guys. The Australians are really organised; I was really surprised by them. I [told the American guys] there, I said, "You want to make this work as a movement? Study the civil rights movement, [and] study the gay rights movement. You know? And study the women's movements from the 1960s and 1970s." You have to study what worked and believe me, if the gay rights movement could work, you can make this work because that was a tough sell. That was a really tough sell and they have gone from being brutalised to being one of the most powerful lobbyists in the nation. They listened to me, the guys that were organizing this … and we will have to see what happens.

Jay, another respondent, echoes the need for greater organisation among fathers' rights activists by pointing to the tactics pursued by other social movements in the 1960s. More specifically, women and Black Americans engaged in effective protest strategies by most importantly 'getting on the street' with their grievances.

> Well, from where I stand, the more people I talk to and I associate with, they all feel that something needs to be done. Injustice has been going on for too long. [Fathers' rights] should be a movement just like, you know, I compare it with the women's movement. Women did not have [many] rights until the 1940s, 1950s, and 1960s. They got on the street, they became active and they got their rights. So did the Blacks [through] the Civil Rights Movement. They got their rights, they got what they were supposed to [get]. Men, who are 50 per cent of the population, and I am not saying that every man gets divorced and has child custody fights, but a lot of them do … Those men, unfortunately, a lot of them, after they lose, they just pack up and go away … That's not the right way [to behave]; they should fight not even for themselves, but for the future.

A major debate among fathers' rights groups is exactly how far these protests should go. Jay reveals his support for public demonstrations, but Ethan, another activist, argues that these 'street activities' might not be enough to achieve the desired effects.

In the 1960s, during the [Black Civil Rights] Movement and riots, there [was] a growing awareness that something was wrong and we won't stand for it ... [Now] people
realise the constitution isn't being followed and people are starting to act on it ... It's
not a good thing to discriminate ... We're seeing the social pathology that has come up
[by] not having parents involved, especially dads now, we've seen enough of this stuff
going on. We see the bad things happen and we need to do things about it. I've been
involved in protesting; other people are doing it. This fall I'm starting a major protest
right at the homes and offices of lawyers.

As Ethan declares, fathers must learn the important lessons of the Black Civil
Rights Movement where people gradually came to the conclusion that discrimination was wrong. In this view, riots played an important role in demonstrating
to others that there was a serious racial problem plaguing American society. While
not explicitly endorsing riots, Ethan claims that only through their own carefully
orchestrated protests against specific individuals—in this case, lawyers, who they
believe are particularly hostile to them in court—will fathers' rights activists be
equally successful in convincing others as to the merits of their cause.

Understanding the nuts and bolts behind protest methods, however, is only
part of the solution for fathers who consider themselves aggrieved. Courage in
executing these tasks also matters. Carey, a father who had to fight for access to his
son and currently has a positive relationship with him, makes this precise argument when he calls for individuals to assume strong leadership roles as they wage
war against current family policy.

The joy that I've experienced by being able to actively participate with my son and be
able to, you know, go through what can be hell as a parent has led me to take the stand
that every parent deserves to be able to do this. There is no right of the government to
come in and tell you no, you can't [be a father]. I joke with the guys who've got the suit
going on in the federal court now challenging [our state's] custody law that I have the
brass ring [of custody arrangements] and I will stay with this until everyone has exactly
what I have ... It is unfortunate, but [it is] becoming the civil rights movement of the
new century versus the Civil Rights Movement that took place in the 1960s. [Far] too
many people [say], I've got what I need [from the courts] and boom, they disappear.
[They say], to heck with everybody else. That is wrong. It takes a few strong people. It
took a few strong people in the 1960s to stand up to get the rights for the Blacks. It is
going to take a few strong people to stand up and get that for all parents.

According to Carey, fathers' rights groups suffer from the same 'free-rider' problem as other social movements. In other words, everyone wants to benefit from
the efforts of the movement, but no one wants to dedicate their own personal
time and resources towards effecting the desired change. As in previous social
movements, fathers' rights groups need individuals to make sacrifices in terms of
planning and participating in new strategies if they truly wish to achieve their
goals.

Prior Movements Teach Fathers' Rights Activists that they Must Protect Themselves Against their Political Foes

Interestingly, while many fathers' rights activists point to previous social movements in American history as models for both planning their own moral arguments and plotting their own mobilisation strategies, other members conceptualise prior movements in a very different way. One of the chief legacies of the activism of the 1960s was that most groups that experienced some form of discrimination had the capacity and legitimacy to organise their members and seek political reform. While for the most part these changes were positive for American society, fathers' rights groups claim that in other cases—most frequently in the women's movement—members went 'too far' in asserting their demands, thereby depriving other citizens of their right to freedom and happiness. Fathers must, therefore, protect themselves by forming a strong, countervailing movement on their own. An activist named Christian articulates this view as he describes the spread of fathers' groups all over the country. In explaining the impetus behind what he views as widespread, father-centered mobilisation, he utilises the metaphor of a 'pendulum' of rights that has swung too far in favour of women's rights.

> [The] information that I get [is that] the same thing [mobilization] is happening all over the place. There is a New Jersey organization just like ours. I have a newsletter that I read once. It was 15–20 pages long. I heard the same sort of horror stories, the same kinds of issues, the same kinds of pleas for help and information about how many people are affected. I am on the internet and I hear from people in Georgia, California, and Arkansas. It is happening everywhere. There are national organizations, there are national speakers, [and] there are national writers who are devoting their careers and their lives to this issue. This is the issue of our time. This is the equal rights [movement] of the 1960s. This is finally equal rights catching up to both genders. Since the 1960s, we [have] had tremendous progress, if you will, in terms of obtaining equal rights between the genders and among the races, but few have realised how much the pendulum has swung the other way in terms of the role women have in the family court system versus what men have. It is high time we put our money where our mouth is in terms of equality in this country.

A respondent named Kip endorses Christian's point on the 'swinging pendulum', but actually goes a step further. He warns all women of the dangers of asking for 'too many rights', because, inevitably, these rights will be rescinded in a political backlash.

> My theory on political science has always been that our political system works on a pendulum system. If the pendulum were to hang straight and true, everything would be rosy, but of course the pendulum never hangs straight and true. There are always forces who are trying to pull it to one side or the other. The further you pull it one way or the other, the more force that pendulum has when it comes back to neutral and swings the other way. My own personal feeling is that the pendulum has swung too far

into the area of women's rights [due to the women's movement] over the past 10–20 years and my fear is that it will swing too far the other way. I have daughters, I have sisters, and [I have] cousins. I don't think we need to go back to the 1950s when women had no rights, but by the same token I don't think we need to live in [the twenty-first century] when men have no rights. I don't think a lot of these women realise that the more they pull that pendulum off to the side, the harder it's going to swing back [with the help of fathers' rights groups] … Eventually, it will swing back, it always does.

Like other activists, Christian and Kip express the idea that social movements can go awry by insisting upon too many benefits at the expense of others. Interestingly, both Christian and Kip also remark that these very same women advocating on behalf of more rights do not yet 'realise' that their demands have gone too far. There has to be a countervailing force, concretely in the form of a strong fathers' rights movement, to help them understand the limitations of their claims.

Other activists agree that the women's movement has placed women in a superior position vis à vis men, but that women are fully cognisant of this power. For example, Barry claims that the women's movement may have produced positive results for society in the past, but now he believes that women have an advantaged position in most areas of life, including work, home and, most importantly for him, family policy.

Well, I think that when the feminist movement of the 1960s and 1970s really took its foothold, that it did a tremendous amount of good. It brought equal wages, opportunities, and, to this day, I've been in high management, and low management, and I've seen women get whatever they want, whenever they want. I don't know, maybe it's just in my area. Maybe things have equaled out, but I also think at the same time, their push to work was a push away from the home … they have pushed themselves out of that primary caretaker role … [Yet the] rules and the laws when it came to court [continue to] be in their favor [and] are kind of outdated. A lot of people are being affected by it, especially the same women that were in the movement back 30 years ago … [Their] husbands are being taken to the cleaners. So, I think that [these affected men are] becoming involved in this men's movement also.

What is noteworthy about Barry's comments is his view that because women consciously 'pushed' themselves in the work force, they must pay a conscious price of reducing their influence in the home. Unfortunately, according to Barry, child support and child custody laws have not exacted this price so far, so men must organise to make sure that the appropriate reforms are implemented. Like Barry, an activist named Jorge draws attention to the advantages women now have in American society due to what he perceives as the fully conscious, overreaching zeal of the women's movement. In his view, fathers face an enormous disadvantage because women are better 'natural organisers' than men.

Listen, [you know about] the women's movement that started in the beginning of the last century. Women have been getting a tremendous amount of rights within society.

> I think just by their behavioural characteristics women tend to be more organised in regards to dealing with these situations … Maybe it is just cultural, maybe it is behavioural. I really don't know, but I do know that women tend to be a bit more vocal in regards to these concerns … Politicians are listening to them.

According to Jorge, women use their talents at organising in order to gain the upper hand in family disputes. He also argues that they have succeeded in their efforts because elected officials are somehow much more attuned to their claims than they are to fathers' concerns. Samuel, another fathers' rights activist, makes a similar case that politicians are now excessively enamoured with furthering women's rights, a cause which he sees as substantively illegitimate given the biological differences between men and women.

> I think what is happening is this. We've talked about this at [our fathers' group] meetings. Probably back in the suffrage times, the 1920s, woman were pretty much like second class citizens. Somehow the women's movement of equal rights [started], or the … burn the bra thing came out. Whatever it was, you know what I mean, everybody wants their freedom. Well, the thing is, let's face it. You have a woman who wants to compete with a man in all arenas—it is not a viable possibility. First of all, like are you going to get on a loading dock and throw 100 pound sacks of flour all day long on a conveyor belt? I don't think you could do it… Not that you're stupid, you're just as intelligent, but you can't do that because you weren't made to do that. So, we were made to be motivated by you and build everything because we were given the testosterone or whatever … You do child bearing, so we each have a role. And this thing about [women saying], "Oh, I need equality"—I can't become equal to a woman! I don't want to be [and] I am not in competition with you. I know I can lift more weight than you, but I don't care. I am supposed to be able to do that. You can have a child; I am not supposed to be able to compete with you … What happens is the women were maybe put behind the eight ball a little bit, [and wanted equal rights] or whatever you want to call it, [but it is now unreasonable] … I don't have to take this without fighting. Just because my name is father, why should I not see my child? … Women are united and they are now a viable body of the United States of America.

To activists like Samuel, then, the women's movement represents a real wake-up call to men's own mobilisation. If fathers do not become organised more quickly, the 'unified' women's movement will continue to strip them of all of their familial rights.

Equality: Is that all they are asking for?

> We are only seeking equality in parenting … That is all we are asking for.[50]

The social turmoil that dominated the 1960s and 1970s brought with it many changes that affected the daily lives of disenfranchised populations across the

---

[50] Ray, interviewee.

United States. Through the politics of protest, both formal and informal, women, Black Americans, and the gay/lesbian community mobilised for equality in the areas of social and economic justice. In doing so, they were successful in promoting change as evidenced by a wide range of socioeconomic indicators, such as additional legal protections, viable options for occupational mobility, and increasing opportunities for higher educational attainment.

More recently, major new family-form related sociodemographic trends detailed at the beginning of this chapter, such as rising divorce rates and single parenthood, and the government's response to these shifts in the form of stricter child support and child custody policies, prompted similar activism by fathers organised into their own 'rights-based' groups. In fact, in many ways as evidenced by the fathers' rights activists interviewed here, these groups have looked to these prior movements for, in social movement language, 'framing' guidance in developing their own plans to enact social change. Indeed, they have learned how to make moral arguments on the basis of equality and have started to devise concrete, tactical strategies for change, both lessons adopted from the successful histories of these prior movements. They have also learned about the need to organise in order to protect themselves from others clamouring for competing rights, most particularly women's groups. Through their group formation, these men aim to shield their interests against what they view as the hostile forces which are mobilised against them, and demand, as they have in other historical moments, a favourable state response. However, one difference between fathers' rights groups and all of their predecessors is striking. Prior social movements that have come before them represented marginalised groups in society who were fighting for power *that they never held*. In contrast, fathers' rights activists are demanding change from a position of already deeply-held power across multiple social domains. Theirs, then, is a defensive struggle against *losing power* in the family dissolution process.[51]

Why is this distinction critical, and what does it mean for the future of public policy? Fathers' rights activists continue to call for 'rule-based' equality, whereby men and women are treated *exactly the same* when the courts consider child support and custody awards.[52] In its prescriptive extreme, this means that each man and each woman should shoulder exactly 50 per cent of these responsibilities with respect to their children. Yet, research has already documented that, even in intact families, women face economic disadvantages in the labour market as well as shoulder a disproportionate share of the childrearing responsibilities in comparison to men. These patterns are difficult to reverse. Upon the breakdown of the

---

[51] RW Connell, *Gender and Power* (Cambridge, Polity, 1987); RW Connell, *Masculinities* (Berkeley, CA, University of California Press, 1995); B Pease, *Recreating Men: Postmodern Masculinity Politics* (London, Sage, 2000); RW Connell, 'Change Among the Gatekeepers: Men, Masculinities, and Gender Equality in the Global Arena' (2005) 30(3) *Signs: Journal of Women in Culture and Society* 1801.

[52] Fineman, above n 4.

traditional family unit, however, some form of corrective action can be taken. More specifically, at these points in time, there is a unique opportunity for governmental intervention to ensure that both the mother-headed and the father-headed halves of the family succeed and prosper.

For the past several decades, legislators and the courts have taken advantage of this opportunity in a variety of different ways. Most prominent have been tougher child support enforcement policies as well as a de facto mother-preference in custody determinations, both of which tend to benefit women disproportionately. Where so much inequality between the genders already exists, leveling the playing field to the greatest extent possible through these laws can therefore be conceived as a worthy goal. That is, it is desirable for the courts to focus on the concept of *outcome-based equality* rather than the *rule-based equality* provisions which fathers' rights groups advocate. Only then will we continue to see the gains that are necessary for women to experience a just and fair society, and consequently best conceptualise the role of men and fathers in this transforming world.

5

Gender Equality, Child Welfare and Fathers' Rights in Sweden

MARIA ERIKSSON AND KEITH PRINGLE

Introduction

In this chapter we outline recent developments in Swedish policy and law on child custody, residence and contact and discuss the role of fathers' rights activists in shaping legal reforms. We argue that, on the one hand, interest groups promoting fathers' rights in Sweden can been seen as highly successful in influencing the policy agenda. In particular, a special non-expert advisory group appointed by the government in 1992—the so-called Daddy-Group[1]—was important in channelling fathers' rights discourses into policy and law. In that sense, reforms to Swedish family law in 1998 can be interpreted as an example of the fathers' rights movement's success.

On the other hand, fathers' rights activists still seem to be relatively few in number, disorganised and—at least in comparison with, for example, the UK—not particularly visible in the media. It would therefore be rather misleading to conclude that these groups constitute a strong and visible fathers' rights movement in Sweden. Furthermore, the 1992 Daddy-Group was clearly linked to broader political attempts to promote gender equality. As a curiosity it can be noted, for example, that one of the former Daddy-Group members—Jens Orback—is at the time of writing himself the minister for gender equality in the current social democratic government.

We argue that to understand the success of a relatively small, disorganised and invisible 'movement', and to explain the patriarchal ethos of policy and legal practice in Sweden in the 1990s, fathers' rights activism must be placed in a broader political and cultural context. Our aim in this chapter is to outline some aspects

---

[1] DS (Departmental Series) 1995:2. *Slutrapport från arbetsgruppen om papporna, barnen och arbetslivet* (Final report from the working group on daddies, children and working life) (Fritzes, Stockholm).

of this context. We start with a description of fathers' rights groups and move on to the dominant discourses in Swedish social policy. Thereafter we detail legal reform in the critical period of the 1990s.

Fathers' Rights Activism in Sweden

So far, there has been very little Swedish research into fathers' rights activism and groups. A recent review of academic and scholarly publications in the last decade on men's practices in Sweden shows that the topic of fathers' rights has not been central to the research agenda.[2] In fact, when searching LIBRIS (the Royal Library's national database) with the key words '*fadersrätt*' (father-rights), '*fäders rätt*' (fathers' rights) and '*faderskap, familjerätt*' (fatherhood, family law), we found one hit that directly mentions the phenomenon of fathers' rights activism—a report authored by a women's shelter activist[3]—but no academic publications and no in-depth discussion of these groups.[4] Therefore, the description below is based upon our own Internet search and review of information that various groups have made available on the web.

Since the late 1980s and early 1990s a number of groups have emerged in Sweden that can be defined as promoting 'fathers' rights'.[5] However, the extent to which these groups explicitly focus on the interests of men and fathers varies. They also tend to present themselves in slightly different ways. Some groups, such as *Söndagsbarn* (Sunday children)[6] and *Föreningen Styvmorsviolen* (an organisation for step-parents/families),[7] tend to frame their work in gender neutral terms and emphasise parental co-operation and agreement after separation or divorce. The focus on the rights of fathers is made clear in various texts published on the web.

---

[2] D Balkmar and K Pringle, *Sweden National Report on Research on Men's Practices*, EU Framework Six Co-ordinated Action on Human Rights (CAHRV, 2005), http://www.cromenet.org. A previous review of Nordic studies on men points in the same direction: see P Folkesson, *Nordisk mansforskning—en kartläggning* (Karlstad, Jämställdhetscentrum/Karlstads universitet, 2000).

[3] G Nordenfors, *Fadersrätt, kvinnofrid och barns säkerhet* (Stockholm, ROKS/Riksorganisationen för kvinno- och tjejjourer i Sverige, 1996).

[4] The most relevant piece of academic work we have found is a report on the voluntary men's hotlines' work with 'men in crisis': C Holmberg and C Bender, *Våld mot kvinnor—män i kris* (Stockholm, Socialstyrelsen, 1998). However, activism to promote the rights of men—including men who are fathers—is not discussed in detail.

[5] According to their websites, *Umgängesrätts Föräldrarnas Riksförening* ('Association for Equal Parenting'; literal translation is 'the national organisation for parents with rights to contact') was founded in 1987, http://www.ufr.org, and *Söndagsbarn. 'Barnets rätt till 2 föräldrar'* (Sunday children. 'The child's right to 2 parents') was founded in 1993, http://www.sondagsbarn.com.

[6] http://www.sondagsbarn.com

[7] http://www.styvmorsviolen.se

For example, when presenting its work on the problems faced by step-families, an organisation for step-parents and families claims that:

> Society has a tendency to value mummies more as parents than daddies, which makes it possible for the mum to use the children as a means to an end in conflicts with the dad.[8]

Other groups are more explicit in their focus on the interests of men and fathers and the problems that they face, especially in relation to separation and divorce and legal conflicts concerning children. One example is the *Mansjouren på webben* (Men's hotline/support on the web), which asks the following on the entry page:

> Have you experienced separation, a conflict about the children, sabotage of contact, duty to repay [child support] ... Are you pushed away from the children by the mummy and/or the social services?[9]

The ways in which these groups relate to feminist perspectives and organisations also differ. While some, like the men's hotline/support quoted above, include a number of feminist organisations in the list of links they publish on the web, others are more openly anti-feminist. For example, the 'Association for Equal Parenting' gives assessments of various organisations and issues a warning against organisations that are labelled 'sexist' and 'chauvinist'. Amongst the latter are the more explicitly feminist national organisations for women's shelters and hotlines in Sweden.[10]

Moreover, the structure of the groups seems to vary. Some are presented as organisations at a national level (like *Söndagsbarn*), whereas others claim to be umbrella organisations for a number of local and/or regional groups (like the national organisations for men's hotlines and the Association for Equal Parenting).[11] It is hard to know what this information represents in practice. In the case of men's hotlines, contact information for 13 local groups is provided. When we follow the links to the three regional groups listed on the website of the Association for Equal Parenting, one (Stockholm) turns out to be a link back to the national level; another (Blekinge) is a link to a web-page where the organisation is seeking a new representative for that area; and the third one (Skåne) leads to nothing at all.[12]

---

[8] http://www.styvmorsviolen.se. Our translation.

[9] http://www.mansjouren.org

[10] *Riksorganisationen för kvinno- och tjejjourer i Sverige*/ROKS, http://www.roks.se. The other organisation, *Sveriges Kvinnojourers Riksförbund*/SKR, is generally perceived, and presents itself, as less feminist, http://www.kvinnojour.com. See also L McMillan, 'Women's Anti-Violence Organisations in Sweden and the UK' in M Eriksson, A Nenola and MM Nilsen (eds), *Gender and Violence in the Nordic Countries. Report from a Conference in Køge, Denmark 23–24 November 2001* (Copenhagen, The Nordic Council of Ministers, 2002).

[11] *Sveriges Mansjourers Riksförbund*, http://www.mansjouren.nu; *Umgängsrätts Föräldrarnas Riksförening* ('Association for Equal Parenting'), http://www.ufr.org.

[12] Some of the organisations make statements about the number of members, eg *Styvmorsviolen* (274) and Association for Equal Parenting (approximately 400, 73% men, 27% women on the national level); others do not provide such information.

As a curiosity, we note that a 'brother' to the UK organisation Fathers 4 Justice has been founded in Sweden (*Fäder för rättvisa*).[13] According to the tabloid newspaper *Aftonbladet*, an incident involving a father in a Spider-Man outfit occurred in Stockholm in August 2005.[14] However, since the media coverage of this event was modest, we were not even aware of it until we carried out the research for this chapter. We also note that the web-page of this organisation is 'under construction' and that very little seems to have happened between September 2005 and March 2006.[15] As with some of the other groups where web-links lead nowhere, it is hard to know if these names and links represent only occasional (web) activities by one or a couple of individuals, or whether they represent more disseminated and sustainable networks.[16]

As regards the activities of the fathers' rights groups, their web-pages tend to include information about various legal matters, literature references, reports by members and useful links to other organisations and/or authorities. Some also describe face-to-face support work, and/or provide support to men/fathers via the web. One example is the men's hotline/support on the web which organises a special 'Daddy-hotline/support', described as a closed e-mail list with 'approximately 25 participants'. Finally, lobbying and attempts to influence legal reform regarding custody, contact, residence and child support form a central activity for at least some of these groups.[17] In particular, family law reforms from the mid-1990s have received a lot of attention. Before moving on to the discussion about the relationship between fathers' rights activists and these legal reforms, we want to outline the broader discursive opportunity structure[18] that forms the context for the framing[19] strategies of activists when trying to influence policy and reform processes.

The Discursive Opportunity Structure

In the study of social movements, it has been argued that the 'cultural resonance' of different framing strategies is key to a movement's success.[20] Yet, as Myra Marx

---

[13] http://www.f4j.se

[14] *Aftonbladet*, 31 August 2005.

[15] http://www.f4j.se

[16] This concerns, for example, *AFAF Aktionsgruppen för Falskt Anklagade Fäder* (Task Force for Falsely Accused Fathers), listed at http://www.ufr.org.

[17] For example, Association for Equal Parenting and *Söndagsbarn*.

[18] MM Ferree, 'Resonance and Radicalism: Feminist Framing in the Abortion Debates of the United States and Germany' (2003) *American Journal of Sociology* 109.

[19] RD Benford and DA Snow, 'Framing Processes and Social Movements: An Overview and Assessment' (2000) *Annual Review of Sociology* 26.

[20] *Ibid.*

Ferree points out, the concept of cultural resonance is problematic, partly because in practice it seems difficult to separate resonance from the outcomes of movement activism: the fact that an idea gains ground may sometimes in itself be interpreted as an indication of its cultural resonance. Moreover, a focus on language could obscure the power relations institutionalised in the hegemonic framing of issues.[21] In addition, the dialogic nature of the interaction between authorities and challengers may be lost. For resonance does not simply reflect properties of the frame itself, but is—at least partly—created through interventions by individual and/or collective actors.

Nevertheless, frames (for example, the ones we use as units for analysis below) exist in a context that is enabling for certain of them, yet restraining as regards others. Discursive opportunities are structured, both in the sense of having pattern and form, and in the sense of being anchored in key political institutions.[22]In our understanding, this context both precedes and is influenced by the framing strategies developed by movement activists. Here, we want to make some suggestions regarding two specific aspects of the discursive opportunity structure contextualising fathers' rights activism in Sweden: discourses regarding gender equality and child welfare respectively.[23]

Gender Equality, the Swedish Way

Before moving any further into a discussion about gender equality ideology and policy we want to point out that Swedish gender equality ideology is often presented as a uniform entity. However, empirically this is not the case. In Sweden two competing discourses have been present: first, gender equality through the promotion of gender as sameness; and secondly, gender equality through the 'celebration' of (complementary) differences between women and men. In the first case, gender difference is presumed to be socially constructed, and therefore possible to reconstruct or transcend; in the second case, differences between women and men are presumed to be (to varying degrees) essential.[24] Empirically, these two discourses intermingle in child and family policy. We would argue that this intermingling creates specific challenges when analysing such policies. As regards fathers, the discourse of sameness tended to be central to the establishment of new policies in the 1960s and 1970s. Later, a discourse centred on the specific 'father

---

[21] Ferree, above n 18, 305.

[22] WH Sewell, 'A Theory of Structure: Duality, Agency, and Transformation' (1992) *American Journal of Sociology* 98, quoted in Ferree, above n 18.

[23] It should be added that, as one of our examples shows, our focus on framing and discourse does not mean that we do not perceive organisational aspects as being of great importance too.

[24] For a more elaborate discussion see eg E Magnusson, 'Party-Political Rhetoric on Gender Equality in Sweden: The Uses of Uniformity and Heterogeneity' (2002) *Nordic Journal of Women's Studies/NORA* 8.

contribution'—reproducing the construction of essential differences—developed. Currently, both can be seen in policy and practice.[25]

Swedish social policy more broadly presupposes that parents share the responsibilities for children. Reforms have been made in a number of areas, for example regarding parental leave insurance which makes it possible for both parents to participate in, and be responsible for, the everyday upbringing and development of young children.[26] Diane Sainsbury argues that the Swedish welfare system is shaped by a gender regime of an individual earner-carer model.[27] The model presumes that fathers and mothers are both responsible for (unpaid) care work as well as for supporting the family financially. This development mirrors broader trends in the Nordic countries.[28] Lis Højgaard argues that since the 1970s and 1980s the focus of Scandinavian gender equality policies has shifted, from attempts to make it possible for women to participate in the labour market to attempts to make men participate in care work at home.[29] While previous social policy measures mainly used women's paid labour to promote gender equality, the later phase is marked by measures making it possible for men to participate in family life under the same conditions as women. Højgaard argues that the latter policy consists of a mixture of measures targeting fathers or mothers specifically, and measures targeting parents in general. Furthermore, she adds that the aim is to give men a legally sanctioned opportunity to take on the role of caregiver in the home.[30]

'Daddy Politics'

The policy concerning custody, contact and residence should be interpreted in the context of these parallel and interlinked political projects where the dismantling of the gender division of work and the transformation of 'traditional' fathers into caring daddies are core ingredients. In Sweden, the political ambition of reshaping

[25] See eg M Eriksson, 'A Visible or Invisible Child? Professionals' Approaches to Children whose Father is Violent Towards their Mother' in M Eriksson, M Hester, S Keskinen and K Pringle (eds), *Tackling Men's Violence in Families: Nordic Issues and Dilemmas* (Bristol, Policy Press, 2005).

[26] See L Bekkengen, *Man får välja—om föräldraskap och föräldraledighet i arbetsliv och familjeliv* (Malmö, Liber, 2002); C Hagström, *Man blir pappa. Föräldraskap och maskulinitet i förändring* (Lund, Nordic Academic Press, 1999); R Klinth, *Göra pappa med barn. Svensk pappa-politik 1960–95* (Umeå, Boréa, 2002); D Sainsbury (ed), *Gender and Welfare State Regimes* (Oxford, Oxford University Press, 1999); J Schiratzki, *Vårdnad och vårdnadstvister* (Stockholm, Nordstedts, 1997).

[27] Sainsbury, *ibid*, 77; cf G Esping-Andersen, *Three Worlds of Welfare Capitalism* (Cambridge, Polity, 1990).

[28] 'Nordic' refers to the five countries Denmark, Finland, Iceland, Norway and Sweden as well as the self-ruling areas: the Faroe Islands (Denmark), Greenland (Denmark) and Åland (Finland). 'Scandinavian' refers to Denmark, Norway and Sweden.

[29] L Højgaard, 'Working Fathers—Caught in the Web of the Symbolic Order of Gender' (1997) *Acta Sociologica* 40. Cf Klinth, above n 26, on how the double emancipatory project of 'getting mam a job and making daddy with child' has developed over time.

[30] Højgaard, *ibid*, 251–2.

fathers' relationships with their children has its roots in the sex-role debate of the early 1960s.[31] In the debate, the gender specific and complementary parental role previously ascribed to fathers became associated with a 'traditional' and 'outdated' male role.[32] The 'new' father was a man who not only supports but also cares for his children.

The importance of the physically and emotionally present and caring father for the psychological and social development of children—and especially boys—was already a central theme in the Swedish debate during the formation of 'daddy politics'[33] at the end of the 1960s and beginning of the 1970s. According to Roger Klinth, psychologists and sociologists at that time painted a picture of the unhealthy and socially destructive man. Klinth is, for example, quoting one of the most influential sociologists in family and gender research of that period, Rita Liljeström, who was professor of sociology at Göteborg University. She portrayed the 'criminality and maladjustment' of men and boys as a consequence of the mother-dominance they were subjected to during childhood.[34] Fatherhood was constructed both as the root of the problem—father absence, and the solution—new fatherhood. Present and caring fathers were presumed to contribute to less destructive, more gender equal men. Here, we see how constructions of gender as 'sameness' and as 'difference' are present simultaneously: fathers are presumed to make a special contribution to the upbringing of (especially boy-) children, and they should therefore become more engaged in caring activities (that is, become more like mothers).

From Grassroots to Central Policy (and Back)

With this background in mind, we want to demonstrate how fathers' rights may be promoted from 'within', rather than from outside of, the governmental system in Sweden. A clear and key example of this is the development of Swedish parental leave insurance and the day care scheme in the late 1960s and early 1970s. Using an interview from a recent large-scale qualitative study of the Swedish child welfare system carried out in 2002,[35] we will illustrate how central the daddy-project has been to the Social Democratic movement itself and to the identity and self-presentation of some of the policy makers in Sweden.

---

[31] See Klinth, above n 26; H Bergman and B Hobson, 'Compulsory Fatherhood: The Coding of Fatherhood in the Swedish Welfare State' in B Hobson (ed), *Making Men into Fathers: Men, Masculinities and the Social Politics of Fatherhood* (Cambridge, Cambridge University Press, 2002).

[32] Klinth, above n 26, 86; Hagström above n 26, 48. A central feature in previous constructions of good fatherhood was the role as breadwinner.

[33] Klinth, above n 26.

[34] R Liljeström, *Jämställdhetens villkor: män och kvinnor i dagens värld* (Stockholm, Sveriges Radio, 1968), quoted in Klinth, above n 26, 79.

[35] ESRC project R000223551. See K Pringle (2002) *Final Report to the ESRC on Project R000223551*, on REGARD DATABASE: http://www.regard.ac.uk/cgi-bin/regardng/showReports.pl?ref=R000223551.

The interviewee in question here used to be a high-ranking civil servant in *Socialstyrelsen* (the National Board for Health and Welfare) from the early 1970s through to the end of the 1990s.[36] In the interview, the respondent identified parental leave insurance and day care policies as originating within discussions among so-called 'study circles' on equality issues, including gender equality. These 'study circles' were local groups of women and men organised in the 1960s by *Arbetarnas Bildningsförbund/ABF* (the Workers Educational Association) and the Social Democratic Party in each area. The interviewee described how the developing interest in broader childcare provision was connected to increased workforce participation by women:

> So the women were pouring out into the labour market and they wanted good child-care for their children. We had circles—circles on equality. We had one at home in 1967/1968. Those study circles on equality were very important. The main material we used was written by Rita Liljeström, a sociology professor from Gothenburg. Her book on equality became widely spread and people discussed the book keenly. Earlier on, the day-care centres had targeted children who had a lone parent or to children and parents who had special needs. The day-care centres were now shifted to be something that you wanted to offer to all children when the parents wanted to work. So there was a shift then in the 1960s over to the 1970s to include other groups of users.

According to this former civil servant, the study circles were used to find ways of suggesting policy changes, to write motions and follow them up politically. This respondent's personal narrative about being involved in all the steps in the reform process around parental leave insurance indicates how efficient the Social Democratic government system can be, and illustrates the centrality of the daddy-project in the Swedish labour movement's attempts to achieve gender equality.[37]

> During that study circle, an idea came up from a good friend [...who was in a job dominated by men]. He suggested that it should be possible for both the man and the woman to stay home with the new born child and that an insurance should cover both of them and they could share it. They could be home in the beginning, both of them; but they could also share it in different ways during the period the child was small. So, inspired by the members of the study circle, I wrote a motion for a parental insurance scheme. I put it forward because I was politically active. It went through the political system and was carried all the way and it turned out eventually to become the parental insurance scheme in Sweden. At that time I was employed at the National Board of Health and Welfare and since part of the parental leave insurance also

---

[36] The Board is a kind of semi-governmental agency which both monitors central government policies on health and welfare in the localities *and* can make suggestions to central government about potential new policies in that field. It is therefore a most important—and huge—central organisation.

[37] It is important to remember that the Social Democratic Party has dominated Swedish politics and government since the 1930s—with only a few very short periods out of power. It came to dominance in the first part of the 20th century after a very bitter class struggle.

entailed other family issues, a Commission called the Family Aid Commission was put into operation to bring the parental leave insurance issue into reality—so that it could be carried through in practice. Other issues like parental education and the whole family situation around the very small child were added. So, day-care centres then needed to be offered to very small children and they had to be of good quality and so we had to penetrate that area as well. I was asked to serve on that Commission as a head secretary ... And so I was on leave of absence for three years from my regular job at the National Board of Health and Welfare. When the reports came out and the parental leave insurance was taken forward and actually initiated, it was then followed up. Suggestions from the report were on the agenda of the National Board of Health and Welfare to help carry it through. Some of the people involved in the work that led to the report had the kind of knowledge needed and they also became involved in the implementation.

The points we want to make here are fourfold. Firstly, according to this narrative a central element of Swedish family policy—the parental leave insurance scheme—was created not through pressure groups or social movements *external to* the government. Instead, it is presented as arising through 'osmosis' from the grassroots party membership, up through the party, into the government, back out of the government to a parliamentary commission; and then from the commission to the semi-governmental authority *Socialstyrelsen* for detailed implementation back at the local level.[38] Secondly, these extracts indicate that the issue of new fatherhood (and the discourse of gender equality as gender sameness) has been at the core of Social Democracy since at least the 1960s. Thirdly, the quotations are marked by a taken-for-granted construction of parenthood as heterosexual and also by an ethos of amicable co-operation between women and men for the benefit of everybody. These are themes that we will discuss further below. Fourthly, the experience described in these quotations suggests that the later success of the non-expert Daddy-Group in the 1990s in shaping policy should (also) be interpreted against a backdrop of historically well-established practices within the governmental system.

Gender — Peace and Harmony?

If well-established discourses of gender equality are a major force in the promotion of fathers' rights, what is the relationship between these discourses and feminist claims? Maud Eduards explores the political-cultural code for what is accepted regarding gender, power and democracy in Sweden. She does so by drawing upon a number of studies and empirical examples of encounters between women's separately organised demands and the defenders of the established

[38] For an overview of policy developments as regards child care see C Kugelberg, *Perceiving Motherhood and Fatherhood. Swedish Working Parents with Young Children* (Uppsala, Uppsala University, 1999).

democratic order in Sweden.[39] She argues that in spite of the reputation for gender equality, it is very difficult to make visible the key differences in interests between women and men in contemporary Sweden; and particularly difficult to make visible the interests of men. To question the established, consensus-oriented and hetero-normative 'normal' way of doing politics, and to name men as a political category, as an interested party in a power relation with women is, according to Eduards, 'the most forbidden' in the Swedish democratic order.[40]

The Welfare and Well-Being of Children

So far, we have focused on the issue of gender and gendered power relations. However, it is necessary also to scrutinise well-established notions of children and child welfare. Not least due to the fact that Sweden was the first country in the world to ban corporal punishment of children in 1979, Sweden has an international reputation for being *barnvänligt* (child friendly). It should be recognised that recent surveys clearly show that physical abuse of children in Sweden has steadily reduced to a low level;[41] and that long-standing Swedish welfare policies geared to broad family support—especially engagement with the labour market—have of course been highly beneficial for children.[42] However, to get a balanced picture of the situation of children in Sweden, it is also important to recognise that, so far, relatively little emphasis has been placed on welfare issues other than economic disadvantage and poverty. For example, one can argue that relatively little attention has been paid to the need to protect children against sexual abuse.[43]

This can be demonstrated in a number of ways. For example, we note that in this research-rich country there has been no thorough national prevalence survey of child sexual abuse since the end of the 1980s. Although physical abuse is almost certainly at relatively low levels in Sweden, there are already sufficient research indications that the same is not true of child sexual abuse.[44] Moreover, this absence of a rather obvious piece of information fits into a broader research picture. For the outcomes of two EC-funded transnational projects clearly show that

---

[39] M Eduards, *Förbjuden handling* (Malmö, Liber, 2002). See also G Gustafsson, M Eduards and M Rönnblom (eds), *Towards a New Democratic Order? Women's Organizing in Sweden in the 1990s* (Stockholm, Publica, 1997).

[40] For a discussion of the tension between claims to 'uniformity' and 'heterogeneity' as regards gendered interests in Sweden, see also Magnusson, above n 24.

[41] SOU 2001:72. *Barnmisshandel. Att förebygga och åtgärda* (Stockholm, Fritzes, 2001).

[42] L Hantrais and M-T Letablier, *Families and Family Policies in Europe* (Harlow, Longman, 1996).

[43] K Pringle, *Children and Social Welfare in Europe* (Buckingham, Open University Press, 1998); K Pringle, 'Hvorfor har vi brug for flere mandlige pædagoger?—Internationale synspunkter' (2005) *VERA* 33.

[44] See eg E Lundgren, G Heimer, J Westerstrand and A-M Kalliokoski, *Captured Queen. Men's Violence Against Women in 'Equal' Sweden—A National Survey* (Umeå, Brottsoffermyndigheten, 2002).

Sweden has carried out far less research on men's violence generally than, say, the UK or Germany—including men's sexual violence towards children.[45] It is worth noting that Sweden and some of the other Nordic countries have been among the European leaders in carrying out research on other aspects of men's practices, such as work and health. It seems that violence features much lower on their list of research priorities.[46]

Turning to examples from the sphere of policy and practice on child protection, it is striking that Sweden lacks central co-ordinated written guidance procedures for professionals about the handling of child sexual abuse. This is despite the fact that *Socialstyrelsen* (the National Board of Health and Welfare) in the last eight years has expended a great deal of its resources on gathering together experts to write extensive information papers on child sexual abuse for its website. As regards practice in relation to the protection of children, the qualitative research project mentioned above also showed that many social workers in Sweden are routinely *not* trained to communicate directly with children. The very same criticism of social work training was also made by a recent Swedish parliamentary committee on child abuse.[47] In making these points, we are not arguing that the 'traditional' family support orientation of services and policy in Sweden is a problem. It is the lack of emphasis on protection of children that is the problem. Child welfare systems can embrace both family support and child protection;[48] the difficulty is that the Swedish system seems to have been massively tilted towards a focus on the former.

It is no doubt possible that the relative success of the ban on corporal punishment in Sweden may have taken some focus off protection issues more generally, especially if social awareness of other forms of abuse—such as sexual abuse or neglect—is so low. However, in explaining this state of affairs in Sweden we want to bring into focus the relative emphasis on both collectivism and consensus which marks Swedish social institutions, including those within the welfare system. We argue that this collectivist and consensual approach has had an impact on the promotion of family support discourses and on the resistance to more conflictual and power-oriented child protective ones. At one level the lack of recognition of child protection issues actually represents resistance to recognising structural inequalities within the family which might impact on its harmonious

---

[45] J Hearn and K Pringle, *European Perspectives on Men and Masculinities* (Houndmills, Palgrave, 2006). The first project was a thematic network on men's practices in eleven European countries that was carried out in 2000–3, co-ordinated by Keith Pringle and funded by the EU Fifth Framework Programme (see http://www.cromenet.org). The second project is a part of a co-ordination action on human rights violations (CAHRV), carried out in 2004–7 and funded by the EU Sixth Framework Programme (see http://www.cahrv.uni-osnabrueck.de).

[46] M Eriksson and K Pringle, 'Introduction: Nordic Issues and Dilemmas' in M Eriksson *et al*, above n 25.

[47] Pringle, above n 43; SOU, above n 41.

[48] N Parton, *Child Protection and Family Support* (London, Routledge, 1997).

functioning, not least inequalities of age and gender.[49] However, it must be conceded that in recent years, more conflictual discourses have gained some ground in Sweden.

Developing, Incompetent and In Need of Heterosexual Parents?

The first law that made it possible for the Swedish state to intervene to protect children came into force in 1926.[50] Thereafter, the issue of children at risk because of abuse or for other reasons was dealt with repeatedly in social policy throughout the rest of the 20th century. Furthermore, the topic gained a new level of attention after the tragic death of four young children due to abuse in the summer of 1990. The year after, *Socialstyrelsen* was given the task of developing more child-centred perspectives in work with children at risk: the so-called *Children in focus project*. Making reference to new research, the 'Child Perspective' was elaborated in the final report of the project. This perspective has since proved influential in Swedish social policy in recent years.

The 'Child Perspective' can be interpreted as a mixture of a welfare discourse and a rights discourse regarding children (drawing upon the United Nations' Convention on the Rights of the Child). In brief, the welfare discourse provides a protective approach whereby children become the object of adults' interventions and control. Here, children are presumed to need care, guidance and protection from adults and it is adults who are presumed to know what is 'in the best interests of the child'.[51] This discourse is thus associated with a 'needs-oriented' approach to children's views, according to which children cannot make decisions about their own lives.[52] According to the second (rights) discourse, children have a right both to society's resources and to participation in proceedings that affect their lives. The rights discourse can also be said to be associated with a 'competence-oriented' approach to children's views, where children's abilities regarding decision-making and participation are emphasised.[53]

---

[49] For further discussion see Balkmar and Pringle, above n 2; D Balkmar, L Iovanni and K Pringle, 'Mäns våld i Danmark och Sverige' (2005) *NIKK Magasin. Temanummer Kön och våld*, No 2; Hearn and Pringle, above n 45: Pringle, 'Hvorfor har vi brug for flere mandlige pædagoger', above n 43; Pringle, *Children and Social Welfare*, above n 43.

[50] The discussion in this section draws mainly upon Prop 1994/95: 224 *Barns rätt att komma till tals* (Stockholm, Fritzes, 1995); Prop 1998/99: 133 *Särskild företrädare för barn* (Stockholm, Fritzes, 1999); Socialstyrelsen *Barn i fokus-projektet. Slutrapport* (Stockholm, Socialstyrelsen, 1996); SOU 1998:31 *Det gäller livet—Stöd och vård till barn och ungdomar med psykiska problem* (Stockholm, Fritzes, 1998); SOU 2000:77 *Omhändertagen. Samhällets ansvar för utsatta barn och unga*. Betänkande från LVU-utredningen (Stockholm, Fritzes, 2000); SOU 2001:14 *Sexualbrotten—ett ökat skydd för den sexuella integriteten och angränsande frågor*. Betänkande från 1998 års Sexualbrottskommitté (Stockholm, Fritzes, 2001); SOU 2001:72, above n 41.

[51] Cf C Smart, B Neale and A Wade, *The Changing Experience of Childhood: Families and Divorce* (Cambridge, Polity, 2001).

[52] See A Singer, *Föräldraskap i rättslig belysning* (Uppsala, Iustus, 2000).

[53] *Ibid*, 83.

Drawing upon a survey of governmental investigation reports and white papers in the 1990s,[54] we conclude that although more conflictual perspectives on the relationships between children and parents seemed to gain some ground in Swedish policies on the protection of children in the 1990s, it is nevertheless possible to claim that in this policy field a welfare discourse and associated construction of the 'child' still dominate. At the core of the 'Child Perspective' is a 'child' that is developing and dependent upon adults to have its needs met.[55]

Furthermore, this child is presumed to need a two-gendered environment to develop in an optimal way. Some documents can be interpreted as a critique of the established family-centredness in the practices of social services.[56] In these reports, statements about children as independent people—not some kind of appendix of their parents—are recurring. However, the family is also portrayed as the 'natural environment' for children when growing up.[57] Here, in addition, we want to point out that Swedish family law takes heterosexual, biological parenthood as its point of departure.[58] Rights and obligations that used to be ascribed to biological parents—which were independent of the actual care of or contact with the child—are today rights and obligations of custodians only.[59] Since most biological parents are presumed to be custodians, the current emphasis on joint custody can be interpreted as a reconstruction of parenthood as fundamentally biological (rather than social or psychological)—that is, of kinship as blood-ties.[60] In line with this naturalisation of heterosexual parenthood, a general need for 'two' parents (a father and a mother complementing each other) becomes the central focus, not particular children's possible need of protection from fathers.[61]

It would seem that, in practice, it is primarily fatherhood that is reconstructed as biological. Even though most separated parents share custody (that is, they share the legally sanctioned decision-making rights as regards children), mothers

---

[54] M Eriksson, *I skuggan av Pappa. Familjerätten och hanteringen av fäders våld* (Stehag, Förlags AB Gondolin, 2003).

[55] Cf A James, C Jenks and A Prout, *Theorizing Childhood* (Cambridge, Polity, 1998).

[56] When the new law on social services (1980:620) came into force in the 1980s, the family was focused upon as a unit. The critique developing in recent years is thus parallel to the critique of earlier family sociology from researchers within the 'new' sociology of childhood. See, for example, L Alanen, *Modern Childhood? Exploring the 'Child Question' in Sociology* (Jyväskylä, Institute for Educational Research, 1992).

[57] See SOU 2000:77, above n 50, 54ff; SOU 2001:72, above n 41, 99ff.

[58] Singer, above n 52.

[59] Schiratzki, above n 26, 344.

[60] Eriksson, above n 54; Cf L Stone, *New Directions in Anthropological Kinship* (Lanham and Oxford, Rowman and Littlefield Publishers, 2001).

[61] Today it is possible for gay/lesbian couples to be assessed for adoption in Sweden. However, the presumption that heterosexual, biological parenthood is more 'natural' and normal is still strong and can also be seen among those who support the new legislation (see eg the parliamentary debate preceding the passing of the law).

are usually the main carers when the parents live apart, especially with regard to very young children.[62] The legally sanctioned decision-making rights of fathers tend, in other words, to be more disconnected from the actual care than are the decision-making rights of mothers. Fatherhood is not connected to constructions of parenthood as child-centred, good-enough caring practices to the same extent as motherhood tends to be.

Not least in combination with the lack of attention paid to child protection issues, the discursive landscape outlined above works against attempts to make visible possible conflicts of interests between, on the one hand, fathers and, on the other hand, children (girls and/or boys). In this sense, the protective welfare perspective on children enables the framing of the interests of fathers as 'general' and identical to the interests of children.

Legal Reform in the 1990s and Fathers' Rights Groups

Swedish family policy today presupposes shared parenting and a high degree of parental co-operation post-separation or divorce. Furthermore, face-to-face contact is generally presumed to be 'in the best interests of the child'. Since the 1970s a series of changes to family law has aimed to reduce conflict between parents and to encourage agreements over contact, custody and residence. In this process, shared custody has increasingly been emphasised.[63] In 1993 the government appointed the *Vårdnadstvistutredningen* (inquiry on custody disputes),[64] which led to changes to family law that came into force in 1998.[65] The 1993 inquiry strongly emphasised joint custody as the preferable option on separation or divorce, and with the 1998 changes it became possible for Swedish courts to award joint custody against the explicit will of one parent.

Swedish fathers and mothers who share custody are defined as jointly responsible for the care of the child, and for ensuring that the child's physical and psychological needs are fulfilled. The parents also share decision-making rights regarding the child and are obliged to make all major decisions jointly—that is,

---

[62] SCB (Statistics Sweden), *Barn och deras familjer 2001* (Stockholm, Statistiska Centralbyrån, 2001).
[63] See G Nordborg, 'Children's Peace? The Possibility to Protect Children by Means of Criminal Law and Family Law' in M Eriksson *et al*, above n 25.
[64] SOU 1995:79 *Vårdnad, boende, umgänge*. Vårdnadstvistutredningen (Stockholm, Fritzes, 1995).
[65] LU 1997/98:12 Lagutskottets betänkande *Vårdnad, boende umgänge* (Fritzes, Stockholm, 1998); Prop 1997/98:7 *Vårdnad, boende, umgänge* (Stockholm, Fritzes, 1998).

everything that goes beyond everyday care (food, clothes, bedtimes, leisure time activities, etc). One parent cannot make any major decision 'of central importance for the child's future' unless the best interests of the child 'apparently demand' this.[66]

The concept of custody—*vårdnad*—was introduced through a law of 1917 regarding children born outside of marriage and a law of 1920 regarding children born within marriage. The word *vårdnad* (custody), which is an abbreviation of *omvårdnad* (care), was used to get away from concepts like parental power and parental authority. Instead, the law was supposed to emphasise parents' responsibility to give children a good upbringing.[67]

Gender Neutral Law?

The language of the Swedish law and preparatory works[68] is for the most part gender neutral and the people discussed are parents (not mothers and fathers) and children (not girls and boys). In the report of the 1993 inquiry on custody disputes, a gender perspective is questioned explicitly. In line with the general guidelines for Swedish public investigations, the government's instruction to the 1993 inquiry states that it should make use of a 'gender equality perspective' in the analysis as well as suggested changes to the law.[69] However, the inquiry chooses to define a gender equality perspective as being irrelevant via the argument that:

> [Q]uestions concerning children and the best interests of children in disputes regarding custody, residence or contact are not an issue of equality between the parents, that is, between the genders. What is best for the child should and must be the deciding factor, regardless of which parent it is that 'wins' or 'loses'. A parent's 'gain' might be equivalent to a loss for the child.[70]

Here, we note the realism in language. The inquiry does not portray the choice to disregard a gender equality perspective as an *interpretation* of what the best interests of the child may be. Instead, the argument is presented as a statement of *fact*. Thereby, it gains more weight than it would do if presented as an interpretation.[71]

---

[66] *Föräldrabalken*, chapter 6, section 13.

[67] See SOU 1995:79, above n 64.

[68] The Nordic idea of law is 'continental' in the sense that written laws are considered to be the primary legal material. In the Nordic courts, the role of preparatory works is quite central in the interpretation of laws. Preparatory works are often rich in statements about the aims of the acts and often also about how they should be interpreted. See K Nousiainen, 'Introductory Remarks in Nordic Law and Gender Identities' in K Nousiainen, Å Gunnarsson, K Lundström and J Niemi-Kiesiläinen (eds), *Responsible Selves: Women in the Nordic Legal Culture* (Aldershot, Ashgate, 2001).

[69] Dir 1993:120 *Handläggning av vårdnadstvister* (Stockholm, Fritzes, 1993).

[70] SOU 1995:79, above n 64, 43. Our translation.

[71] J Potter, *Representing Reality: Discourse, Rhetoric and Social Construction* (London, Sage, 1996).

116   *Maria Eriksson and Keith Pringle*

Similar formulations, where gender equality is associated with a 'winner' and a 'loser', can be found in the government's *proposition* (white paper) that followed the inquiry report. There it is stated that:

> [I]t is important to keep in mind that child custody has nothing to do with justice between the parents and that a decision regarding custody is not a reward or punishment for the parents' behaviour towards each other.[72]

It can be argued that one of the consequences of this explicit disregard of a gender perspective was that the highly gendered issue of violence in heterosexual relationships was marginalised in the reform process. As regards violence, this issue was the object of important law reforms in the 1990s. Moreover, Swedish legislation today acknowledges violence in heterosexual relationships as gendered: primarily violence by men against women.[73] However, the issue of men's violence has been discussed to only a very limited extent in relation to (continued) parental cooperation and the well-being of children post-separation/divorce.[74] In the preparatory works to the law, it is mentioned that there are cases where the general principles of joint custody and unsupervised face-to-face contact do not apply, but until very recently little attention was paid to these exceptions. Despite the growing recognition—in politics and policy—of the gendered features of violence in heterosexual relationships, fathers are still to a large extent constructed as essentially non-violent.[75]

This lack of awareness can also been seen in practice. For example, at the end of March 2005 the central government's Children's Ombudsman published a report on current legal practice concerning custody, contact and residence disputes in cases of violence on family members by a parent.[76] According to this study of all relevant cases in the *tingsrätter* (district courts) from 2002, joint custody is ordered against the wishes of one parent in 49 per cent of the cases where there are some indications of a history of violence (in most cases by the father against the mother). In cases where the father has a previous conviction for a crime against the mother, the district courts award joint custody against the wishes of one parent in 38 per cent of cases. According to the Children's Ombudsman, the study clearly shows that the courts do not see how the issue of violence done to one parent by the other is linked to the well-being of the child.

---

[72] Prop 1997/98:7, above n 65, 35.
[73] See G Nordborg and J Niemi-Kiesiläinen, 'Women's Peace: A Criminal Law Reform in Sweden' in K Nousiainen *et al*, above n 68; Nordborg, above n 63; M Wendt-Höjer, *Rädslans politik. Våld och sexualitet i den svenska demokratin* (Malmö, Liber, 2002).
[74] M Eriksson and M Hester, 'Violent Men as Good-Enough Fathers? A look at England and Sweden' (2001) *Violence Against Women* 7.
[75] *Ibid.*
[76] Barnombudsmannen, *När tryggheten står på spel* (Stockholm, Barnombudsmannen, 2005). See also Eriksson and Hester, *ibid*; Nordborg, above n 63.

This is in spite of the fact that research on the links between men's violence against adult women and men's violence to children in the family is well known and quoted at the policy level in Sweden.[77] As regards contact and residence, the awareness of safety issues also seems to be low.

It can thus be argued that in the family law area (civil law) Swedish policy and practice have until recently been marked by a 'rule of optimism'.[78] In the wake of severe criticism of both family law and its implementation in cases involving violence, the government appointed (in 2002) a parliamentary committee to review the family law—again. This time, the situation of children who experience violence in their families was one of the topics to be given special attention. We will return to this recent development in our concluding remarks.

Gendered Interests: Fathers' Rights

The principle of gender neutrality is not consistent in all parts of the 1993 inquiry. In the report it is explicitly stated that there are gender specific motives for the suggested changes to the law that will make it possible for the courts to award joint custody against the wishes of one parent. It is stated that the *father* should be able to get some form of custody even if the *mother* does not want joint custody.[79] This is because:

> [I]n practice it is impossible for a father who at the child's birth is not married to the child's mother to get joint custody if the mother does not want it.[80]

One way to amend this problem would have been to adopt the principle of automatic joint custody at the child's birth. However, this solution was rejected by the 1993 inquiry on the grounds that such legislation might cause some mothers to obstruct the establishing of paternity. This 'would be much worse for the child than the parents not getting automatic joint custody'.[81] Instead, the inquiry suggests the possibility of enforcing joint custody against the wishes of one parent (but not both parents) at a later stage. The inquiry is thus promoting measures that will undermine possibilities for (unmarried) mothers to exclude fathers, measures that will *equalise the position of fathers with the position of mothers.*

---

[77] See, for example, the report from the parliamentary 1993 *Kvinnovåldskommissionen*, SOU 1995:60 *Kvinnofrid* (Stockholm, Fritzes, 1995).

[78] R Dingwall, 'Some Problems about Predicting Child Abuse and Neglect' in O Stevenson (ed), *Child Abuse: Professional Practice and Public Policy* (Hemel Hempstead, Harvester Wheatsheaf, 1989).

[79] For example, SOU 1995:79, above n 64, 9.

[80] *Ibid*, 84. This was because with the previous legislation the court had to make a choice between the parents if one of the parents opposed joint custody.

[81] *Ibid*, 79.

Both the inquiry report and the government's white paper quote cases from *Högsta Domstolen* (the Supreme Court) stating that neither parent is more fit than the other to be the custodian as a result of gender.[82] The background to these cases is a previous presumption that the mother is the best carer of small children if nothing speaks against it. Until the beginning of the 20th century, a father-presumption prevailed in Sweden. From the 1920s until the 1970s a mother-presumption can be found in legal practice to varying degrees, even though—unlike many other countries—the mother-presumption has never been codified in Swedish law. In a case from the end of the 1980s, *Högsta Domstolen* made it clear that no parent should be presumed to be better because of their gender.[83]

Against this backdrop, unmarried mothers' 'monopoly' on custody may be interpreted as being unjust. In the 1993 inquiry report, mothers are simply presented as having unfair advantages in comparison with unmarried fathers.[84] According to a norm that gender should be (formally) irrelevant, the gender-specific aim that fathers should gain access to custody against the wishes of mothers becomes reasonable and fair. In this way, fathers' rights can be constructed as promoting gender equality. In spite of the 1993 inquiry's explicit rejection of a 'gender equality perspective' implying rights for parents, the inquiry report can thus be interpreted as expressing a concern for justice—mainly for fathers.[85]

However, the suggested changes to the law are not framed as being about the rights of fathers, but as being about the rights, needs and interests of children. The needs and interests of children and fathers are said 'generally' to coincide when joint custody is ensured:

> Joint custody is in general of such an importance for the *child*, and also the *parents* that it must be possible for a *father* to achieve joint custody also against the wishes of the mother.[86]

Through such portrayals of the interests of children, parents and fathers as 'general', the interests of mothers are constructed as 'particular'.[87]

The point of departure for the 1993 inquiry on custody disputes seems to be that (unmarried) mothers have an illegitimate and dominant position as compared to fathers and therefore measures to redeem this alleged injustice are necessary. As regards the power of fathers, such power is actually mentioned in one passage of the report—but only as power over children within marriage before the regulation of parent-child relationships by law in 1734.[88] In the text, this

---

[82] *Ibid*, 50; Prop 1997/98:7, above n 65, 32.
[83] See Schiratzki, above n 26.
[84] This is also portrayed as an increasing problem since more and more children are born outside of marriage: SOU 1995:79, above n 64, 54.
[85] Eriksson, above n 54.
[86] SOU 1995:79, above n 64, 84. Our emphasis.
[87] Cf Eduards, above n 39.
[88] SOU 1995:79, above n 64, 47.

passage provides a contrast which is used to emphasise an (unmarried) father's supposedly limited 'possibilities to get custody of their children' in modern times.

In summary, our conclusion is that the preparatory works to the 1998 changes to Swedish family law can be seen as being marked by a concern for the position of fathers and a fathers' rights agenda. We also note that the suggested changes to the law, intended to promote the interests and rights of fathers, are framed as being about either the promotion of gender equality or children's interests and well-being. The frames constructing fathers' rights as 'gender equality', 'parental co-operation', or as 'children's interests' thus seem to be of central importance to this legal reform process. Here, the concept of frames refers to 'schemata of interpretation' that enable individuals to locate, perceive, identify and label occurrences within their life space and in the world at large.[89] They render events meaningful and thereby function to organise experience and guide action. It can be argued that with the 'cultural turn' in social movement theory, the focus has shifted to how issues are framed discursively. Furthermore, meaning-work and discursive politics are defined as core ingredients in social movement activities and success.[90] Drawing on such perspectives, we suggest that fathers' rights activists' meaning-work might be a key to their apparent success and we move on to look more closely at the role of fathers' rights groups' in the framing of fathers' rights and interests as gender equality, parental co-operation and/or children's interests.

The Daddy-Group

Like all interested parties, fathers' rights groups are incorporated in the consultative framework characteristic of the Swedish policy reform process. As regards the 1993 inquiry on custody disputes, their presence was actually quite strong at the inquiry's consultative meeting with voluntary organisations that took place in November 1994. At this meeting only one of the six participating non-governmental organisations/groups had a clear focus on women's interests.[91] The other five can to varying degrees be defined as concerned with fathers' rights agendas.[92]

---

[89] E Goffman, *Frame Analysis: An Essay on the Organization of Experience* (New York, Harper Colophon, 1974). See also Benford and Snow, above n 19.

[90] See Benford and Snow, above n 19; Ferree, above n 18; R Eyerman and A Jamison, *Social Movements: A Cognitive Approach* (Cambridge, Polity, 1991). On discursive politics see M Katzenstein, *Faithful and Fearless: Moving Feminism into the Church and the Military* (Princeton, NJ, Princeton University Press, 1998).

[91] The National Organisation for Women's Shelters in Sweden (ROKS).

[92] The others were: *Föreningen Barns rätt till 2 föräldrar* (Association for children's right to two parents); *Sveriges Mansjourers Riksorganisation* (National organisation for men's hotlines in Sweden); *Föreningen Söndagsförälder i Malmö* (Association of Sunday parents in Malmö); *Umgängsrätts Föräldrarnas Riksförening* (Association for equal parenting); *Mullvadarnas Riksorganisation* (National organisation for moles [sic!]).

However, we would argue that the rather small and new (as they were then) and disparate fathers'/men's groups outside of the governmental system were not the most important agents when it came to the framing of fathers' rights in the preparatory works to the 1998 law reform. Instead, we want to turn our focus to a special non-expert group appointed by the Minister of Gender Equality in 1992: *Arbetsgruppen (S 1993:C) om papporna, barnen och arbetslivet* (The Working Group on Daddies, Children and Working Life).[93] This so-called *Pappa-gruppen* (Daddy-Group) consisted of 'a handful of men' who originally were asked to investigate obstacles to men's use of parental leave insurance and make suggestions for policy changes to promote men's parental leave. Of central importance to our argument here is that it was the Daddy-Group that explicitly and by its own initiative connected the issue of daddies' parental leave with rights to custody and contact. Previously, these topics had been separated in the debates on family and gender equality policy.[94]

The Daddy-Group argued strongly for, among other things: the abolition of single custody as a concept; a 'ban' on the possibility of mothers 'vetoing' the father as a custodian; that major decisions regarding the child should be made jointly and in agreement between both parents; and that such reforms would not just improve the position of fathers, but also benefit children.[95] Furthermore, we note that some of the group's suggestions are quoted directly in the 1993 inquiry report.[96] It is thus possible to trace to the Daddy Group the discourse of disadvantaged fathers and the framing of fathers' rights as being about gender equality, parental co-operation and children's interests. It lies beyond the scope of this chapter to investigate the origins of the frames in detail. However, it can be argued that this group was a key agent in channelling, and/or strengthening the impact of, these frames in the reform process.

In their final report, the seven self-proclaimed 'ambassadors for the vision of the caring daddy'[97] state that 'we have not perceived it as our task to initiate a large modern men's movement; it is already developing by itself'.[98] However, at the same time they identify a link between their own government-assigned tasks and a broader movement. In this sense, they present themselves as, if not part of a fathers' rights movement, at least being connected to a broader pattern of collective action by men. However, in spite of this group's self-presentation, we would

[93] DS 1995:2, above n 1.
[94] Klinth, above n 26. A similar link between 'new' fatherhood and custody issues was also made in other contexts in the early 1990s: see R Collier, *Masculinity, Law and the Family* (London, Routledge, 1995); M Hester and L Harne, 'Fatherhood, Children and Violence: Placing England in an International Context' in S Watson and L Doyal (eds), *Engendering Social Policy* (Buckingham, Open University Press, 1999).
[95] DS 1995:2, above n 1, 113–14.
[96] Eg SOU 1995:79, above n 64, 77 and 91.
[97] DS 1995:2, above n 1, 14. Our translation.
[98] DS 1995:2, above n 1, 13. Our translation.

argue that it is too simplistic to regard this working group as a clear-cut example of successful fathers' rights activism in Sweden. As indicated by the fact that this group was actually appointed by the minister for gender equality, the Daddy-Group is clearly linked to broader political attempts to achieve gender equality in Sweden. Here lies an important key to a more complex understanding of the relationship between fathers' rights agendas and the Swedish state. For, as we have seen earlier, the discursive framing of fathers' rights by the groups discussed here—including the Daddy-Group—clearly resonates with dominant discourses in Swedish social policy more broadly.

Concluding Remarks

We have argued in this chapter that in current legal practice in Sweden violent fathers are granted rights at the expense of children and co-parents/mothers. It can be added that this pattern in cases involving violence seems to form part of a broader picture. In a comparative perspective the Swedish 'fatherhood regime' is characterised by strong rights to custody and contact, and weak obligations (responsibilities for child support and alimony), according to Barbara Hobson and David Morgan.[99] How are we to understand the strong position of fathers—including violent fathers—in Sweden? How are we to explain that they may be granted stronger rights than fathers in some other (Western) contexts? Can efforts by fathers' rights activists, like the interventions in the reform process preceding the 1998 changes to the law, at least partly explain this pattern?

Our answer to the last question is both yes and no. In the broad Swedish landscape which we have portrayed, it becomes easier to see why a fathers' rights movement can be perceived as both relatively marginal *and* relatively successful in advancing the rights of fathers. We have argued that this is because the reform processes have operated in a collectivist and (age and gender) consensual manner and because measures promoting fathers' rights have largely been adopted from *within* the governmental system and Social Democratic Party. Furthermore, we suggest that the discursive opportunity structure dominant within the Swedish state is itself highly enabling as regards the framing of fathers' rights in terms of gender equality, parental co-operation, and children's interests respectively. Therefore, the framing strategies adopted by activists such as the Daddy-Group can be defined as having a high degree of 'cultural resonance'. For example, the backdrop of the consensual and hetero-normative ethos within the Swedish political

---

[99] B Hobson and D Morgan, 'Introduction: Making Men into Fathers' in B Hobson (ed), *Making Men into Fathers: Men, Masculinities and the Social Politics of Fatherhood* (Cambridge, Cambridge University Press, 2002).

domain makes it easier to see why the framing of fathers' rights as gender equality and parental co-operation might be perceived as a more fruitful strategy by fathers' rights advocates than the more conflictual and individual rights (that is, for men/fathers) frames that can be seen in, for example, the UK.[100]

A strong commitment to consensus in social institutions seems to make it extremely difficult for mainstream Swedish society to recognise and address social divisions other than class.[101] In terms of conceptualising the Swedish welfare system, what this in effect means is that historically it has been extremely successful in ameliorating the impact of poverty.[102] That is why Sweden rates relatively highly on mainstream comparative welfare measures—such as that developed by Gøsta Esping-Andersen—which also tend to be based upon a class analysis.[103] However, the Swedish welfare system has been rather poor at addressing other forms of disadvantage, such as violations of what we might call a person's 'bodily integrity': for instance, men's violence to women, or sexual violence to children, or racism.[104] From this perspective it is perhaps unsurprising to find the unintended consequences of the 1998 family law reform: that in practice even violent fathers are granted rights to custody and contact at the expense of children and co-parents/mothers. For this to happen, a fathers' rights movement might not even be needed in Sweden.

The question is whether this will also be the case in the future. As we have hinted at above, Sweden is going through a period of change. After consulting a number of actors in the field and after carrying out some studies of its own, the 2002 parliamentary committee on custody came to share previous criticisms of both law and practice. In the report—published in June 2005—the committee suggests a number of changes to improve the situation regarding cases involving violence. In contrast to its predecessor, it acknowledges that violence in heterosexual relationships is a gendered phenomenon, which implies that the associated risks for children are also tied to gender, that is to men/fathers.[105] Perhaps even

---

[100] J Hearn and K Pringle, with members of Critical Research on Men in Europe, *European Perspectives on Men and Masculinities* (Houndmills, Palgrave, 2006); K Pringle, *Men, Masculinities and Social Welfare* (London, UCL Press, 1995); K Pringle, 'Neglected Issues in Swedish Child Protection Policy and Practice: Age, Ethnicity and Gender' in M Eriksson *et al*, above n 25. However, it should be noted that formal equality and gender neutral individualism also play an important role in Swedish gender equality ideology and policy.

[101] See Balkmar and Pringle, above n 2; Hearn and Pringle, *ibid*; Pringle, *ibid*.

[102] Even if cracks are now appearing in this edifice; see A Gould, 'Sweden: The Last Bastion of Social Democracy' in V George and P Taylor-Gooby (eds), *European Welfare Policy: Squaring the Welfare Circle* (Houndmills, Macmillan, 1996).

[103] Esping-Andersen, above n 27. Cf W Arts and J Gelissen, 'Three Worlds of Welfare Capitalism or More? A State of the Art Report' (2002) 12 *Journal of European Social Policy* 137–58.

[104] Balkmar and Pringle, above n 2; Pringle, above n 100; Hearn and Pringle, above n 100.

[105] As could be expected, some of the fathers' rights groups discussed earlier express criticism of this framing of violence; see eg Föreningen Styvmorsviolen, *Yttrande över Betänkandet SOU 2005:43. Vårdnad, Boende, Umgänge* (Föreningen Styvmorsviolen, Järfälla, 2005), http://www.styvmorsviolen.se.

more importantly, the changes to the law proposed by the recent committee are primarily intended to limit the possibility of violent fathers acquiring custody and contact. In the middle of March 2006 the government suggested changes to the law emphasising the issues of risk. In the white paper it is stated that if a parent is violent to the child or another member of the family, it is 'in principle in the best interests of the child' that the violent parent is not awarded custody.[106] Will this shift result in a critical focus on father-power more broadly in policy and practice? And if so, could this contribute to an expansion and radicalisation of existing fathers' rights groups in Sweden? We will have to wait and see.

---

[106] Prop 2005/06:99 *Nya vårdnadsregler* (Stockholm, Fritzes, 2006), 50–51. Our translation.

6

Yearning for Law: Fathers' Groups and Family Law Reform in Australia

HELEN RHOADES

Introduction

A major battle is being waged in Australia over the best way to manage the effects of relationship breakdown where children are involved.[1] As in other jurisdictions, fathers' demands for increased parenting rights have been central to this struggle. To some observers, this phenomenon is a gender war and the fathers' lobby is the cause of the extensive policy changes that are being wrought.[2] This chapter explores this assessment in the context of the Australian government's recently proposed 'New Family Law System' reforms, which are the end product of a 2003 inquiry into the law governing post-separation parenting arrangements. Fathers' groups were 'the prime movers and shakers' behind this inquiry,[3] and the Prime Minister's act of initiating it was said to have won him 'a new legion of fans amongst separated dads'.[4] Many of the proposals for change are also informed by perspectives which fathers' groups purport to support. Yet the question of ultimate responsibility for this shift is a story of complex and shifting influences.

This chapter attempts to trace and tease out the meaning of fathers' groups' fluctuating fortunes in their campaign for custody law reform from their initial success in triggering the parliamentary investigation, through the failure to secure their law

---

[1] The imagery of battle is common in media stories of post-divorce parenting. See, for example, M Cosic, 'Uncivil War', *The Australian Magazine*, 21–22 August 1999; J van Tiggelen, 'Dads' Army', *The Age Good Weekend Magazine*, 21 May 2005; L Mitchell, 'Caught in a Crossfire', *The Age*, 11 July 2005.

[2] See, eg, N Bala, 'A Report From Canada's "Gender War Zone": Reforming the Child-Related Provisions of the *Divorce Act*' (1999) 16 *Canadian Journal of Family Law* 163.

[3] Standing Committee on Family and Community Affairs, *Official Committee Hansard* (13 October 2003) 23–24 (Mr Quick, Committee). Hereafter '*Official Committee Hansard*'.

[4] Fatherhood Foundation, 'Howard's Betrayal', *Dads on the Air*: http://www.dadsontheair.com/index.php?page=showcomments&id=209.

reform goal from that process, to their later victory in achieving critical last minute amendments to the government's draft legislation. The first part of the chapter focuses on some of the key rhetorical devices used by the groups during the 2003 inquiry and the relative influence of these and other factors, (including the empirical research on post-separation life), on its outcome. The next section goes on to explore the ways in which advocates for fathers responded to the inquiry's report and their continued demand for a parental equality rule in the face of its child-focused recommendations. The final section looks at the 'father friendly' changes[5] to the government's draft legislation that occurred during the parliamentary review process and its transformation from an evidence-based approach to an ideological framework for dealing with post-separation parenting disputes.

Before moving on to look at their claims and discursive strategies, the next section provides some background information about fathers' groups in Australia.

Australia's Fathers' Lobby and the 2003 'Equal Parenting' Inquiry

As Richard Collier describes in this volume, debates around men's behaviour and identities as fathers have become commonplace in recent years, and, as in the UK, the relationship between law and men's parenting practices has become increasingly politicised in Australia. Recent empirical studies suggest that Australian fathers are more interested than ever in being active parents,[6] and many are reportedly taking advantage of 'the opening up of gender roles' generated by the women's movement to become involved fathers.[7] At the same time, though, Australia's workplace environment has become less not more family-friendly, with employed men now working longer hours outside the home,[8] and men's identities continue to be critically linked to their paid labour.[9] For an increasing number of men, extended working hours have meant rising stress levels and 'negative spillover' into family life, particularly for those on low pay.[10] While these factors

---

[5] This characterisation of the relevant amendments comes from A Horin and N Jamal, 'Push for Equal Custody a Win for Fathers' Groups', *The Age*, 8 December 2005.

[6] K Hand and V Lewis, 'Fathers' Views on Family Life and Paid Work' (2002) 61 *Family Matters* 26; G Russell and L Bowman, *Work and Family: Current Thinking, Research and Practice* (Department of Family and Community Services, 2000).

[7] M Flood, *Fatherhood and Fatherlessness* (ACT, The Australia Institute, Discussion Paper No 59, 2003), 34.

[8] R Weston, L Qu and G Soriano, 'Implications of Men's Extended Work Hours for their Personal and Marital Happiness' (2002) 61 *Family Matters* 18.

[9] Flood, above n 7, 58.

[10] Weston, Qu and Soriano, above n 8, 25.

impede fathers' relationships with their children irrespective of their family status,[11] their meaning becomes especially significant at the point of family separation, when many find themselves (relatively) poorly prepared for sole parenthood. As a result, the government has found itself increasingly occupied with policy issues affecting divorced fathers, not those in intact families.

Reflecting this emphasis, the groups with which this chapter is concerned can be distinguished from other men's networks by their identification of the (legal, financial and health) position of fathers following relationship breakdown as an urgent social problem, and their agitation for law reform as a strategy of redress. Unlike the members of other social support groups for fathers, men who join these groups are typically divorced or separated and have often experienced a painful legal battle over their children.[12] Michael Flood, who has written extensively on the men's movement in Australia, suggests that fathers' groups can also be distinguished by their attitude to feminism.[13] Like their counterparts in other countries,[14] Australian fathers' groups have female members, including co-founders.[15] However, some draw a sharp distinction between such 'ordinary women' and feminists, suggesting that the latter are 'anti-male'[16] and have little to offer the 'vast majority' of women who are not tertiary educated.[17] Most relevant for this chapter, fathers' groups differ from other organisations in the sector in their lobbying function: while their primary function may be to support individual men in negotiating the divorce transition (offering grief counselling, support meetings, and information about the legal system), they are also critically engaged in a campaign to change the family law system.

Activism around family policy issues affecting fathers has a long history in Australia, and its fathers' rights community now comprises a diverse range of organisations that vary in size and emphasis. The most longstanding group—the Lone Fathers Association (Australia) Inc (LFA)—was formed in 1973 and has been operating nationally since 1975, the year Australia's no-fault divorce legislation was first enacted. Alongside more recently formed advocacy groups such as Dads in Distress (DiDs), which focuses on men's health issues, the LFA works to

---

[11] Recent studies show that fathers are typically the 'back-up' carers in intact families, helping out rather than taking responsibility for parenting activities: J Baxter and M Weston, 'Women's Satisfaction with the Domestic Division of Labour' (1997) 47 *Family Matters* 16.

[12] Flood, above n 7, 36.

[13] M Flood, 'Men's Movements' (1998) 46 *Community Quarterly* 62.

[14] See Crowley, this volume.

[15] M Kaye and J Tolmie, 'Fathers' Rights Groups in Australia' (1998) 12 *Australian Journal of Family Law* 19, 22.

[16] *Official Committee Hansard* (24 September 2003) 79 (Mrs Bawden, Shared Parenting Council of Australia). See also Boyd, this volume for a description of Canadian fathers' groups' anti-feminist rhetoric.

[17] The Men's Rights Agency, for example, argues that the 'utopia promised by modern-day gender feminism' is 'an illusion' for the 'vast majority' of women who have 'limited academic skills and limited opportunities': http://www.mensrights.com.au/AppdX%20A%20FL_pathways.pdf.

maintain '"family" as an issue of government social policy' and achieve 'fairer' laws for fathers.[18] Miranda Kaye and Julia Tolmie, who conducted a study of Australia's fathers' rights lobby in the late 1990s, noted the high turnover of this kind of group and suggested that the 'stayers' were those who relied on 'the tireless efforts of one or more key individuals'.[19] In this vein, the longevity of the LFA owes much to the dedication of its leader, Barry Williams, who has been the organisation's President since its inception. Both DiDs and the LFA appear to have good working relationships with government, and have been invited to represent fathers' interests on family law reform reference groups.[20]

Other groups, such as those that were formed in the wake of Australia's child support reforms, are more strongly characterised by an anti-discrimination agenda and more closely exhibit the kind of 'backlash' perspective described by Susan Boyd.[21] As fathers are the main payers of child support,[22] the introduction of the Child Support Scheme in the late 1980s disproportionately affected men's income and many saw this as the point at which family law policies swung too far in favour of mothers. Reflecting this sense of injustice, groups such as the Men's Rights Agency (MRA) and Dads Against Discrimination (DADs), which date from this time, express their policy goals in terms of achieving gender equality. The MRA's website, for example, suggests there has been an 'over-reaction' to calls for equality for women and that its key aim is to secure 'equal rights and a level playing field for all men'.[23] But the organisation that is perhaps most relevant to the present topic is the Shared Parenting Council of Australia (SPCA), an umbrella group of around 30 fathers' groups which incorporated in September 2002 with the shared aim of prescribing into law 'every child's fundamental human right to an equal relationship with both their mother and father following separation or divorce'.[24]

The 'equal parenting' campaign was a response to what these groups saw as the failure of the Family Law Reform Act 1995 (the Reform Act) to bring about a normative shift in post-separation parenting practices.[25] Despite exhorting parents to 'share' their parenting duties,[26] and providing children with a right to be cared for

---

[18] http://www.lonefathers.com.au/index.html

[19] Kaye and Tolmie, above n 15, 22.

[20] The leaders of both organisations were members of the 2005 Child Support Review Reference Group. Barry Williams was also a member of the 1980s Child Support Consultative Committee.

[21] SB Boyd, 'Backlash Against Feminism: Canadian Custody and Access Reform Debates of the Late Twentieth Century' (2004) 16(2) *Canadian Journal of Women and the Law* 255.

[22] The vast majority of sole parent households in Australia are female-headed: B Cass, 'The Changing Face of Poverty in Australia: 1972–1982' (1985) 1 *Australian Feminist Studies* 67.

[23] http://www.mensrights.com.au//src/MissionStatement.php

[24] http://www.spca.org.au. Its executive comprises leaders of other fathers' rights groups.

[25] The Family Law Reform Act 1995 (Cth) came into operation on 11 June 1996. For a description of this legislation, which was modelled on the private law provisions of the UK Children Act, see J Dewar, 'The Family Law Reform Act 1995 (Cth) and the Children Act 1989 (UK) Compared—Twins or Distant Cousins?' (1996) 10 *Australian Journal of Family Law* 18.

[26] Family Law Act 1975 (Cth), s 60B(2)(c).

by both of their parents,[27] genuine shared care arrangements remain rare.[28] Disappointed fathers blamed this situation on the discretionary nature of the Reform Act's approach, which encouraged rather than mandated joint responsibility for children, and, as they saw it, left too much power in the hands of the legal profession. The crux of the problem, according to this view, was summarised in the following statement by DADs:

> DADs Australia *refuses* to use the term 'shared parenting'. Some non-profit community groups mistakenly believe that shared parenting is the answer. However, under the current existing legislation, shared parenting is exactly what our community and children are forced to suffer: 75% to the mother and 25% to the father. *Equal Parenting* is what all children and most parents are now demanding as the *default* starting point that as a society we should accept after family separation. The *default* standard for children after separation should be 50:50 parenting, that is, 50% of the time with mum and 50% of time with dad.[29]

The campaign for an equal parenting rule therefore focused on the amount of time children should spend with their parents (ie, physical rather than legal custody) and was designed to force lawyers and judges to make joint residence orders, which the earlier reforms had failed to achieve. In late 2002, the SPCA began to lobby government backbenchers to this end, resulting in the creation of a 'Back Bench Committee' which supported their shared residence objective and brought pressure to bear on the Prime Minister to change the law.[30] In June 2003 John Howard announced a parliamentary inquiry into the law governing 'custody' arrangements, citing the concern that 'too many boys are growing up without proper role models'[31] and giving the House of Representatives Standing Committee on Family and Community Affairs (the Committee) six months to investigate the merits of enacting an 'equal time' presumption.[32]

Discursive Strategies in the 2003 Inquiry

In their 1990s study, Kaye and Tolmie found that the fathers' groups they surveyed relied on a 'surprising commonality' of rhetorical devices when presenting their

[27] *Ibid*, s 60B(2)(a). This right is subject to the 'best interests of the child' principle.

[28] B Smyth (ed), *Parent-Child Contact and Post-Separation Parenting Arrangements* (Research Report No 9, Australian Institute of Family Studies, 2004).

[29] Emphasis in original.

[30] Shared Parenting Council of Australia, 'Federal Government Recognises Shared Parenting is the Way Forward for Australian Children of Divorce', Press Release, 18 November 2002.

[31] P Hudson, 'PM Orders Inquiry on Joint Custody', *The Age*, 25 June 2003.

[32] Commonwealth, House of Representatives, Standing Committee on Family and Community Affairs, *Every Picture Tells a Story: Report on the Inquiry Into Child Custody Arrangements in the Event of Family Separation* (Australian Government Publishing Service, 2003) xvii. Hereafter '*Every Picture* report'.

concerns publicly.[33] These included appeals to the principle of equality, claims to victim status, the use of anecdotes, reliance on rights language, and the conflation of children's and fathers' interests.[34] Fathers' submissions to the 2003 inquiry were likewise notably consistent. Yet although their reform goal had not changed since the 1990s, the ways in which they framed their claim for a joint custody presumption had evolved somewhat, and a number of the strategies Kaye and Tolmie documented had been re-worked or abandoned by the time of the later investigation. Of course, as Carol Smart has shown, the discursive ground around parenting practices shifted considerably in that period, effectively constraining the kinds of argument that parents could raise. [35]

Whereas pre-Reform Act policies in Australia focused on ensuring the child's attachment to its primary carer, the current dominant discourse is one of responsible parenting, which is synonymous with parental co-operation.[36] As a result, arguments emphasising women's history of care for their children were rarely made during the 2003 hearings, and those that were raised were deftly deflected.[37] But the ascendancy of the responsible parent discourse also challenged the ways in which fathers were able to make their claim for custody reform. In contrast with the strategies reported in Kaye and Tolmie's study, fathers' groups in 2003 made a concerted effort to be mother-friendly and were careful to construct mothers and fathers as co-beneficiaries of an equal parenting approach, detailing its material and health benefits for women.[38] Although victim stories continued to be told, this time around it was lawyers and judges, not mothers, who were cast as the cause of fatherless families.[39] Fathers offered no arguments blaming mothers for men's violence, which Kaye and Tolmie had found in their 1990s survey,[40] and instead of accusing women of hostility to contact, some urged the Committee to encourage mothers to take enforcement action against 'irresponsible fathers' who failed to exercise contact with their children.[41]

---

[33] Kaye and Tolmie, above n 15, 27–28.

[34] M Kaye and J Tolmie, 'Discoursing Dads: The Rhetorical Devices of Fathers' Rights Groups' (1998) 22 *Melbourne University Law Review* 162.

[35] C Smart, 'The Legal and Moral Ordering of Child Custody' (1991) 18 *Journal of Law and Society* 485; C Smart, 'Losing the Struggle for Another Voice—The Case of Family Law' (1995) 18 *Dalhousie Law Journal* 173.

[36] F Kaganas and SD Sclater, 'Contact Disputes: Narrative Constructions of 'Good' Parents' (2004) 12 *Feminist Legal Studies* 1; H Reece, 'The Paramountcy Principle: Consensus or Construct' (1996) 49 *Current Legal Problems* 267.

[37] See eg *Official Committee Hansard* (13 October 2003) 16 and 17 (Mrs Hull, Committee Chair).

[38] See eg DADs' argument that mothers would better able to participate in the paid workforce and that the 'present regime of awarding sole custody can easily overload many mothers': *Official Committee Hansard* (1 September 2003) 12 (Mr Hardwick, Dads Against Discrimination); and DADs' written submission, Submission 494, to the House of Representatives Standing Committee on Family and Community Affairs, http://www.aph.gov.au/house/committee/fca/childcustody/subs.htm.

[39] *Official Committee Hansard* (1 September 2003) 18 (Mr Marsh, Fatherhood Foundation).

[40] Compare Kaye and Tolmie, above n 15, 57.

[41] See *Official Committee Hansard* (27 October 2003) 55 (Mr Lenton, Dads in Distress).

Essentially fathers' groups' submissions reflected three discursive themes. Their primary argument was a child welfare one, which proposed that equal time with parents produces the best outcomes for children while sole custody arrangements are dangerous to their development. Different groups supported this claim with references to various research studies which, as DADs suggested, purported to prove that children living in joint custody arrangements 'outperform children who are raised by a single parent across all social indicators'.[42] As Michael Flood has described elsewhere,[43] however, such arguments often failed to indicate whether the cited studies were based on voluntary or imposed custody arrangements or acknowledge the many other significant variables that influence children's well-being following parental separation (such as the impact of economic (in)security). On some occasions, fathers' groups simply alluded to the existence of empirical support for their position without naming any particular study, suggesting broadly that 'all the research available indicates that children require both their mother and their father to become balanced adults',[44] or that 'most countries' have 'found from research studies that it is the sole custody regime that damages children the most'.[45]

Fathers also bolstered their child welfare claims by telling stories about their own child's desire to live with both parents—or as one father put it, to 'see you and mum fairly'[46]—and at other times they invoked 'common sense' arguments, implying that the truth of their position was intuitively evident and needed no empirical backup. The latter technique was particularly used in response to the submission (offered by opponents of the presumption) that children should be given an opportunity to say what arrangement they would prefer, with advocates arguing that it was already obvious that 'equal parenting is what children want',[47] or suggesting that '70 per cent of children say they would like to have equal time with their parents',[48] or, to use the SPCA's submission:

You ask a five-year-old child and he will tell you, 'I want mum and dad'. They all will.[49]

A second discursive thread involved a justice claim, which portrayed the discretionary approach to determining parenting arrangements as unfair to fathers. According to this argument, the demand for an equality presumption was about

---

[42] *Official Committee Hansard* (1 September 2003) 11 (Mr Hardwick, Dads Against Discrimination).

[43] See for a discussion of the use of 'bogus statistics' by fathers' rights groups Flood, above n 7, 21–23. See also Kaye and Tolmie, above n 34, 177.

[44] *Official Committee Hansard* (24 September 2003) 73 (Mr Greene, SPCA).

[45] DADs, Submission No 494, above n 38, 6.

[46] See eg *Official Committee Hansard* (29 August 2003) 27 (Private witness).

[47] *Official Committee Hansard* (1 September 2003) 11 (Mr Hardwick, Dads Against Discrimination).

[48] *Official Committee Hansard* (17 October 2003) 54 (Mr Carter, Lone Fathers Association).

[49] *Official Committee Hansard* (24 September 2003) 77 (Mr Greene, SPCA).

132   *Helen Rhoades*

giving men 'a rightful place' in their children's lives after separation so they would no longer have to go 'begging for a minute' with their children.[50] This perspective was in some ways a reprise of the equal rights strategies of the 1990s, but with an emphasis on the *meaning* of being a non-resident parent rather than the *percentage* of residence orders made in favour of women. In the earlier version, men claimed that the imbalance of custody awards to mothers was evidence of gender discrimination by the judiciary. In 2003, judges were not so much biased as out-of-touch with changing social attitudes and burdened with 'some rather old-fashioned ideas' about men's ability to care for children.[51] As noted above, what counts as a parent in modern family law is not the history of care but the promise of it.[52] In line with this development, fathers did not produce any research data about men's care giving work in families, but used a (profoundly moving) storytelling approach to illustrate the painful emotional terrain of life as a contact parent and suggest the harmful effects of a legal system that frustrates their relationships with their children.[53]

The third and related strategy involved an 'anti-professionals' discourse and a plea for 'people power'. By contrast with Kaye and Tolmie's 1998 finding that a 'couple of groups' saw lawyers as problematic,[54] antipathy towards the legal profession (and the court system) was a major feature of men's submissions during the later reform process. These submissions made it clear that fathers did not see solicitors' practices as simply misguided or uninformed, but as a product of vested interests and a reluctance to yield power to parents. Lawyers were accused of deliberately exacerbating hostilities between parents and 'making a lot of money' out of divorce work.[55] More to the point, they had 'failed to follow the directions of parliament'[56] and were 'thumbing their noses' at the law.[57] Thus a presumption

[50] *Official Committee Hansard* (27 October 2003) 53 (Mr Lenton, Dads in Distress).

[51] *Official Committee Hansard* (17 October 2003) 54 (Mr Carter, Lone Fathers Association). Note that this more generous construction was not applied to the then Chief Justice of the Family Court, Alastair Nicholson, who was attacked by fathers' groups for making 'political comments' in the lead up to and during the inquiry: see Shared Parenting Council of Australia, 'Is the Family Court a Political or a Judicial Institution?', Media Release, 30 October 2002; D Wroe, 'Judge Claims Intimidation in Row over Child Custody', *The Age*, 2 December 2003.

[52] Smart, 'The Legal and Moral Ordering of Child Custody', above n 35.

[53] See for these narratives in media representations of divorce 'The Coping Strategies of Divorced Dads', *The Sunday Age Magazine*, 24 April 2005 (regarding divorced men's loneliness), and 'Caught in a Crossfire', *The Age*, 11 July 2005 (regarding the failure of schools to provide information to divorced fathers).

[54] Kaye and Tolmie, above n 15, 64.

[55] *Official Committee Hansard* (1 September 2003) 18 (Mr Marsh, Fatherhood Foundation).

[56] *Official Committee Hansard* (1 September 2003) 10 and 14 (Mr Hardwick, Dads Against Discrimination). This distrust was also evident during the later legislative review process when the SPCA urged parliament to 'legislate away' the courts' ability to develop case law guidelines that might qualify the new legislative provisions: House of Representatives Legal and Constitutional Affairs Committee, *Report on the Exposure Draft of the Family Law Amendment (Shared Parental Responsibility) Bill 2005* (Canberra, August 2005) [8.61] and [8.62]. Hereafter '*Exposure Draft* report'.

[57] This claim was made by the Men's Rights Agency in their written submission to the House of Representatives Legal and Constitutional Affairs Committee regarding the government's draft legislation, 24 February 2006, http://www.mensrights.com.au/mra%20submit%20to%20Senate%20L&C.pdf.

was needed to wrest control from them and 'spell it out' that shared parenting represents 'the wishes of the people'.[58]

This kind of criticism, however, was not confined to lawyers, and a number of other professional groups associated with the family law system were targeted, including family counsellors, academic researchers, and government bureaucrats. The SPCA, for example, complained that welfare reports prepared by social workers were 'skewed because of feminist ideology, because that is what is taught in our universities',[59] while the MRA were critical of the 'domestic violence industry', claiming that the research on this issue was 'heavily influenced by academics, who are at the forefront of an anti-male, anti-father network that seeks to deconstruct and reconstruct men as if being a man is a pathology'.[60] According to the SPCA, the whole problem with the family law system was that it had been 'built up by professionals for professionals'.[61]

This rhetorical strategy forms part of a broader cultural dynamic in Australia that centres on a growing antipathy towards university-educated professionals with 'progressive opinions'[62] and a distrust of their values, interests and policy preferences.[63] Marian Sawer and others have described how this antipathy, which has been nurtured by the present federal government, has become normalised in Australian society in recent years, with derogatory references to 'café society intellectuals' and 'special interest groups' appearing regularly in the opinion pages of the broadsheet and tabloid press.[64] Central to this new populism is a suspicion of the kinds of 'expert' knowledge cultivated in courts, universities and other public institutions, and the belief that such 'knowledge elites' are contemptuous of the values of 'ordinary people'.[65] One consequence of this has been to recast advocacy

---

[58] *Official Committee Hansard* (1 September 2003) 10 and 14 (Mr Hardwick, Dads Against Discrimination).

[59] *Official Committee Hansard* (24 September 2003) 79 (Mrs Bawden, Shared Parenting Council of Australia).

[60] http://www.mensrights.com.au/AppdX%20A%20FL_pathways.pdf. See also Men's Rights Agency written submission to the Standing Committee on Family and Community Affairs, http://www.mensrights.com.au/MRA_submit.pdf, 28.

[61] *Official Committee Hansard* (24 September 2003) 78 (Mrs Bawden, Shared Parenting Council of Australia).

[62] See M Sawer and B Hindess (eds), *Us and Them: Anti-Elitism in Australia* (Perth, API Network, 2004); M Simons, 'Ties that Bind' (2005) 8 *Griffith Review* 13; K Betts, 'People and Parliamentarians: The Great Divide' (2004) 12 *People and Place* 64.

[63] T Dymond, 'A History of the "New Class" Concept in Australian Public Discourse' in Sawer and Hindess, above n 62, 57–58.

[64] S Scalmer and M Goot, 'Elites Constructing Elites: News Limited's Newspapers 1996–2002' in Sawer and Hindess, above n 62; M Sawer, 'Populism and Public Choice in Australia and Canada: Turning Equality-Seekers into "Special Interests"' in Sawer and Hindess, above n 62.

[65] M Sawer, *Populism and Public Choice: The Construction of Women as a 'Special Interest'*, paper presented at the Australasian Political Studies Association Conference, University of Tasmania, Hobart, 29 September–1 October 2003.

for social justice agendas as patronising and out of touch with mainstream Australia,[66] limiting 'what can be heard' in public policy debates.[67] As described above, fathers' groups' submissions to the 2003 inquiry were strongly imbued with this kind of resentment of the scope provided by the legal system for professional intrusion into personal lives, and a conviction that 'strong law' could overcome this problem. In the words of DADs:

> Equal parenting takes power back from the state and gives it to those to whom it rightly belongs, the people—not the judges; not the solicitors; not the small letterhead, self-interest groups of the misandrist movement, but the people.[68]

Failure to Secure an 'Equal Time' Presumption from the Inquiry

> The hopes of many fathers, who were encouraged by the positive reception they and fathers' groups received from the Committee to believe they might shortly be regarded as important in their children's lives, have now been dashed.[69]

The Committee did not deliver the equality rule that fathers' groups had hoped for. Although its members were clearly sympathetic to their cause,[70] in the end they concluded that there were 'dangers in a one size fits all approach' to children's living arrangements and expressed concern that the focus on time had 'turned the debate away' from children's need for involved parenting.[71] Instead of the presumption men sought, the Committee's *Every Picture* report recommended that orders be determined according to 'the best interests of the child concerned and on the basis of what arrangement works for that family'.[72] The Committee's main interest lay with reshaping the system's dispute resolution processes, not the law, and with finding ways to create *peaceful* rather than *equal* post-separation parents.[73] This section explores the reasons for this outcome and the forces that proved influential in shaping the inquiry's recommendations.

[66] D Cahill, 'New-Class Discourse and the Construction of Left-Wing Elites' in Sawer and Hindess, above n 62, 78; Scalmer and Goot, above n 64, 150.
[67] B Hindess and M Sawer, 'Introduction', in Sawer and Hindess, above n 62, 2.
[68] *Official Committee Hansard* (1 September 2003) 11 (Mr Hardwick, Dads Against Discrimination).
[69] Men's Rights Agency, Press Release, 29 December 2003.
[70] See eg *Official Committee Hansard* (29 August 2003) 24 (Mr Pearce); *Official Committee Hansard* (29 August 2003) 27 (Mrs Irwin); *Official Committee Hansard* (13 October 2003) 23–24 (Mr Quick).
[71] *Every Picture* report, above n 32, paras 2.39 and 2.4.
[72] *Ibid*, para 2.44.
[73] *Ibid*, paras 4.5 and 4.47.

Children and Research

The Committee gave a number of reasons for deciding against an equal time presumption. These focused primarily on the risks to children of adopting any one particular model of care arrangement, and included references to 'the diversity of family situations', the 'changing needs of children' as they develop, the adverse consequences of exposing children to parental conflict, children's need for stability, and the 'many practical hurdles' that parents need to overcome to make shared parenting work.[74] Such justifications reveal the impact of the empirical evidence presented to the Committee by opponents of the presumption, and suggests that, like the British government, Australia's rejection of an equality rule was informed by the insights of the burgeoning socio-legal research of post-divorce life.[75] During the parliamentary inquiry that preceded the 1995 reforms, this kind of research was at 'a very preliminary stage'.[76] But by the time the 2003 hearings were convened there was a relative wealth of empirical material for the Committee to draw on, including evidence of children's perspectives on divorce, which contradicted some of the key claims made by fathers' groups.

At a superficial level, the research on children appeared to bear out men's child welfare arguments. It demonstrated, as fathers' groups submitted, that children value a continuing relationship with both of their parents and that many would like—or would have liked—to spend substantially equal amounts of time with each of them.[77] But contrary to fathers' claims, these findings did not support a clear link between a child's well-being and the *form* of their living arrangements.[78] They suggested, rather, that children's understanding of shared parenting depends on the *quality* of the care they receive, not the amount of contact they have with each parent.[79] The Committee heard that children prefer flexible arrangements that can be adapted as circumstances change,[80] and are more interested in 'fairness' than equality.[81] Researchers also provided evidence that shared parenting is

---

[74] *Ibid*, ch 2, especially para 2.39.

[75] See Collier, this volume.

[76] Kaye and Tolmie, above n 15, 33.

[77] M Gollop, A Smith and N Taylor, 'Children's Involvement in Custody and Access Arrangements after Parental Separation' (2000) 12 *Child and Family Law Quarterly* 383; P Parkinson, J Cashmore and J Single, *Adolescents' Views on the Fairness of Parenting and Financial Arrangements After Separation* (Sydney, University of Sydney, 2003).

[78] J Pryor and B Rodgers, *Children in Changing Families: Life after Parental Separation* (Oxford, Blackwell, 2001) 214; J Hunt, *Researching Contact* (London, National Council for One Parent Families, 2003) 7.

[79] PR Amato and JG Gilbreth, 'Nonresident Fathers and Children's Well-Being: a Meta-Analysis' (1999) 61 *Journal of Marriage and the Family* 557; C Smart, 'From Children's Shoes to Children's Voices' (2002) 40 *Family Court Review* 305, 314; JB Kelly, 'Changing Perspectives on Children's Adjustment Following Divorce' (2003) 10 *Childhood* 237, 247.

[80] C Smart, B Neale and A Wade, *The Changing Experience of Childhood: Families and Divorce* (Cambridge, Polity, 2001) 122 and 167; B Smith, NJ Taylor and P Tapp, 'Rethinking Children's Involvement in Decision-Making after Parental Separation' (2003) 10 *Childhood* 201, 207.

[81] Parkinson, Cashmore and Single, above n 77.

'developmentally risky' for some children, including infants and toddlers (who are at risk of developing a disorganised attachment) and children exposed to intense or protracted conflict between their parents (who are at increased risk of mental health problems and poor educational achievement),[82] and showed that young people can find living across two homes difficult to manage as they grow older.[83]

The divorce research also revealed to the Committee the importance of allowing children to influence the shape of their own post-divorce lives—that children feel disempowered when they are not consulted about their care arrangements and that they value the chance to participate in the decision-making process.[84] On the basis of this work researchers submitted that an equal parenting presumption was 'disrespectful' to children by assuming in advance what is best for them, and suggested that family law needs to provide increased avenues for children's agency.[85] Other aspects of fathers' claims also proved problematic in light of the empirical data. Fathers' groups had spoken of shared living arrangements as though these could be easily managed. Yet studies of such arrangements revealed the existence of a number of logistical obstacles to making them work, including the need for geographical proximity, financial capacity, workplace flexibility, and mutual emotional support,[86] and even fathers' advocates who appeared before the Committee conceded that such factors would prevent many men from implementing a 50/50 care arrangement for their children.[87]

Balancing Stakeholder Interests

In similar fashion to Susan Boyd's description of the Canadian custody reform process in this volume,[88] the *Every Picture* report suggests that the Australian Committee was conscious of the political need to negotiate the competing claims of the system's various consumer groups.[89] Fathers' submissions had focused on

---

[82] *Official Committee Hansard* (20 October 2003) 3 and 9 (Dr McIntosh).

[83] Smart, above n 79; B Neale, J Flowerdew and C Smart (2003) 'Drifting Towards Shared Residence?' *Family Law* 904, 905.

[84] Smart, Neale and Wade, above n 80, 122; Smith, Taylor and Tapp, above n 80, 207.

[85] Submission of L Moloney, Submission 748, to the Standing Committee on Family and Community Affairs, http://www.aph.gov.au/house/committee/fca/childcustody/subs.htm, 7; *Official Committee Hansard* (20 October 2003) 15 (L Moloney). See also A James and MPM Richards, 'Sociological Perspectives, Family Policy, Family Law and Children: Adult Thinking and Sociological Tinkering' (1999) 21 *Journal of Social Welfare and Family Law* 23; A James and A James, 'Pump Up the Volume: Listening to Children in Separation and Divorce' (1999) 6 *Childhood* 189; C Smart, 'Towards an Understanding of Family Change: Gender Conflict and Children's Citizenship' (2003) 17 *Australian Journal of Family Law* 20.

[86] *Official Committee Hansard* (13 October 2003, Canberra) 8 (A Sanson and B Smyth, Australian Institute of Family Studies).

[87] See below, n 130.

[88] See also SB Boyd, 'Walking the Line: Canada's Responses to Child Custody Law Reform Discourses' (2003) 21 *Canadian Family Law Quarterly* 397.

[89] H Rhoades and SB Boyd, 'Reforming Custody Laws: A Comparative Study' (2004) 18 *International Journal of Law, Policy and the Family* 119.

the ways in which the law and the legal profession were depriving men of time with their children. Women's groups, on the other hand, were more concerned about the system's treatment of intimate partner violence and the impact that a shared residence presumption would have on women's and children's safety. Representatives from these organisations pointed to the need for a specially targeted response to disputes involving violence, in which protection from harm and not maintenance of contact would guide outcomes.[90] A third position was articulated by advocates for children, including child welfare organisations, developmental psychologists, and researchers. These submissions called for a more child-focused approach to negotiating post-separation arrangements which would recognise the damage caused by parental conflict and the benefits of including children in the decision-making process.

In light of these disparate demands, the Committee's report can be read as a careful exercise in diplomacy, designed to strike a balance between the interests of the different constituencies. Its recommendations reveal the Committee's attempt to address both men's equality desires and women's safety concerns, as well as children's wish to be consulted about their living arrangements. The essence of its solution was the creation of a bifurcated system which would enable 'the majority' of children to 'grow up with meaningful and positive relationships' with their parents, while ensuring that 'families and children subject to abuse are not exposed to further risk'.[91] There were a number of overtures to fathers' campaign goals, including a presumption of 'equal shared parental responsibility' for making decisions about major issues in children's lives,[92] and the committee suggested that '50/50 shared residence (or "physical custody") should be considered as a starting point for discussion and negotiation'.[93] On the other hand, it recommended that there be a presumption *against* shared parenting in families affected by violence,[94] and proposed the establishment of child-inclusive decision-making processes within the system.[95]

Mediators and Self-Governance

While the Committee's rejection of the equal time presumption reflected the influence of both the socio-legal studies and its desire to balance the interests of competing lobby groups, its proposal to reduce the reach of the legal profession reflects the coalescence of other forces. Fathers' criticisms of the family law system

---

[90] See eg *Official Committee Hansard* (28 August 2003) 23 (A Bailey, Domestic Violence and Incest Resource Centre).

[91] *Every Picture* report, above n 32, para 2.8.

[92] *Ibid*, paras 2.82 and 2.84.

[93] *Ibid*, paras 2.38 and 2.43.

[94] *Ibid*.

[95] *Ibid*, paras 2.66 and 4.158.

resonated with a number of Committee members who had 'been through it personally as well'[96] and who shared their distrust of lawyers.[97] But the Committee opted for a different response to this problem from the one proposed by fathers. Instead of devising legislative formulae about the amount of contact children should have with their parents, its preference was to replace the court-centred model of dispute resolution with a non-adversarial approach 'where involvement of lawyers is the exception rather than the rule'.[98] In part, then, this reform direction was informed by the complaints of fathers' groups, but it also reflected the interests of stakeholders with quite different agendas, including mediation professionals and their supporters and government itself.

Advocates of alternative dispute resolution processes were among those who opposed the call for an equal time presumption. Nevertheless, they agreed with the fathers' argument that there was a pressing need for 'lawyer reform',[99] and suggested that the government should replace legal advisers with social-science trained practitioners who have 'an in-depth understanding of child development'.[100] Their critiques of the legal profession's practices rested on a series of dichotomies which operated discursively and ideologically to drive the Committee's recommendations.[101] Lawyers were said to resort to 'adversarial' tactics that drew parents 'into a vortex of ambit claims and mutual denigration'[102] and left them 'estranged from one another',[103] and artificially created 'legal matters' out of what were 'really' human relationship issues.[104] Mediators, by contrast, focused on conflict reduction and collaboration building, and their practices were child-focused and therapeutic.[105] This rhetoric reinforced fathers' arguments about the disempowering practices of legal professionals and aligned mediators with the notion of 'people power': where lawyers 'took over' negotiations and

---

[96] See eg *Official Committee Hansard* (29 August 2003) 24 (Mr Pearce).

[97] *Official Committee Hansard* (13 October 2003) 43 (Mr Dutton).

[98] *Every Picture* report, above n 32, para 4.47.

[99] *Official Committee Hansard* (20 October 2003) 3 (L Moloney); *Official Committee Hansard* (13 October 2003) 30–47 (Professor Parkinson and Dr Cashmore); Family Mediation Centre, Submission 755, and Dr L Moloney, Submission 748, to the Standing Committee on Family and Community Affairs, http://www.aph.gov.au/house/committee/fca/childcustody/subs.htm. See also L Moloney and J McIntosh, 'Child-Responsive Practices in Australian Family Law: Past Problems and Future Directions' (2004) 10 *Journal of Family Studies* 71.

[100] *Official Committee Hansard* (20 October 2003) 3 (L Moloney).

[101] See generally M Fineman, 'Dominant Discourse, Professional Language, and Legal Change in Child Custody Decisionmaking' (1988) 101 *Harvard Law Review* 727.

[102] Moloney and McIntosh, above n 99, 73. Compare R Hunter, 'Adversarial Mythologies: Policy Assumptions and Research Evidence in Family Law' (2003) 30 *Journal of Law and Society* 156.

[103] *Official Committee Hansard* (20 September 2003) 2 (L Moloney). See also N Webb and L Moloney, 'Child-Focused Development Programs for Family Dispute Professionals: Recent Steps in the Evolution of Family Dispute Resolution Strategies in Australia' (2003) 9 *Journal of Family Studies* 23, 27; and Moloney and McIntosh, above n 99, 73.

[104] See T Fisher, 'Family Mediators and Lawyers Communicating about Children: PDR-Land and Lawyer-Land' (2003) 9(2) *Journal of Family Studies* 201, 203.

[105] See on this, A Diduck, *Law's Families* (London, LexisNexis, 2003) 119.

prevented parents from speaking for themselves,[106] mediation practitioners engaged 'respectfully with family members' and allowed parents to

> ...say what they need to say, not in a manner filtered by a barrister through legally modified language but directly and in their own language.[107]

These submissions chimed with the government's already well-established policy goal of 'encouraging people to take responsibility for resolving disputes themselves'.[108] Over the past decade, the Australian government has shown an increasing interest in promoting the use of 'private ordering' in family law,[109] and in shifting funding away from the courts and into non-litigation dispute resolution pathways.[110] As a consequence, a wide range of alternative conflict management services has commenced in Australia, intervening at various points in the family law system. These include the establishment of mediation services within Legal Aid bodies,[111] and the use of parenting support programs to enhance compliance with contact orders,[112] which share a goal of fostering the parental alliance between separated spouses. More recently the federal Attorney-General's Department has implemented professional development programs for legal practitioners to encourage the use of child-focused dispute resolution practices.[113] Fathers' groups' anti-lawyer rhetoric thus struck a chord with members of the Committee, both personally (for some) and ideologically, while submissions of mediation advocates offered an antidote and a chance to reinforce the government's existing policy agenda.

Responses and Rhetoric after the Inquiry

Fathers' groups responded angrily to the Committee's report and their press statements from the time reveal a deep sense of betrayal at the government's acceptance

---

[106] *Every Picture* report, above n 32, para 4.66 (testimony of L Moloney).

[107] *Official Committee Hansard* (20 September 2003) 2 and 3 (L Moloney). See also L Moloney, T Love, T Fisher and S Ferguson, 'The Words to Say It—Clients' Own Experiences of Family Mediation' (1996) 10 *Australian Journal of Family Law* 53.

[108] Family Law Amendment (Shared Parental Responsibility) Bill 2005, Explanatory Statement, Introduction.

[109] See generally M Neave, 'Resolving the Dilemma of Difference: A Critique of "The Role of Private Ordering in Family Law"' (1994) 44 *University of Toronto Law Journal* 97.

[110] Family Law Pathways Advisory Group, *Out of the Maze: Pathways to the Future for Families Experiencing Separation* (Commonwealth of Australia, 2001).

[111] J Dewar, J Giddings and S Parker, 'The Impact of Legal Aid Changes on Family Law Practice' (1999) 13 *Australian Journal of Family Law* 33.

[112] See Commonwealth Attorney-General's Department, *The Contact Orders Program: A Summary of the Independent Evaluation of the Contact Orders Pilot* (Canberra, 2003); H Rhoades, 'Contact Enforcement and Parenting Programs—Policy Aims in Confusion?' (2004) 16 *Child and Family Law Quarterly* 1.

[113] Webb and Moloney, above n 103.

of its dispute resolution emphasis. The MRA suggested that the inquiry had been 'an elaborate ploy to silence the growing anger of disenfranchised fathers',[114] and the SPCA declared that it had all been 'a cruel hoax to separated parents who took the Prime Minister at his word',[115] while the Fatherhood Foundation described the government's response as displaying a 'sneering and contemptuous attitude to separated fathers'.[116] This section looks at the rhetoric emanating from fathers' advocates in the wake of the *Every Picture* recommendations and at what these and the discursive arguments they employed throughout the reform process reveal about their law reform desires.

Children's Citizenship and Adults' Injured Feelings

As the previous section outlined, the Committee's report suggested that it had been compelled by the empirical research to conclude that no one living arrangement is appropriate for all families and that children should be afforded opportunities to influence their own post-divorce lives. A striking feature of some groups' responses to the Committee's report was their rejection of this focus on children's perspectives. Despite employing a child-welfare discourse during the hearings, their post-inquiry rhetoric suggested that family law needed to be re-moralised in a way that de-emphasises children's wishes and brings parents' authority back into rightful focus.

For some groups, the reticence to cede citizenship status to children was already evident during the inquiry. DiDs, at one point, had suggested to the Committee that it was placing 'too much emphasis on what children think',[117] and DADs and the MRA were critical of the law's conferral of parental *responsibilities* rather than *rights*.[118] As noted earlier, several groups had also resisted the arguments for consulting children about their preferences and opted to speak on their behalf, suggesting that it was obvious what children would choose. But the marginalisation of children's agency gained momentum after the *Every Picture* report was handed down, when groups like the LFA which had previously supported the child's right to 'have a say in the matter' began to attack the 'best interests' principle, the apparent stumbling block to achieving their law reform goal.[119] Instead of reflecting on

[114] Men's Rights Agency, 'Disenfranchised Fathers Still Unequal When it Comes to Child Custody', http://www.mensrights.com.au/, posting dated 6 September 2004.
[115] Shared Parenting Council of Australia, 'Howard's Family Law Amendments a Cruel Failure', Media Release, 24 June 2005.
[116] Fatherhood Foundation, above n 4.
[117] *Official Committee Hansard* (27 October 2003) 53 (Mr Lenton, Dads in Distress).
[118] *Official Committee Hansard* (1 September 2003) 12 (Mr Hardwick, Dads Against Discrimination); *Official Committee Hansard* (4 September 2003) 14 (Mrs Price, Men's Rights Association). The MRA's written submission to the inquiry devoted an entire section to the problems created by the best interests principle: see http://www.mensrights.com.au/MRA_submit.pdf.
[119] *Official Committee Hansard* (17 October 2003) 57 (Mr Williams, Lone Fathers Association).

children's desire for flexibility and an independent voice, some advocates intensified their demand for the 'best interests' principle to be 'redefined' as a 'right' to equal parenting,[120] insisting that parental rights be restored[121] and described 'in terms of time expectations'.[122]

This parent-focused approach was given 'scholarly' expression in this period by John Hirst, a professor of history who publicly supported fathers' campaign for law reform.[123] Hirst's published attack on the family law system accused judges of excessive piety in their 'purist pursuit of the "best interests of the child"',[124] and proposed that the 'best way' to secure children's well-being was to recognise 'the parents' interest in the child'.[125] Echoing the sentiments of fathers' groups who posted his work on their websites, he argued that the legal system's fixation on children's interests 'offends our sense of what is right',[126] and called for the re-introduction of a fault-based model which would acknowledge the meaning of relationship breakdown for the adults affected by it. As Hirst described this view:

> The difficulty of managing no-fault divorce is that most of the parties involved strenuously believe in fault. When they have children, they are urged most earnestly to put aside their injured feelings and concentrate on what is best for their children. Why should they?[127]

Care Work and Moral Claims

Other clues in the arguments made by of fathers' advocates suggest that their reform campaign had more to do with gaining legal recognition of fathers' moral worth than changing children's care patterns. Men who appeared before the Committee took umbrage at the legal profession's assumption that women are the primary carers of children in families. Fathers' groups suggested that this approach was quaint and 'old-fashioned' and implied that major social changes had rendered men and women equal carers of children in modern family relationships, which

---

[120] B Williams, 'Systems Failing Fathers: A Fatherless Society in Waiting', address to the Lone Fathers Association National Conference, 22–23 June 2005, Canberra.

[121] Men's Rights Agency, Submission to the Legal and Constitutional Committee, 24 February 2006, http://www.mensrights.com.au/mra%20submit%20to%20Senate%20L&C.pdf.

[122] Shared Parenting Council of Australia, 'Protecting the Child's Rights is Paramount to their Welfare and Best Interests', Media Release, 30 July 2004; Shared Parenting Council of Australia, 'Government Shared Parenting Announcement a Courageous and Small Step Forward', Media Release, 30 July 2004.

[123] See for a critique of Hirst's argument A Genovese, 'States of Contempt and Equality: The Family Court, John Hirst and Feminism' (2006) 21 *Australian Feminist Studies* (forthcoming).

[124] J Hirst, 'Kangaroo Court: Family Law in Australia' (2005) 17 *Quarterly Essay* 17–19.

[125] *Ibid*, 22.

[126] *Ibid*, 76.

[127] J Hirst, 'Court Rule Offensive to Families', *The Australian*, 21 March 2005.

judges had failed to notice.[128] This understanding of contemporary family life resonated with a number of Committee members, who roundly criticised submissions which dared to suggest that women were still the primary carers of children.
As the Chair of the Committee noted in an exchange with one researcher:

> I have said this before, but, as a parent and grandmother, I know that my sons have a far
> different role in their children's lives than my husband had in our children's lives. They
> go out to work through the day as the primary breadwinners, but I would not consider
> their mothers to be the primary care givers at all. I would consider that my sons are the
> primary care givers, even though they are the primary breadwinners as well.[129]

A closer look at men's submissions, however, belies their belief in the changed
practices argument. In fact, both during the inquiry hearings and in later
responses to the government's draft legislation, representatives of fathers' groups
conceded that many of their members were unlikely to avail themselves of an
equal time offer.[130] As DiDs expressed it:

> Most guys will not take 50-50. Most guys will be working and will not be able to take
> that equal time.[131]

Rather than providing the impetus for actual arrangements, fathers' groups suggested that the presumption they sought was 'more a mental mind-set',[132] a way of
enfranchising fathers so that they do not have to 'beg' for time with their children,[133] and ensuring that they are 'regarded as being equally important to their
children'.[134] In fact, as the MRA suggested in a post-inquiry submission to parliament, the equality presumption was needed *because* men do relatively little care
work in intact families:

> It is nonsense to talk of prior interaction with children as being the guide to whether a
> parent can continue to have contact after separation (sought by some women's advo-
> cates). Are we to punish the father who has worked long hours, sometimes in the most
> dreadful locations away from his family, in order to provide for their every need?[135]

---

[128] See eg *Official Committee Hansard* (17 October 2003) 54 (Mr Carter, Lone Fathers Association).
[129] *Official Committee Hansard* (13 October 2003) 16 and 17 (Mrs Hull, Committee Chair).
[130] *Official Committee Hansard* (17 October 2003) 57 (Mr Carter, Lone Fathers Association); Men's
Rights Agency written submission to the Standing Committee on Family and Community Affairs,
http://www.mensrights.com.au/MRA_submit.pdf, 23; *Exposure Draft* report, above n 56, para 2.49
(Dads in Distress) and para 2.50 (Lone Fathers Association).
[131] *Exposure Draft* report, above n 56, para 2.49.
[132] *Official Committee Hansard* (24 September 2003) 74 (Mr Greene, Shared Parenting Council of
Australia).
[133] *Official Committee Hansard* (27 October 2003) 53 (Mr Miller, Dads in Distress).
[134] Men's Rights Agency, written submission to the Standing Committee on Family and Community
Affairs, http://www.mensrights.com.au/MRA_submit.pdf, 23.
[135] Men's Rights Agency, submission to the Legal and Constitutional Committee, 24 February 2006,
http://www.mensrights.com.au/mra%20submit%20to%20Senate%20L&C.pdf

These acknowledgements of men's relative powerlessness are not simply about the effects of a prejudicial legal system, but reflect an understanding that mothers' primary care work has rendered them the gatekeepers of children's daily lives, and a fear that they may lose their child's affections once the mother is no longer motivated to facilitate their relationship with the child. But they also suggest that men's desire for law reform was not concerned with creating a genuine cultural change in family practices that might afford them greater opportunities to care for their children than they have so far been able to enjoy. Indeed it is notable that fathers' groups have not lobbied for flexible workplace arrangements that might enable this to occur.[136] Instead they argued for recognition of a 'different but equal' expression of parental worth:

> Even though a father may not be at home as often as the mother, the children still feel his presence and know to expect him back after work. They know he is away from them working to provide support for them. This is the way he shows his love for his family.[137]

What men sought, then, was the law's power to shape their value as parents in the post-separation context. Seen from this perspective, the demand for an equal time presumption was in essence a campaign to gain legal recognition of fathers as parents of equal importance with mothers,[138] regardless of their past inexperience as carers or their future inability to spend significant periods of time with their children, and thereby overcome the historical 'primary-secondary' framework which prioritises care work over financial provision.[139] In John Hirst's version of this argument, viability as a post-separation parent should be linked to the moral conduct of the parents while their relationship was a going concern, not their nurturance of children. Harking back to the days of fault-based divorce, Hirst suggests that the equal time demand is about fairness to fathers who have 'done nothing wrong':

> Men who have these [unequal] settlements imposed upon them stagger from the court buildings feeling that they have been in a nightmare world where all the usual standards have been inverted. They are driven to unfashionable declarations of their moral worth: I am not a wife beater; I have been a good provider; I have been a faithful husband; I love my kids; I am a good worker for the community. They cannot believe that there is a place, an official institution, where all this counts for nothing.[140]

[136] Fathers' advocates also attacked a government report that was aimed at improving the work/life balance for families: see P Goward, 'Revision of Labour', *The Weekend Australian*, 25–26 June 2005; F Farouque, 'The Male Backlash', *The Age*, 25 June 2005.

[137] Men's Rights Agency, Submission to the Legal and Constitutional Committee, 24 February 2006, http://www.mensrights.com.au/mra%20submit%20to%20Senate%20L&C.pdf.

[138] See Men's Rights Agency, Press Release, 29 December 2003; and *Official Committee Hansard* (27 October 2003) 53 (Mr Miller, Dads in Distress).

[139] See for this language, *Official Committee Hansard* (17 October 2003) 56 (Mr Williams, Lone Fathers Association), and *Official Committee Hansard* (27 October 2003) 53 (Mr Lenton, Dads in Distress).

[140] Hirst, above n 124.

Subsequent Developments and Expedient Processes

> Today the light of democracy beamed out across this land as the Government took deci-
> sive action to strengthen children's right to an opportunity for equal or substantially
> equal relationships with both their parents.[141]

Australia's proposals for overhauling the family law system evolved somewhat
after the Committee's report was handed down, becoming less child-focused and
more adult-centred in the process. The federal government released an Exposure
Draft of its planned legislation—the Family Law Amendment (Shared Parental
Responsibility) Bill (SPRB)—in July 2005, inviting public comment and sending
it to the House of Representatives Legal and Constitutional Affairs Committee for
review. The SPRB incorporated significantly more legislative changes than had
been recommended by the Committee and signalled a major departure from the
Committee's evidence-based suggestions. For example, children's views, instead of
taking centre-stage, were demoted to a secondary consideration in the 'best interests' checklist, subsidiary to their need for a continuing relationship with both
parents (which reflects the concerns of fathers' groups) and the need for arrangements to be safe (which reflects the submissions of women's organisations).[142]

The Legal and Constitutional Committee went further than this. Although it
rejected men's demands for a 50/50 presumption, as the inquiry Committee had
done before it, its report expressed 'sympathy with the submissions' of fathers'
groups and recommended a number of amendments that brought the law closer
to delivering the kind of equality recognition fathers' groups desired.[143] If
implemented, as they seem likely to be, these changes will require judges to consider making 'equal time' orders in the majority of cases, and where this
arrangement is not appropriate, to consider orders that will allow the child to
spend 'substantial and significant time' with each parent and enable both of
them to be involved in the child's daily routines.[144] The current language of 'residence' and 'contact' will be removed from the law, to be replaced by the single
concept of 'parenting time',[145] creating a legislative assumption of equally
involved (or equally worthy) parenting.

The Legal and Constitutional Committee thus took one month to substantially
alter reform recommendations that had evolved out of a considered inquiry

---

[141] Shared Parenting Council of Australia, 'Family Law Amendment (Shared Parental Responsibility)
Bill 2005: The Fourth Pillar to the Family Reform Measures is a Solid Piece of Work', Media Release, 9
December 2005.

[142] Proposed Family Law Act 1975 (Cth), s 68F(1A).

[143] *Exposure Draft* report, above n 56, para 2.56.

[144] Proposed Family Law Act 1975 (Cth), s 65DAA(1), (2) and (3).

[145] House of Representatives, Family Law Amendment (Shared Parental Responsibility) Bill 2005,
Explanatory Memorandum, para 921.

process and a wealth of empirical evidence on post-separation family practices. Although it invited written submissions on the draft legislation (giving respondents just three weeks to make these), it received only 88, providing it with a significantly smaller pool of information to draw from than was available to the inquiry Committee, which received over 1,700 submissions and heard evidence from 166 witnesses in public hearings across the country. During the earlier process, fathers' groups were faced with an overwhelming obstacle in the shape of research findings that contradicted their claimed benefits for children. Based on this evidence, the 2003 inquiry concluded that the focus on time was 'misguided' and that there were 'dangers' in attempting to define a child's welfare in this way.[146] In stark contrast, the later Committee saw 'merit' in men's fairness arguments, agreeing with them that 'the provisions related to the time each parent spends with their child' are the 'key aspect of shared parenting'.[147]

Conclusion

At the time the 1995 Reform Act was introduced, it represented the most significant legislative change to Australia's custody laws in the Family Law Act's then twenty-year history. In large part its replacement of the traditional custody and access division of responsibility for children with a shared parenting approach was influenced by the demands of divorced fathers who were tired of 'languishing' as access parents.[148] The establishment of the 2003 inquiry into children's post-separation arrangements was likewise a response to lobbying by their advocates, initiated by a Prime Minister who was sympathetic to their plight. But the inquiry did not deliver the legislative presumption men had hoped for, and a close reading of the *Every Picture* report suggests that key elements of their submissions failed to impress and that a range of other forces played a significant role in shaping its recommendations.

Fathers' groups linked their equality claim to children's well-being, but failed to marry the rhetoric to the empirical reality of children's lives. They pleaded for justice for men, telling powerful personal stories of loss and loneliness, but the divorce research conveyed a more complex picture of post-separation families and convinced the Committee that a 'one size fits all' approach was dangerously simplistic and logistically unworkable. Their submissions were peppered with hostility towards lawyers and 'the system' and challenged the Committee to craft new

---

[146] *Every Picture* report, above n 32, paras 2.4, 2.41 and 2.44.
[147] *Exposure Draft* report, above n 56, paras 2.37, 2.11, 2.12, 2.42, 2.55, 2.56 and 2.57.
[148] This description comes from P Nygh, 'The New Part VII—An Overview' (1996) 10 *Australian Journal of Family Law* 4, 16. Note that Kaye and Tolmie were reluctant to assign complete responsibility for this reform to the fathers' lobby: see Kaye and Tolmie, above n 15.

ways of managing parental disputes. Yet the Committee focused on processes rather than law, and set about reducing conflict, not inequality.

The government accepted the thrust of the *Every Picture* recommendations and proceeded to construct a new-look system which is intended to 'encourage a culture of agreement making' among separating parents.[149] In the process, however, the inquiry Committee's careful balancing of stakeholder interests shifted towards greater recognition of fathers' equality demands, demoting the importance of children's complex views in the 'best interests' hierarchy and winning back for government the approval of the fathers' lobby. The Legal and Constitutional Committee's report reveals how compelling it found the SPCA's equality arguments, in marked contrast to the earlier Committee's warnings about the dangers of using law to privilege particular forms of parenting arrangement. The story of Australia's latest parenting law reform process thus suggests that fathers' groups are likely to have limited success in public inquiry processes that rely on research evidence to inform legal change, but that they appear to wield significant power 'behind the scenes' and their justice claims hold significant appeal for policy makers who are not familiar with the socio-legal research on children and divorce.

---

[149] House of Representatives, Family Law Amendment (Shared Parental Responsibility) Bill 2005, Explanatory Memorandum, para 81.

Bibliography

ALANEN, I., *Modern Childhood? Exploring the 'Child Question' in Sociology* (Jyväskylä, Institute for Educational Research, 1992).

ALBERTS, S, 'Class-Action Suit Threatened over Suffering by Children of Divorce' *National Post*, 20 July 1999.

AMATO, PR and JG GILBRETH, 'Nonresident Fathers and Children's Well-Being: A Meta-Analysis' (1999) 61 *Journal of Marriage and the Family* 557.

ARDITTI, J and K ALLEN, 'Distressed Fathers' Perceptions of Legal and Relational Inequities Post-Divorce' (1993) 31 *Family and Conciliation Courts Review* 461.

ARENDELL, T, 'The Social Self as Gendered: A Masculinist Discourse of Divorce' (1992) 15 *Symbolic Interactionism* 151.

—— *Fathers and Divorce* (Thousand Oaks, CA, Sage, 1995).

ARTS, W and J GELISSEN, 'Three Worlds of Welfare Capitalism or More? A State of the Art Report' (2002) 12 *Journal of European Social Policy* 137.

ASHE, M, 'Postmodernism, Legal Ethics, and Representation of "Bad Mothers"' in M FINEMAN and I KARPIN, *Mothers in Law: Feminist Theory and the Legal Regulation of Motherhood* (New York, Columbia University Press, 1995).

BACKETT, K, 'The Negotiation of Fatherhood' in C LEWIS and M O'BRIEN (eds), *Reassessing Fatherhood: New Observations on Fathers and the Modern Family* (London, Sage, 1987).

BAILEY, MJ and M GIROUX, *Relocation of Custodial Parents: Final Report* (Ottawa, Status of Women Canada, 1998).

BAILEY-HARRIS, R, J BARRON and J PEARCE, 'From Utility to Rights? The Presumption of Contact in Practice' (1999) 13 *International Journal of Law, Policy and the Family* 111.

BAINHAM, A, 'Contact as a Fundamental Right' (1995) 54 *Cambridge Law Journal* 255.

BAKER-FLETCHER, GK (ed), *Black Religion after the Million Man March* (Maryknoll, NY, Orbis, 1998).

BALA, N, 'A Report from Canada's "Gender War Zone": Reforming the Child Related Provision in the Divorce Act' (1999) 16 *Canadian Journal of Family Law* 163.

BALKMAR, D, L IOVANNI and K PRINGLE, 'Mäns våld i Danmark och Sverige' *NIKK Magasin. Temanummer Kön och våld* ('Men's violence in Denmark and Sweden', NIKK Magazine, special issue on gender and violence) No 2 (2005) 22.

BALKMAR, D and K PRINGLE, *Sweden National Report on Research on Men's Practices* (2005) EU Framework 6 Co-ordinated Action on Human Rights (CAHRV), http://www.cromenet.org.

BANDES, SA (ed), *The Passions of Law* (New York, New York University Press, 1999).

BARNOMBUDSMANNEN, *När tryggheten står på spel* (When safety is at stake) (Stockholm, Barnombudsmannen, 2005).

BAUMAN, Z, *Intimations of Postmodernity* (London, Routledge, 1992).

BAUMLI, F (ed), *Men Freeing Men: Exploding the Myth of the Traditional Male* (Jersey City, NJ, New Atlantis, 1985).

BAXTER, J and M WESTON, 'Women's Satisfaction with the Domestic Division of Labour' (1997) 47 *Family Matters* 16.

BECK, U, *Risk Society: Towards a New Modernity* (London, Sage, 1992).

BECK, U and E BECK GERNSHEIM, *The Normal Chaos of Love* (Cambridge, Polity, 1995).

—— *Individualisation* (London, Sage, 2002).

BEKKENGEN, L, *Man får välja—om föräldraskap och föräldraledighet i arbetsliv och familjeliv* (Man/one may choose—on parenthood and parental leave at work and in family life) (Malmö, Liber, 2002).

BENFORD, R and D SNOW, 'Framing Processes and Social Movements: An Overview and Assessment' (2000) 26 *Annual Review of Sociology* 611.

BENTLY, L and L FLYNN (eds), *Law and the Senses* (London, Pluto, 1996).

BERGMAN, H and B HOBSON, 'Compulsory Fatherhood: The Coding of Fatherhood in the Swedish Welfare State' in B HOBSON (ed), *Making Men into Fathers: Men, Masculinities and the Social Politics of Fatherhood* (Cambridge, Cambridge University Press, 2002).

BERNARD, J, 'The Good-Provider Role: Its Rise and Fall' (1981) 36 *American Psychologist* 1.

BERTOIA, C, 'An Interpretative Analysis of the Mediation Rhetoric of Fathers' Rightists: Privatization versus Personalization' (1998) 16(1) *Mediation Quarterly* 15.

BERTOIA, C and J DRAKICH, 'The Fathers' Rights Movement: Contradictions in Rhetoric and Practice' (1993) 14(4) *Journal of Family Issues* 592.

BETTS, K, 'People and Parliamentarians: The Great Divide' (2004) 12 *People and Place* 64.

BIANCHI, SM, L SUBAIYA and J KAHN, 'The Gender Gap in the Economic Well-being of Nonresident Fathers and Custodial Mothers' (1999) 36 *Demography* 195.

BLANKENHORN, D, *Fatherless America: Confronting our Most Urgent Social Problem* (New York, Basic Books 1995).

BOURQUE, DM, '"Reconstructing" the Patriarchal Nuclear Family: Recent Developments in Child Custody and Access in Canada' (1995) 10(1) *Canadian Journal of Law and Society* 1.

BOYD, S, 'Backlash and the Construction of Legal Knowledge: The Case of Child Custody Law' (2001) 20 *Windsor Yearbook of Access to Justice* 141.

—— *Child Custody, Law and Women's Work* (Oxford, Oxford University Press, 2003).

—— 'Walking the Line: Canada's Responses to Child Custody Law Reform Discourses' (2003) 21 *Canadian Family Law Quarterly* 397.

—— 'Backlash Against Feminism: Custody and Access Reform Debates of the Late 20th Century' (2004) 16(2) *Canadian Journal of Women and the Law* 255.

—— 'Demonizing Mothers: Fathers' Rights Discourses in Child Custody Law Reform Processes' (2004) 6(1) *Journal of the Association for Research in Mothering* 52.

BOYD, S and C YOUNG, 'Who Influences Family Law Reform? Discourses on Motherhood and Fatherhood in Legislative Reform Debates in Canada' (2002) 26 *Studies in Law, Politics & Society* 43.

—— 'Feminism, Fathers' Rights, and Family Catastrophes: Parliamentary Discourses on Post-Separation Parenting, 1966–2003' in DE CHUNN, SB BOYD and H LESSARD (eds), *Feminism, Law, and Social Change: (Re)Action and Resistance* (forthcoming).

BRANNEN, J, G MESZAROS, P MOSS and G POLAND, *Employment and Family Life: A Review of Research in the UK (1980–1994)*, Department of Employment Research Series No 4 (London, University of London, 1994).

BRAVER, S and D O'CONNELL, *Divorced Dads: Shattering the Myths* (New York, Tarcher-Putnam, 1998).

BRITTAN, A, *Masculinity and Power* (Oxford, Blackwell, 1989).

BROWN, J and S DAY SCLATER, 'Divorce: A Psychodynamic Perspective' in S DAY SCLATER and C PIPER (eds), *Undercurrents of Divorce* (Aldershot, Ashgate, 1999).

BROWN, S, 'Changes in Laws Governing Divorce: An Evaluation of Joint Custody Presumptions' (1984) 5 *Journal of Family Issues* 200.

BRUCH, C, 'Parental Alienation Syndrome and Alienated Children—Getting it Wrong in Child Custody Cases' [2002] 14 (4) *Child and Family Law Quarterly* 381.

CAHILL, D, 'New-Class Discourse and the Construction of Left-Wing Elites' in M SAWER and B HINDESS (eds), *Us and Them: Anti-Elitism in Australia* (Perth, API Network, 2004).

CANADA, Department of Justice, *Response to the Report of the Special Joint Committee on Child Custody and Access: Strategy for Reform* (Ottawa, Department of Justice, 1999).

CANADA, Department of Justice, *Custody, Access and Child Support in Canada: Report on Federal-Provincial-Territorial Consultations* (Ottawa, IER Planning, Research and Management Services, presented to the Federal-Provincial-Territorial Family Law Committee, 2001).

CANADA, Department of Justice, *Post-Separation Visitation Disputes: Differential Interventions* by R Birnbaum and W McTavish (paper prepared for the Family, Children and Youth Section, 2001).

CANADA, Department of Justice, *Final Federal-Provincial-Territorial Report on Custody and Access and Child Support: Putting Children First* (Custody and Access Project of the Federal-Provincial-Territorial Family Law Committee, 2002).

CANADA, Department of Justice, *An Overview of the Risks and Protectors for Children of Separation and Divorce* by SC Bernardini and JM Jenkins (paper prepared for the Family, Children and Youth Section, 2002).

CANADA, Special Joint Committee on Child Custody and Access, *For the Sake of the Children* (Ottawa, Parliament of Canada, 1998).

CARRIGAN, T, R CONNELL and J LEE, 'Towards a New Sociology of Masculinity' (1985) 14 *Theory and Society* 551.

CASS, B, 'The Changing Face of Poverty in Australia: 1972–1982' (1985) 1 *Australian Feminist Studies* 67.

CHUNN, DE, SB BOYD and H LESSARD (eds), *(Re)Action and Resistance: Feminism, Law and Social Change* (Vancouver, UBC Press, forthcoming).

COBBS, C, 'The Custody Fight on the Hill' *Ottawa Citizen,* 12 October 1998.

—— 'A Bill of Rights for Divorced Parents' *Ottawa Citizen,* 9 December 1998.

COHEN, J and N GERSHBAIN, 'For the Sake of the Fathers? Child Custody Reform and the Perils of Maximum Contact' (2001) 19 *Canadian Family Law Quarterly* 121.

COLLIER, R, *Masculinity, Law and the Family* (London, Routledge, 1995).

—— '"Coming Together?": Post-Heterosexuality, Masculine Crisis and the New Men's Movement' (1996) 4(1) *Feminist Legal Studies* 3.

—— 'Feminising the Workplace? (Re)constructing the "Good Parent" in Employment Law and Family Policy' in A MORRIS and T O'DONNELL (eds), *Feminist Perspectives on Employment Law* (London, Cavendish, 1999).

—— 'From "Women's Emancipation" to "Sex War"?: Beyond the Masculinized Discourse of Divorce' in SD SCLATER and C PIPER (eds), *Undercurrents of Divorce* (Aldershot, Dartmouth, 1999).

—— 'Men, Heterosexuality and the Changing Family: (Re)constructing Fatherhood in Law and Social Policy' in C WRIGHT and G JAGGAR (eds), *Changing Family Values* (London, Routledge, 1999).

—— 'A Hard Time to be a Father?: Law, Policy and Family Practices' (2001) 28 *Journal of Law and Society* 520.

—— 'Reflections on the Relationship Between Law and Masculinities: Rethinking the "Man Question" in Legal Studies' (2003) 56 *Current Legal Problems* 345.

—— 'Fathers 4 Justice, Law and the New Politics of Fatherhood' (2005) 17(4) *Child and Family Law Quarterly* 1.

COLLIER, R and S SHELDON, *Fatherhood: A Socio-Legal Study* (Oxford, Hart, forthcoming).

COLTRANE, S, 'Marketing the Marriage Solution: Misplaced Simplicity in the Politics of Fatherhood' (2001) 44 *Sociological Perspectives* 387.

COLTRANE, S and N HICKMAN, 'The Rhetoric of Rights and Needs: Moral Discourse in the Reform of Child Custody and Child Support Laws' (1992) 39 *Social Problems* 400.

Commonwealth Attorney-General's Department, *The Contact Orders Program: A Summary of the Independent Evaluation of the Contact Orders Pilot* (Canberra, 2003).

Commonwealth, House of Representatives, Standing Committee on Family and Community Affairs, *Every Picture Tells a Story: Report on the Inquiry into Child Custody Arrangements in the Event of Family Separation* (Australian Government Publishing Service, 2003).

CONELL, C and S COHN, 'Learning from Other People's Actions: Environmental Variation and Diffusion in French Coal Mine Strikes, 1890–1935' (1995) 101 *American Journal of Sociology* 366.

CONNELL, RW, 'Change among the Gatekeepers: Men, Masculinities, and Gender Equality in the Global Arena' (2005) 30(3) *Signs: Journal of Women in Culture and Society* 1801.

—— *Gender and Power* (Cambridge, Polity, 1987).

—— *Masculinities* (Berkeley, CA, University of California Press, 1995).

COSIC, M, 'Uncivil War' *The Australian Magazine*, 21–22 August 1999.

COSSMAN, B, 'Family Feuds: Neo-Liberal and Neo-Conservative Visions of the Reprivatization Project' in B COSSMAN and J FUDGE (eds), *Privatization, Law and the Challenge to Feminism* (Toronto, University of Toronto Press, 2002).

COVER, R, 'Nomos and Narrative' (1983) 97 *Harvard Law Review* 4.

—— 'Violence and the Word' (1986) 95 *Yale Law Review* 1601.

CROWLEY, JE, 'Supervised Devolution: The Case of Child Support Enforcement' (2000) 30 *Publius: The Journal of Federalism* 99.

—— 'Who Institutionalizes Institutions? The Case of Paternity Establishment in the United States' (2001) 82 *Social Science Quarterly* 312.

—— 'The Rise and Fall of Court Prerogatives in Paternity Establishment' (2002) 23 *Justice System Journal* 363.

—— 'The Gentrification of Child Support Enforcement Services, 1950–1984' (2003) 77 *Social Services Review* 585.

—— *The Politics of Child Support in America* (New York, Cambridge University Press, 2003).

—— 'Organizational Responses to the Fatherhood Crisis: The Case of Fathers' Rights Groups in the United States' (forthcoming 2006) 39 *Marriage and Family Review.*

—— book manuscript on Fathers' Rights Groups in the United States, in preparation.

CZAPANSKIY, K, 'Volunteers and Draftees: The Struggle for Parental Equality' (1991) 38 *UCLA Law Review* 415.

DANIELS, CR, 'Introduction' in CR DANIELS (ed), *Lost Fathers* (New York, St Martin's Press, 1998).

DAY SCLATER, S, 'Divorce—Coping Strategies, Conflict and Dispute Resolution' [1998] *Family Law* 150.

—— *The Psychology of Divorce: A Research Report to the ESRC* (London, University of East London, 1998).

—— *Divorce: A Psycho-Social Study* (Aldershot, Ashgate, 1999).

—— 'Families Reunited' (2003) *FQ: The Magazine For Modern Dads* (Winter) 56.

DAY SCLATER, S and F KAGANAS, 'Contact: Mothers, Welfare and Rights' in A BAINHAM, B LINDLEY, M RICHARDS and L TRINDER (eds), *Children and Their Families* (Oxford, Hart, 2003).

DAY SCLATER, S and C PIPER, 'Re-Moralising the Family? Family Policy, Family Law and Youth' [2000] 12 (3) *Child and Family Law Quarterly* 135.

DAY SCLATER, S and C YATES, 'The Psycho-Politics of Post Divorce Parenting' in A BAINHAM, S DAY SCLATER and M RICHARDS (eds), *What is a Parent? A Socio-Legal Analysis* (Oxford, Hart, 1999).

DE HAAN, W and I LOADER, 'On the Emotions of Crime and Punishment and Social Control' (2002) 6(3) *Theoretical Criminology* 243.

DEKESEREDY, W, 'Tactics of the Antifeminist Backlash Against Canadian National Woman Abuse Surveys' (1999) 5(11) *Violence Against Women* 1258.

DELOREY, AM, 'Joint Legal Custody: A Reversion to Patriarchal Power' (1989) 3(1) *Canadian Journal of Women and the Law* 33.

DENCH, D, *Exploring Variations in Men's Family Roles: Joseph Rowntree Foundation Social Policy Research Findings No 99* (York, Joseph Rowntree Foundation, 1996).

DENNIS, N and G ERDOS, *Families Without Fatherhood* (London, Institute of Economic Affairs, 1993).

DEWAR, J, 'The Family Law Reform Act 1995 (Cth) and the Children Act 1989 (UK) Compared—Twins or Distant Cousins?' (1996) 10 *Australian Journal of Family Law* 18.

—— 'The Normal Chaos of Family Law' (1998) 61 *Modern Law Review* 467.

—— 'Family Law and its Discontents' (2000) 14 *International Journal of Law, Policy and Family* 59.

DEWAR, J, J GIDDINGS and S PARKER, 'The Impact of Legal Aid Changes on Family Law Practice' (1999) 13 *Australian Journal of Family Law* 33.

DIAMOND, B, 'The Special Joint Committee on Custody and Access: A Threat to Women's Equality Rights' (1999) 19 *Canadian Woman Studies* 182.

DIDUCK, A, *Law's Families* (London, LexisNexis, 2003).

DINGWALL, R, 'Some Problems about Predicting Child Abuse and Neglect' in O STEVENSON (ed), *Child Abuse: Professional Practice and Public Policy* (Hemel Hempstead, Harvester Wheatsheaf, 1989).

DIR (Sweden) (Committee instructions) 120. *Handläggning av vårdnadstvister* (The handling of custody disputes) (Stockholm, Fritzes, 1993).

DOUGLAS, M, 'Emotion and Culture in Theories of Justice' (1993) 22(4) *Economy and Society* 501.

DOWD, N, *Redefining Fatherhood* (New York, New York University Press, 2000).

DS (Sweden) (Departmental Series) 2. *Slutrapport från arbetsgruppen om papporna, barnen och arbetslivet* (Final report from the working group on daddies, children and working life) (Stockholm, Fritzes, 1995).

DUNCAN, S, A CARLING and R EDWARDS (eds), *Analysing Families: Morality and Rationality in Policy and Practice* (London, Routledge, 2002).

DUNCAN, S and R EDWARDS, *Lone Mothers, Paid Work and Gendered Moral Rationalities* (Basingstoke, Palgrave Macmillan, 1999).

DUNN, J, 'Contact and Children's Perspectives on Parental Relationships' in A BAINHAM, B LINDLEY, M RICHARDS and L TRINDER (eds), *Children and Their Families* (Oxford, Hart, 2003).

DUNNE, JE, EW HUDGINS and J BABCOCK, 'Can Changing the Divorce Law Affect Post-Divorce Adjustment?' (2000) 33 *Journal of Divorce and Remarriage* 35.

DYMOND, T, 'A History of the "New Class" Concept in Australian Public Discourse' in M SAWER and B HINDESS (eds), *Us and Them: Anti-Elitism in Australia* (Perth, API Network, 2004).

EDUARDS, M, *Förbjuden Handling* (Forbidden Action) (Malmö, Liber, 2002).

ELLIS, E, *Divorce Wars: Interventions with Families in* Conflict (Washington, DC, American Psychological Association, 2000).

ELROD, LD, *Child Custody, Practice and Procedure* (Clark Boardman Callaghan, 1993 and Supp 2002).

ERIKSSON, M, *I skuggan av Pappa. Familjerätten och hanteringen av fäders våld* (In the shadow of Daddy. Family law and the handling of fathers' violence) (Stehag, Gondolin, 2003).

—— 'A Visible or Invisible Child? Professionals' Approaches to Children whose Father is Violent towards their Mother' in M ERIKSSON, M HESTER, S KESKINEN and K PRINGLE (eds), *Tackling Men's Violence in Families. Nordic Issues and Dilemmas* (Bristol, Policy Press, 2005).

ERIKSSON, M and M HESTER, 'Violent Men as Good-Enough Fathers? A Look at England and Sweden' (2001) 7 *Violence Against Women* 779.

ERIKSSON, M, M HESTER, S KESKINEN and K PRINGLE (eds), *Tackling Men's Violence in Families. Nordic Issues and Dilemmas* (Bristol, Policy Press, 2005).

ERIKSSON, M and K PRINGLE, 'Introduction: Nordic Issues and Dilemmas' in M ERIKSSON, M HESTER, S KESKINEN and K PRINGLE (eds), *Tackling Men's Violence in Families. Nordic Issues and Dilemmas* (Bristol, Policy Press, 2005).

ESPING-ANDERSEN, G, *The Three Worlds of Welfare Capitalism* (Cambridge, Polity, 1990).

EYERMAN, J and A JAMISON, *Social Movements: A Cognitive Approach* (Cambridge, Polity, 1991).

FALCONER, C, C CLARKE and P HEWITT, 'Ministerial Forward' in *Parental Separation: Children's Needs and Parents' Responsibilities*, Cm 6273 (London, HMSO, 2004).

FALUDI, S, *Backlash: The Undeclared War Against Women* (London, Chatto and Windus, 1991).

—— *Stiffed: The Betrayal of the Modern Man* (London, Chatto and Windus, 1999).

FAROUQUE, F, 'The Male Backlash', *The Age*, 25 June 2005.

FARRELL, W, *The Myth of Male Power: Why Men are the Disposable Sex* (New York, Simon & Schuster, 1993).

FATHERHOOD FOUNDATION, 'Howard's Betrayal', *Dads on the Air*: http://www.dadsontheair.com/index.php?page=showcomments&id=209.

FEATHERSTONE, B, 'Taking Fathers Seriously' (2003) 33 (2) *British Journal of Social Work* 239.

FERREE, MM, 'Resonance and Radicalism: Feminist Framing in the Abortion Debates of the United States and Germany' (2003) 109 *American Journal of Sociology* 304.

FINEMAN, M, 'Dominant Discourse, Professional Language, and Legal Change in Child Custody Decisionmaking' (1988) 101 *Harvard Law Review* 727.

—— *The Illusion of Equality: The Rhetoric and Reality of Divorce Reform* (Chicago, University of Chicago Press, 1991).

—— *The Neutered Mother, the Sexual Family and other Twentieth Century Tragedies* (New York and London, Routledge, 1995).

FISHER, T, 'Family Mediators and Lawyers Communicating about Children: PDR-Land and Lawyer-Land' (2003) 9(2) *Journal of Family Studies* 201.

FLOOD, M, 'Men's Movements' (1998) 46 *Community Quarterly* 62.

—— *Fatherhood and Fatherlessness* (ACT, The Australia Institute, Discussion Paper No 59, 2003).

—— 'Backlash: Angry Men's Movements' in SE ROSSI (ed), *The Battle and Backlash Rage On: Why Feminism Cannot be Obsolete* (Philadelphia, Xlibris Press, 2004).

—— 'Separated Fathers and the Fathers' Rights Movement' presented at *Feminism, Law and the Family*, workshop held at Melbourne Law School, 24 February 2006.

FOLKESSON, P, *Nordisk mansforskning—en kartläggning* (Nordic studies on men—an overview) (Karlstads universitet, Karlstad, Jämställdhetscentrum, 2000).

FUREDI, F, *Paranoid Parenting* (London, Allen Lane, 2002).

FURSTENBERG, G, 'Good Dads—Bad Dads: Two Faces of Fatherhood' in AJ CHERLINE (ed), *The Changing American Family and Public Policy* (Washington, DC, The Urban Institute Press, 1988).

GADD, D, 'Masculinities, Violence and Defended Psycho-Social Subjects' (2000) 4 *Theoretical Criminology* 429.

GARFINKEL, I, DR MEYER and SS MCLANAHAN, 'A Brief History of Child Support Policies in the United States' in I GARFINKEL, SS MCLANAHAN, DR MEYER and JA SELTZER (eds), *Fathers Under Fire: The Revolution in Child Support Enforcement* (New York, Russell Sage, 1998).

GAVANAS, A, 'The Fatherhood Responsibility Movement: The Centrality of Marriage, Work and Male Sexuality in Reconstructions of Masculinity and Fatherhood' in B HOBSON (ed), *Making Men into Fathers: Men, Masculinities and the Social Politics of Fatherhood* (Cambridge, Cambridge University Press, 2002).

GELDOF, B, 'The Real Love that Dare Not Speak its Name' in A BAINHAM, B LINDLEY, M RICHARDS and L TRINDER (eds), *Children and Their Families* (Oxford, Hart, 2003).

GENOVESE, A, 'States of Contempt and Equality: The Family Court, John Hirst and Feminism' (2006) 21 *Australian Feminist Studies* (forthcoming).

GERSON, K, *No Man's Land: Men's Changing Commitments to Family and Work* (New York, Basic Books, 1993).

GIBB, F, 'Fathers Winning Battle to have Custody Hearing in Public' *The Times,* 10 January 2005.

GIDDENS, A, *The Transformations of Intimacy* (Cambridge, Polity, 1992).

GOFFMAN, E, *Frame Analysis: An Essay on the Organization of Experience* (New York, Harper Colophon, 1974).

GOLDBERG, H, *The Hazards of Being Male: Surviving the Myth of Masculine Privilege* (New York, Signet, 1976).

GOLLOP, M, A SMITH and N TAYLOR, 'Children's Involvement in Custody and Access Arrangements after Parental Separation' (2000) 12 *Child and Family Law Quarterly* 383.

GORDON, M, 'No Anti-Male Bias in the Tragic White Family Case' *Edmonton Journal,* 7 April 2000.

GOULD, A, 'Sweden: The Last Bastion of Social Democracy' in V GEORGE and P TAYLOR-GOOBY (eds), *European Welfare Policy: Squaring the Welfare Circle* (Houndmills, Macmillan, 1996).

GOWARD, P, 'Revision of Labour', *The Weekend Australian,* 25–26 June 2005.

GRALL, T, *Custodial Mothers and Fathers and their Child Support: 2001* (Current Population Reports, US Census Bureau, 2003).

GRAYCAR, R, 'Law Reform by Frozen Chook: Family Law Reform for the New Millennium?' (2000) 24 *Melbourne University Law Review* 737.

GRBICH, C, 'Male Primary Caregivers and Domestic Labour: Involvement or Avoidance?' (1995) 1(2) *Journal of Family Studies* 114.

GREATBATCH, D and R DINGWALL, 'The Marginalization of Domestic Violence in Divorce Mediation' (1999) 13(2) *International Journal of Law, Policy and the Family* 174.

GRIFFITHS, M, *Feminisms and the Self: The Web of Identity* (London, Routledge, 1995).

GUSTAFSSON, G, M EDUARDS and M RÖNNBLOM (eds), *Towards a New Democratic Order? Women's Organizing in Sweden in the 1990s* (Stockholm, Publica, 1997).

HAGSTRÖM, C, *Man blir pappa. Föräldraskap och maskulinitet i förändring* (Man/one becomes a daddy. Parenthood and masculinity in change) (Lund, Nordic Academic Press, 1999).

HAND, K and V LEWIS, 'Fathers' Views on Family Life and Paid Work' (2002) 61 *Family Matters* 26.

HANTRAIS, L and M-T LETABLIER, *Families and Family Policies in Europe* (Harlow, Longman, 1996).

HATTEN, W, L VINTER and R WILLIAMS, *Dads on Dads: Needs and Expectations at Work and Home* (Manchester, Equal Opportunities Commission, 2002).

HEARN, J, 'A Crisis in Masculinity, or New Agendas for Men?' in S WALDBY (ed), *New Agendas For Women* (London, Macmillan, 1999).

HEARN, J and K PRINGLE with members of Critical Research on Men in Europe, *European Perspectives on Men and Masculinities* (Houndmills, Palgrave, 2006).

HEARN, J, K PRINGLE, U MÜLLER, E OLEKSY, E LATTU, J CHERNOVA, H FERGUSON, ØG HOLTER, V KOLGA, I NOVIKOVA, C VENTIMIGLIA, E OLSVIK and T TALLBERG, 'Critical Studies on Men in Ten European Countries: (1) the State of Academic Research' (2002) 4 *Men and Masculinities* 380.

HESTER, M and L HARNE, 'Fatherhood, Children and Violence: Placing England in an International Context' in S WATSON and L DOYAL (eds), *Engendering Social Policy* (Buckingham, Open University Press, 1999).

HINDESS, B and M SAWER, 'Introduction' in M SAWER and B HINDESS (eds), *Us and Them: Anti-Elitism in Australia* (Perth, API Network, 2004).

HIRST, J, 'Court Rule Offensive to Families' *The Australian*, 21 March 2005.

—— 'Kangaroo Court: Family Law in Australia' (2005) 17 *Quarterly Essay.*

HOBSON, B (ed), *Making Men into Fathers: Men, Masculinities and the Social Politics of Fatherhood* (Cambridge, Cambridge University Press, 2002).

HOBSON, B and D MORGAN, 'Introduction: Making Men into Fathers' in B HOBSON (ed), *Making Men into Fathers: Men, Masculinities and the Social Politics of Fatherhood* (Cambridge, Cambridge University Press, 2002).

HØJGAARD L, 'Working Fathers—Caught in the Web of the Symbolic Order of Gender' (1997) 40 *Acta Sociologica* 245.

HOLDEN, KC and PJ SMOCK, 'The Economic Costs of Marital Dissolution: Why do Women Bear a Disproportionate Cost?' (1991) 17 *Annual Review of Sociology* 51.

HOLMBERG, C and C BENDER, *Våld mot kvinnor—män i kris* (Violence against women—men in crisis) (Stockholm, National Board of Health and Welfare, 1998).

HORIN, A and N JAMAL, 'Push for Equal Custody a Win for Fathers' Groups', *The Age*, 8 December 2005.

HORN, WF, 'Did You Say "Movement"?' in WF HORN, D BLANKENHORN and MB PEARLSTEIN (eds), *The Fatherhood Movement: A Call to Action* (Lanham, MD, Lexington Books, 1999).

HORN, WF, D BLANKENHORN and MB PEARLSTEIN, *The Fatherhood Movement: A Call to Action* (Lexington MD, Lexington Books, 1999).

HUDSON, P, 'PM Orders Inquiry on Joint Custody', *The Age*, 25 June 2003.

HUNT, J, *Researching Contact* (London, National Council for One Parent Families, 2003).

HUNTER, R, 'Adversarial Mythologies: Policy Assumptions and Research Evidence in Family Law' (2003) 30 *Journal of Law and Society* 156.

JAMES, A and A JAMES, 'Pump up the Volume: Listening to Children in Separation and Divorce' (1999) 6 *Childhood* 189.

JAMES, A, C JENKS and A PROUT, *Theorizing Childhood* (Cambridge, Polity, 1998).

JAMES, A and MPM RICHARDS, 'Sociological Perspectives, Family Policy, Family Law and Children: Adult Thinking and Sociological Tinkering' (1999) 21 *Journal of Social Welfare and Family Law* 23.

JENKS, C, *Childhood* (London, Routledge, 1996).

JOHNSON, SD, 'Who Supports the Promise Keepers?' (2001) 61 *Sociology of Religion* 93.

KAGANAS, F and S DAY SCLATER, 'Contact Disputes: Narrative Constructions of "Good Parents"' (2004) 12(1) *Feminist Legal Studies* 1.

KAGANAS, F and A DIDUCK, 'Incomplete Citizens: Changing Images of Post-Separation Children' (2004) 67(6) *Modern Law Review* 959.

KAGANAS, F and C PIPER, 'Contact and Domestic Violence: The Winds of Change?' [2000] *Family Law* 630.

KAGANAS, F and C PIPER, 'Shared Parenting—A 70% Solution?' [2002] 14 (4) *Child and Family Law Quarterly* 365.

KATZENSTEIN, M, *Faithful and Fearless: Moving Feminism into the Church and the Military* (Princeton, NJ, Princeton University Press, 1998).

KAYE, M and J TOLMIE, 'Discoursing Dads: The Rhetorical Devices of Fathers' Rights Groups' (1998) 22 *Melbourne University Law Review* 162.

—— 'Fathers' Rights Groups in Australia and their Engagement with Issues in Family Law' (1998) 12(1) *Australian Journal of Family Law* 19.

—— '"Lollies at a Children's Party" and Other Myths: Violence, Protection Orders and Fathers' Rights Groups' (1998) 10(1) *Current Issues in Criminal Justice* 52.

KELLY, JB, 'Changing Perspectives on Children's Adjustment Following Divorce' (2003) 10 *Childhood* 237.

KENEDY, RA, *Fathers For Justice: The Rise of a New Social Movement in Canada as a Case Study of Collective Identity Formation* (Ann Arbor, MI, Caravan Books, 2004).

KING, M, 'Foreword' in S DAY SCLATER and C PIPER (eds), *Undercurrents of Divorce* (Aldershot, Ashgate, 1999).

KING, M and C PIPER, *How the Law Thinks About Children* (2nd edn, Aldershot, Arena, 1995).

KLINTH, R, *Göra pappa med barn. Svensk pappa-politik 1960–95* (Making daddy with child: Swedish daddy-politics 1960–95) (Umeå, Boréa, 2002).

KURKI-SUONIO, K, 'Joint Custody as an Interpretation of the Best Interests of the Child in Critical and Comparative Perspective' (2000) 14(3) *International Journal of Law, Policy and the Family* 183.

LAING, M, 'For the Sake of the Children: Preventing Reckless New Laws' (1999) 16 *Canadian Journal of Family Law* 229.

LAROSSA, R, *The Modernization of Fatherhood: A Social and Political History* (Chicago, University of Chicago Press, 1997).

LASTER, K and P O'MALLEY, 'Sensitive New-Age Laws: the Reassertion of Emotionality in Law' (1996) 24 *International Journal of the Sociology of Law* 21.

LAVILLE, S, 'Batman and Robin Quit Protest Group' *The Guardian*, 9 June 2005.

LAWRENCE, S, 'Feminism, Consequences, Accountability' (2004) 42(4) *Osgoode Hall Law Journal* 583.

LESSARD, H, 'Mothers, Fathers, and Naming: Reflections on the Law Equality Framework and *Trociuk v British Columbia (Attorney General)*' (2004) 16(1) *Canadian Journal of Women and the Law* 165.

LEWIS, C, *A Man's Place in the Home: Fathers and Families in the UK* (York, Joseph Rowntree Foundation, 2000).

LEWIS, C, A PAPACOSTA and J WARIN, *Cohabitation, Separation and Fatherhood* (York, YPS/Joseph Rowntree Foundation, 2002).

LEWIS, J, 'The Decline of the Male Breadwinner Model Family' (2001) 8 *Social Politics* 152.

—— *The End of Marriage? Individualism and Intimate Relations* (Cheltenham, Edward Elgar, 2001).

LILJESTRÖM, R, *Jämställdhetens villkor: män och kvinnor i dagens värld* (The conditions of gender equality: Men and women today) (Stockholm, Sveriges Radio, 1968).

LU (Reports from the civil law committee) 12. Lagutskottets betänkande *Vårdnad, boende umgänge* (Custody, residence, contact) (Stockholm, Fritzes, 1997/98).

LUEPNITZ, DA, *Child Custody* (Lexington, MD, DC Heath and Company, 1982).

LUNDGREN, E, G HEIMER, J WESTERSTRAND and A-M KALLIOKOSKI, *Captured Queen. Men's Violence Against Women in 'Equal' Sweden—A National Survey* (Umeå, Brottsofermyndigheten, 2002).

LUPTON, D and L BARCLAY, *Constructing Fatherhood: Discourses and Experiences* (London, Sage, 1997).

MCADAM, D and D RUCHT, 'Cross National Diffusion of Social Movement Ideas' (1993) 528 *The Annals of the American Academy of Political and Social Science* 56.

MCMILLAN, L, 'Women's Anti-Violence Organisations in Sweden and the UK' in M ERIKSSON, A NENOLA and MM NILSEN (eds), *Gender and Violence in the Nordic Countries. Report from a Conference in Køge, Denmark, 23–24 November 2001*. TemaNord 2002: 545 (Copenhagen, Nordic Council of Ministers, 2002).

MACLEAN, M, 'The Contribution of the International Research Community to UK Law Reform re Child Contact', paper presented at the Annual Meeting of the Research Committee of the Sociology of Law, ISA, Paris, 11–13 June 2005.

MACLEAN, M and J EEKELAAR, *The Parental Obligation: A Study of Parenthood Across Households* (Oxford, Hart, 1997).

MAGNUSSON, E, 'Party-Political Rhetoric on Gender Equality in Sweden: The Uses of Uniformity and Heterogeneity' (2000) 8 *Nordic Journal of Women's Studies/NORA* 78.

MARSIGLIO, W (ed), *Fatherhood: Contemporary Theory, Research and Social Policy* (London, Sage, 1995).

MASON, MA, *The Custody Wars: Why Children are Losing the Legal Battle and What We Can Do About It* (New York, Basic Books, 1999).

MASSON, J, 'Parental Alienation Syndrome' [2002] *Family Law* 568.

MATAS, R, 'The Pain Behind a Suicide' *The Globe and Mail*, 8 April 2000.

MAY, S, 'Child Custody and Visitation' (2001) 2 *Georgetown Journal of Gender and the Law* 382.

MELLI, MS, 'Guideline Review: Child Support and Time-sharing by Parents' (1999) 33 *Family Law Quarterly* 219.

MELVILLE, A and R HUNTER, 'As Everybody Knows: Countering Myths of Gender Bias in Family Law' (2001) 1(1) *Griffith Law Review* 124.

MEN'S RIGHTS AGENCY, 'Disenfranchised Fathers Still Unequal When it Comes to Child Custody': http://www.mensrights.com.au/, posting dated 6 September 2004.

MESSNER, MA, *Politics of Masculinities: Men in Movements* (Thousand Oaks, CA, Sage, 1997).

MEYER, DS and N WHITTIER, 'Social Movement Spillover' (1994) 41 *Social Problems* 277.

MITCHELL, L, 'Caught in a Crossfire', *The Age*, 11 July 2005.

MOLONEY, L, T LOVE, T FISHER and S FERGUSON, 'The Words to Say It—Clients' Own Experiences of Family Mediation' (1996) 10 *Australian Journal of Family Law* 53.

MOLONEY, L and J MCINTOSH, 'Child-Responsive Practices in Australian Family Law: Past Problems and Future Directions' (2004) 10 *Journal of Family Studies* 71.

MORGAN, D, *Family Connections: An Introduction to Family Studies* (Cambridge, Polity, 1996).

MOSS, P (ed), *Father Figures: Fathers in the Families of the 1990s* (London, HMSO, 1995).

NAFFINE, N, *Law and the Sexes* (Sydney, Allen and Unwin, 1990).

NEALE, B, J FLOWERDEW and C SMART, 'Drifting Towards Shared Residence?' [2003] *Family Law* 904.

NEALE, B and C SMART, 'Experiments with Parenthood?' (1997) 31(2) *Sociology* 201.

—— 'In Whose Best Interests? Theorising Family Life following Parental Separation or Divorce' in S DAY SCLATER and C PIPER (eds), *Undercurrents of Divorce* (Aldershot, Ashgate, 1999).

NEAVE, M, 'Resolving the Dilemma of Difference: A Critique of "The Role of Private Ordering in Family Law"' (1994) 44 *University of Toronto Law Journal* 97.

NEILSON, LC, 'Demeaning, Demoralizing and Disenfranchising Divorced Dads: A Review of the Literature' (1999) 31(3/4) *Journal of Divorce and Remarriage* 129.

—— 'Putting Revisions to the Divorce Act through a Family Violence Filter: The Good, the Bad and the Ugly' (2003) 20(1) *Canadian Journal of Family Law* 11.

NORDBORG, G and J NIEMI-KIESILÄINEN, 'Women's Peace: A Criminal Law Reform in Sweden' in K NOUSIAINEN, Å GUNNARSSON, K LUNDSTRÖM and J NIEMI-KIESILÄINEN (eds), *Responsible Selves. Women in the Nordic Legal Culture* (Aldershot, Ashgate, 2001).

NORDBORG, G, 'Children's Peace? The Possibility to Protect Children by Means of Criminal Law and Family Law' in M ERIKSSON, M HESTER, S KESKINEN and K PRINGLE (eds), *Tackling Men's Violence in Families. Nordic Issues and Dilemmas* (Bristol, Policy Press, 2005).

NORDENFORS, G, *Fadersrätt, kvinnofrid och barns säkerhet* (Father-rights, women's peace and children's safety) (ROKS/Riksorganisationen för kvinno- och tjejjourer i Sverige, Stockholm, 1996).

NOUSIAINEN, K, 'Introductory Remarks in Nordic Law and Gender Identities' in K NOUSIAINEN, Å GUNNARSSON, K LUNDSTRÖM and J NIEMI-KIESILÄINEN (eds), *Responsible Selves. Women in the Nordic Legal Culture* (Aldershot, Ashgate, 2001).

NUSSBAUM, M, *Hiding from Humanity: Disgust, Shame and the Law* (Princeton, NJ, Princeton University Press, 2004).

NYGH, P, 'The New Part VII—An Overview' (1996) 10 *Australian Journal of Family Law* 4.

O'BRIEN, M, *Shared Caring: Bringing Fathers into the Frame* (Manchester, Equal Opportunities Commission, 1995).

O'DONOVAN, K, *Family Law Matters* (London, Pluto, 1993).

OLSON, M, *The Logic of Collective Action: Public Goods and the Theory of Groups* (Cambridge, MA, Harvard University Press, 1965).

PARKE, R, *Fatherhood* (Cambridge MA, Harvard University Press, 1996).

PARKINSON, P, J CASHMORE, and J SINGLE, *Adolescents' Views on the Fairness of Parenting and Financial Arrangements After Separation* (Sydney, University of Sydney, 2003).

PARTON, N (ed), *Child Protection and Family Support* (London, Routledge, 1997).

PEASE, B, *Recreating Men: Postmodern Masculinity Politics* (London, Sage, 2000).

PHILLIPS, A, 'Most Fathers get Justice' *The Guardian*, 13 October 2004.

PHILLIPS, M, *The Sex-Change Society: Feminised Britain and the Neutered Male* (London, The Social Market Foundation, 1999).

PIPER, C, *The Responsible Parent* (Hemel Hempsted, Harvester Wheatsheaf, 1993).

—— 'Divorce Reform and the Image of the Child' (1996) 23(3) *Journal of Law and Society* 364.

—— 'Assumptions About Children's Best Interests' (2000) 22 *Journal of Social Welfare and Family Law* 261.

POTTER, J, *Representing Reality: Discourse, Rhetoric and Social Construction* (London, Sage, 1996).

PRINGLE, K, *Men, Masculinities and Social Welfare* (London, UCL Press, 1995).

—— *Children and Social Welfare in Europe* (Milton Keynes, Open University Press, 1998).

—— *Final Report to the ESRC on project R000223551* (2002) on REGARD DATABASE website: http://www.regard.ac.uk/cgi-bin/regardng/showReports.pl?ref=R000223551

—— 'Hvorfor har vi brug for flere mandlige pædagoger?—Internationale synspunkter' (Why do we need more men as pedagogues?—International perspectives) (2005) 33 *VERA* 30.

—— 'Neglected Issues in Swedish Child Protection Policy and Practice: Age, Ethnicity and Gender' in M ERIKSSON, M HESTER, S KESKINEN and K PRINGLE (eds), *Tackling Men's Violence in Families. Nordic Issues and Dilemmas* (Bristol, Policy Press, 2005).

PROP (Swedish government white paper) 1994/95:224 *Barns rätt att komma till tals* (Children's right to voice) (Stockholm, Fritzes).

—— 1997/98:7 *Vårdnad, boende, umgänge* (Custody, living, rights of access) (Stockholm, Fritzes).

—— 1998/99:133 *Särskild företrädare för barn* (Special representative for children) (Stockholm, Fritzes).

—— 2005/06:99 *Nya vårdnadsregler* (New custody rules) (Stockholm, Fritzes).

PRYOR, J and B RODGERS, *Children in Changing Families: Life after Parental Separation* (Oxford, Blackwell, 2001).

QUICKE, A and K ROBINSON, 'Keeping the Promise of the Moral Majority: A Historical Critical Comparison of the Promise Keepers and the Christian Coalition, 1989–1998' in DS CLAUSSEN (ed), *The Promise Keepers: Essays on Masculinity and Christianity* (Jefferson, NJ, McFarland and Company, 2000).

REECE, H, 'The Paramountcy Principle: Consensus or Construct' (1996) 49
    Current Legal Problems 267.
—— *Divorcing Responsibly* (Oxford, Hart Publishing, 2003).
REPUTATION INTELLIGENCE, *F4J Heralds a New Era in Political Campaigning:
    Media Report* (London, Reputation Intelligence, 2004).
RHOADES, H, 'Posing as Reform? The Case of the Family Law Reform Act' (2000)
    14(2) *Australian Journal of Family Law* 142.
—— 'The "Non Contact Mother": Reconstructions of Motherhood in the Era of the
    New Father' (2002) 16 *International Journal of Law, Policy and the Family* 72.
—— 'The Rise and Rise of Shared Parenting Laws: A Critical Reflection' (2002)
    19(1) *Canadian Journal of Family Law* 75.
—— 'Contact Enforcement and Parenting Programs—Policy Aims in Confusion?'
    (2004) 16 *Child and Family Law Quarterly* 1.
RHOADES, H and SB BOYD, 'Reforming Custody Laws: A Comparative Study'
    (2004) 18 *International Journal of Law, Policy and the Family* 119.
RHOADES, H, R GRAYCAR and M HARRISON, *The Family Law Reform Act 1995:
    The First Three Years* (University of Sydney/Family Court of Australia, 2000).
ROBSON, K, *Wrapped in the Flag of the Child: Post-Divorce Parenting Experiences
    in an Era of Guidelines and Privatization* (PhD Thesis, Department of
    Sociology, Queen's University, defended 11 November 2005).
RUSSELL, G and L BOWMAN, *Work and Family: Current Thinking, Research and
    Practice* (Department of Family and Community Services, 2000).
SAINSBURY, D (ed), *Gender and Welfare State Regimes* (Oxford, Oxford University
    Press, 1999).
SANDBERG, JF and SL HOFFERTH, 'Changes in Children's Time with Parents:
    United States, 1981–1997' (2001) 38 *Demography* 423.
SAWER, M, *Populism and Public Choice: The Construction of Women as a
    'Special Interest'*, paper presented at the Australasian Political Studies
    Association Conference, University of Tasmania, Hobart, 29 September–1
    October 2003.
—— 'Populism and Public Choice in Australia and Canada: Turning Equality-
    Seekers into "Special Interests"' in M Sawer and B Hindess (eds), *Us and Them:
    Anti-Elitism in Australia* (Perth, API Network, 2004).
SAWER, M and B HINDESS (eds), *Us and Them: Anti-Elitism in Australia* (Perth,
    API Network, 2004).
SAYER, LC, SM BIANCHI and JP ROBINSON, 'Are Parents Investing Less Time in
    Children?' (2004) 110 *American Journal of Sociology* 1.
SCALMER, S and M GOOT, 'Elites Constructing Elites: News Limited's Newspapers
    1996–2002' in M SAWER and B HINDESS (eds), *Us and Them: Anti-Elitism in
    Australia* (Perth, API Network, 2004).
SCB (Statistics Sweden), *Barn och deras familjer 2001* (Children and their families
    2001) (Stockholm and Örebro, Statistiska centralbyrån, 2003).

SCHIRATZKI, J, *Vårdnad och vårdnadstvister* (Custody and custody disputes) (Stockholm, Nordstedts, 1997).

SCLATER, SD and F KAGANAS, 'Contact: Mothers, Welfare and Rights' in A BAINHAM, B LINDLEY, M RICHARDS and L TRINDER (eds), *Children and Their Families* (Oxford, Hart, 2003).

SEVENHUIJSEN, S, *Citizenship and the Ethics of Care: Feminist Considerations about Justice, Morality and Politics* (London, Routledge, 1998).

SEWELL, WH, 'A Theory of Structure: Duality, Agency, and Transformation' (1992) 98 *American Journal of Sociology* 1.

SHARED PARENTING COUNCIL OF AUSTRALIA, 'Is the Family Court a Political or a Judicial Institution?', Media Release, 30 October 2002.

—— 'Federal Government Recognises Shared Parenting is the Way Forward for Australian Children of Divorce', Press Release, 18 November 2002.

—— 'Government Shared Parenting Announcement a Courageous and Small Step Forward', Media Release, 30 July 2004.

—— 'Protecting the Child's Rights is Paramount to their Welfare and Best Interests', Media Release, 30 July 2004.

—— 'Howard's Family Law Amendments a Cruel Failure', Media Release, 24 June 2005.

—— 'Family Law Amendment (Shared Parental Responsibility) Bill 2005: The Fourth Pillar to the Family Reform Measures is a Solid Piece of Work', Media Release, 9 December 2005.

SHELDON, S, 'Fragmenting Fatherhood: The Regulation of Reproductive Technologies' (2005) 68(4) *Modern Law Review* 523.

SIMONS, M, 'Ties that Bind' (2005) 8 *Griffith Review* 13.

SINGER, A, *Föräldraskap i rättslig belysning* (Parenthood according to the law) (Uppsala, Iustus, 2000).

SMART, C, 'Feminism and Law: Some Problems of Analysis and Strategy' (1986) 14 *International Journal of the Sociology of Law* 109.

—— *Feminism and the Power of Law* (London, Routledge, 1989).

—— 'The Legal and Moral Ordering of Child Custody' (1991) 18 *Journal of Law and Society* 485.

—— 'Losing the Struggle for Another Voice—The Case of Family Law' (1995) 18 *Dalhousie Law Journal* 173.

—— 'Wishful thinking and harmful tinkering? Sociological Reflections on Family Policy' (1997) (26) 3 *Journal of Social Policy* 1.

—— 'The "New" Parenthood: Fathers and Mothers After Divorce' in E SILVA and C SMART (eds), *The New Family?* (London, Sage, 1999).

—— 'From Children's Shoes to Children's Voices' (2002) 40 *Family Court Review* 305.

—— 'Introduction: New Perspectives on Childhood and Divorce' (2003) 10(2) *Childhood* 123.

—— 'Towards an Understanding of Family Change: Gender Conflict and Children's Citizenship' (2003) 17 *Australian Journal of Family Law* 20.

—— 'Equal Shares: Rights for Fathers or Recognition for Children?' (2004) 24(4) *Critical Social Policy* 484.

—— 'The Ethic of Justice Fights Back: Family Law and the Rise of the New Paternity', paper presented at the Canadian Law and Society Association Annual Meeting, 'Law's Empire', 26–29 June 2005.

SMART, C, V MAY, A WADE and C FURNISS, *Residence and Contact Disputes in Court: Research Report 6/2003* (London, Department for Constitutional Affairs, 2003).

SMART, C and B NEALE, 'Arguments Against Virtue: Must Contact be Enforced?' [1997] *Family Law* 332.

—— 'Good Enough Morality? Divorce and Postmodernity' (1997) 17(4) *Critical Social Policy* 3.

—— *Family Fragments?* (Cambridge, Polity, 1999).

—— '"I Hadn't Really Thought About It": New Identities/New Fatherhoods' in J SEYMOUR and P BAGGULEY (eds), *Relating Intimacies: Power and Resistance* (Basingstoke, Palgrave Macmillan, 1999).

—— '"It's My Life Too"—Children's Perspectives on Post-Divorce Parenting' [2000] *Family Law* 163.

SMART, C, B NEALE and A WADE, *The Changing Experience of Childhood: Families and Divorce* (Cambridge, Polity, 2001).

SMART, C and P STEPHENS, *Cohabitation Breakdown* (York, Family Policy Studies Centre/Joseph Rowntree Foundation, 2000).

SMEATON, D and A MARSH, *Maternity and Paternity Benefits: Survey of Parents 2005: Employment Relations Research Series No 50* (London, Department of Trade and Industry, 2006).

SMITH, B, NJ TAYLOR and P TAPP, 'Rethinking Children's Involvement in Decision-Making after Parental Separation' (2003) 10 *Childhood* 201.

SMOCK, PJ, 'Gender and the Short-Run Economic Consequences of Marital Disruption' (1994) 73 *Social Forces* 243.

SMYTH, B (ed), *Parent-Child Contact and Post-Separation Parenting Arrangements* (Research Report No 9, Australian Institute of Family Studies, 2004).

SOCIALSTYRELSEN, *Barn i fokus-projektet. Slutrapport* (The Children in focus-project. Final report) (Stockholm, Socialstyrelsen, 1996).

SOMMERS, CH, *Who Stole Feminism? How Women Have Betrayed Women* (New York, Simon and Schuster, 1994).

SOU (Swedish Public Investigations) 1995:60 *Kvinnofrid. Kvinnovåldskommissionens huvudbetänkande* (Women's Peace. Main report from the commission on violence against women) (Stockholm, Fritzes, 1995).

—— 1995:79 *Vårdnad, boende, umgänge*. Vårdnadstvistutredningen (Custody, residence, contact. The inquiry on custody disputes) (Stockholm, Fritzes, 1995).

—— 1998:31 *Det gäller livet—Stöd och vård till barn och ungdomar med psykiska problem* (Concerning life—Support to and care of children and young people with psychiatric problems) (Stockholm, Fritzes, 1998).

—— 2000:77 *Omhändertagen. Samhällets ansvar för utsatta barn och unga.* Betänkande från LVU-utredningen (Taken into care. Society's responsibility for children and young people at risk. Report from the inquiry on the law on young people in care) (Stockholm, Fritzes, 2000).

——2001:14 *Sexualbrotten—ett ökat skydd för den sexuella integriteten och angränsande frågor.* Betänkande från 1998 års Sexualbrottskommitté (Sexual crimes—increased protection of the sexual integrity and associated issues. Report from the 1998 Committee on sexual crimes) (Stockholm, Fritzes, 2001).

—— 2001:72. *Barnmisshandel. Att förebygga och åtgärda* (Child abuse—Prevention and protection. Final Report from the parliamentary committee against child abuse) (Stockholm, Fritzes, 2001).

—— 2005:43 *Vårdnad—Boende—Umgänge. Barnets bästa, föräldrars ansvar.* Betänkande från 2002 års Vårdnadskommitté (Custody, residence, contact. The best interests of children, parents' responsibility. Report from the 2002 parliamentary committee on custody) (Stockholm, Fritzes, 2005).

SPELMAN, E, *Inessential Woman* (Boston, Beacon Press, 1990).

STACEY, J, 'Dada-ism in the 1990s: Getting Past Baby Talk About Fatherlessness' in CR DANIELS (ed), *Lost Fathers: The Politics of Fatherlessness in America* (New York, St Martin's Press, 1998).

STATUS OF WOMEN CANADA, *Setting the Stage for the Next Century: The Federal Plan for Gender Equality* (Ottawa, Status of Women Canada, 1995).

STONE, L (ed), *New Directions in Anthropological Kinship* (Lanham, MD and Oxford, Rowman and Littlefield, 2001).

STRAUSS, A and J CORBIN, *Basics of Grounded Theory: Grounded Theory Procedures and Techniques* (Newbury Park, CA, Sage, 1990).

TARROW, S, 'Modular Collective Action and the Rise of the Social Movement: Why the French Revolution Was Not Enough' (1993) 21 *Politics and Society* 69.

—— *Power in Movement: Social Movements, Collective Action and Politics* (New York, Cambridge University Press, 1994).

TEUBNER, G, 'How the Law Thinks: Toward a Constructivist Epistemology of Law' (1989) 23 *Law & Society Review* 727.

TORR, J, *Is there a Father in the House: A Handbook for Health and Social Care Professionals* (Oxford, Radcliffe Medical Press, 2003).

TRONTO, JC, 'Women and Caring: What Can Feminists Learn about Morality from Caring?' in A JAGGAR and S BORDO (eds), *Gender, Body, Knowledge* (Newark, NJ, Rutgers University Press, 1989).

—— *Moral Boundaries: A Political Argument for an Ethic of Care* (London, Routledge, 1993).

VAN TIGGELEN, J, 'Dads' Army', *The Age Good Weekend Magazine*, 21 May 2005.

VENOHR, J and RG WILLIAMS, 'The Implementation and Periodic Review of State Child Support Guidelines' (1999) 33 *Family Law Quarterly* 7.

WADE, A, B NEALE and C SMART, *The Changing Experience of Childhood: Families and Divorce* (Cambridge, Polity, 2001).

WADE, A and C SMART, *Facing Family Change: Children's Circumstances, Strategies and Resources* (York, YPS/Joseph Rowntree Foundation, 2002).

WALLER, M, *My Baby's Father: Unmarried Parents and Paternal Responsibility* (Ithaca, NY, Cornell University Press, 2002).

WARIN, J, Y SOLOMON, C LEWIS and W LANGFORD, *Fathers, Work and Family Life* (York, Joseph Rowntree Foundation/Family Policy Studies Centre, 1999).

WEBB, N and L MOLONEY, 'Child-Focused Development Programs for Family Dispute Professionals: Recent Steps in the Evolution of Family Dispute Resolution Strategies in Australia' (2003) 9 *Journal of Family Studies* 23.

WENDT-HÖJER, M, *Rädslans politik. Våld och sexualitet i den svenska demokratin* (The Politics of fear. Violence and sexuality in the Swedish democracy) (Malmö, Liber, 2002).

WESTON, R, L QU and G SORIANO, 'Implications of Men's Extended Work Hours for their Personal and Marital Happiness' (2002) 61 *Family Matters* 18.

WILLIAMS, B, 'Systems Failing Fathers: A Fatherless Society in Waiting', Address to the Lone Fathers Association National Conference, 22–23 June 2005, Canberra.

WILLIAMS, C, 'Parental Alienation Syndrome' [2002] *Family Law* 410.

WILLIAMS, GI and RH WILLIAMS, 'All We Want is Equality: Rhetorical Framing in the Fathers' Rights Movement' in J BEST (ed), *Images of Issues: Typifying Contemporary Social Problems* (New York, Aldine de Gruyter, 1995).

WROE, R, 'Judge Claims Intimidation in Row over Child Custody', *The Age*, 2 December 2003.

Index